Teacher's Resource Book

D1242537

Houghton Mifflin

Spelling and Vocabulary

Level 2

Houghton Mifflin Company   Boston

Atlanta   Dallas   Geneva, Illinois   Palo Alto   Princeton

How to Use This Resource Book

Introduction

This Resource Book provides a variety of student and teacher support materials that can be used with this level of *Houghton Mifflin Spelling and Vocabulary*.

Section 1
Unit Resources

Practice Masters

The materials for each Basic Unit include three Practice Masters designed to provide three levels of practice. These pages include meaning-based activities as well as many motivating gamelike activities that mix practice with fun.

● **Practice A** can be used for reteaching or practice. It includes the Summing Up statement from the Basic Unit and one activity that reinforces the unit spelling principle. Practice A pages deal with the first column of five Basic Words as well as any Elephant Words listed on the Part A page. By dealing with only part of the Basic Word list, this page provides an easy practice for students who may be having difficulty with the word list or who have limited English proficiency.

● **Practice B** provides extra practice for all of the Basic and Elephant Words listed on the Basic Unit Part A page. Many Practice B masters use the Basic Words in proofreading activities to remind students of the importance of checking for correct spelling whenever they write.

● **Practice C** provides extra practice and extension activities for students who are working with the two Challenge Words listed in the Teacher's Edition and with the Theme Vocabulary Words listed on the Part E page of each Basic Unit.

Tests

Placement

The **Prebook Test** can help you evaluate each student's general level of spelling ability. The test

consists of twenty-five items that include seventy-five Basic and Elephant Words drawn from all of the Basic Units in this level. Students who score between 50 and 85 percent generally can be assigned the complete Basic and Elephant Word list for each unit. Students who score above 85 percent might also attempt to work with the Challenge Words. Students who score below 50 percent could be assigned only the first column of Basic Words and the Elephant Words in each unit.

Note: You may also want to use the **Pretest** in your Teacher's Edition or the **Unit Test** in this Resource Book to determine each student's spelling assignment on a unit-by-unit basis.

Unit-by-Unit Evaluation

The **Unit** and **Review Tests** provide alternatives to the Pretest and the Unit Evaluation included in your Teacher's Edition. The Teacher's Resource Book Unit and Review Tests can help you evaluate your students' spelling skills as well as provide practice with many of the formats used on standardized tests. They can be used as either pretests or posttests.

   Unit Tests: Each Unit Test evaluates every Basic and Elephant Word in that unit. The words from the first column of the Basic Word list are tested first, followed by the words from the second column. The words are in a sequence different from that used in the student book word lists.

   Review Tests: There are two Review Tests for each Review Unit.

● **Review Test A** evaluates the Basic Words in the first column of each Basic Unit word list in that cycle as well as some of the Elephant Words. (One cycle comprises five Basic Units and the following Review Unit.)

● **Review Test B** evaluates the Basic Words in the second column of each Basic Unit word list in that cycle as well as some of the Elephant Words.

Houghton Mifflin Spelling and Vocabulary. Copyright © Houghton Mifflin Company. All rights reserved.

Note: Not all of the words tested in Review Tests A and B are practiced in the pupil book Review Unit exercises. To review all of the Basic and Elephant Words in preparation for Review Tests A and B, have students complete the Extra Practice exercises in their pupil books and the Review Unit exercises.

Cumulative Tests

The **Midyear Test** and the **End-of-Year Test** are intended to be used after Review Units 18 and 36 respectively. Each test consists of twenty-five items that include seventy-five Basic and Elephant Words. The Midyear Test draws on Basic and Elephant Words from all Basic Units in Cycles 1–3. The End-of-Year Test draws both on Basic and Elephant Words from all Basic Units in Cycles 1–6.

Bulletin Boards

A **Bulletin Board** suggestion has been provided for each cycle of units. Each bulletin board idea can be used with every unit in that cycle.

Spelling Newsletters

A **Spelling Newsletter** for students and their families is available for each cycle of units. The letter appears in two languages, English and Spanish. Each letter includes a simple cooperative family activity that reinforces the importance of correct spelling in an enjoyable way.

Spelling Games

A **Spelling Game** master has been provided for each cycle of units. Some games work specifically with the spelling words in the cycle. Other games encourage students to work with any words that meet the game criteria in order to build their interest in words and language as a whole. Students can use these game masters independently.

When the game instructions direct students to use spelling words, they specify Basic and Elephant Words. Depending on students' skills,

you may want to direct some or all students to use Review, Challenge, or Theme Vocabulary Words as well.

Prewriting Ideas

A **Prewriting Ideas** master has been provided for use with Step 1 of the Writing Process assignment in the Literature and Writing lesson in each Review Unit. This master provides structured, yet open-ended, activities that will help students choose their writing topics and plan the organization and content of their compositions before they begin to write.

Section 2
Additional Resources

This section provides **Individual** and **Class Progress Charts** for record keeping. These charts are especially useful during meetings with parents or school administrators.

Note: The **Class Progress Chart** provides record-keeping space for one cycle of units. Make duplicate copies to cover all six cycles. You may want to write students' names on one copy and use that page to make the additional copies.

The **Proofreading Marks** and the **Proofreading Checklist** masters can be duplicated for each student to use as handy references for writing.

The **Handwriting Models** masters provide examples of four different handwriting styles. You may want to duplicate specific models for each student to use as a reference.

Section 3
Practice Master and
Test Answers

This section includes annotated copies of **Practice Masters A**, **B**, and **C**. It also includes annotated copies of the **Prebook**, **Midyear**, **End-of-Year**, **Unit**, and **Review Tests**. These materials are organized sequentially by unit.

Houghton Mifflin Spelling and Vocabulary. Copyright © Houghton Mifflin Company. All rights reserved.

Contents

Unit Resources

Placement and Cumulative Evaluation
Prebook Test (Unit 1)
Midyear Test (Unit 18)
End-of-Year Test (Unit 36)
Basic Units
Practice Masters
Practice A (Easy)
Practice B (Average)
Practice C (Challenging)
Unit Test
Review Units
Bulletin Board Idea
Spelling Newsletter (English and Spanish)
Spelling Game
Tests
Review Test A
Review Test B
Prewriting Ideas

Prebook Test

There are three words beside each number. One of the words is spelled wrong. Mark the letter next to that word.

Sample:
(a) bat
● digg
(c) job

1. (a) sad
   (b) wishes
   (c) fout

2. (a) hoam
   (b) dress
   (c) much

3. (a) give
   (b) batted
   (c) nite

4. (a) was
   (b) foxx
   (c) read

5. (a) whitch
   (b) baby
   (c) found

6. (a) nut
   (b) slo
   (c) for

7. (a) swimm
   (b) great
   (c) yes

8. (a) start
   (b) yuo
   (c) warm

9. (a) pin
   (b) cloc
   (c) draw

10. (a) thank
    (b) plain
    (c) maibe

Houghton Mifflin Spelling and Vocabulary. Copyright © Houghton Mifflin Company. All rights reserved.

(continued)

Prebook Test (continued)

11. (a) we've
    (b) teling
    (c) road

12. (a) saim
    (b) been
    (c) glad

13. (a) keep
    (b) than
    (c) childrin

14. (a) only
    (b) has'nt
    (c) am

15. (a) gos
    (b) hand
    (c) kind

16. (a) your
    (b) making
    (c) wach

17. (a) som
    (b) not
    (c) ask

18. (a) call
    (b) breng
    (c) coat

19. (a) down
    (b) after
    (c) siks

20. (a) lawg
    (b) told
    (c) could

21. (a) undre
    (b) chased
    (c) well

22. (a) went
    (b) these
    (c) playe

23. (a) when
    (b) bels
    (c) try

24. (a) witout
    (b) shopping
    (c) five

25. (a) rain
    (b) food
    (c) morening

Houghton Mifflin Spelling and Vocabulary. Copyright © Houghton Mifflin Company. All rights reserved.

PRACTICE A
Spelling the Short a Sound

Summing Up

The vowel sound in **hat** and **as** is called the short **a** sound. The short **a** sound may be spelled **a**.

Basic Words
1. hat
2. bag
3. as
4. am
5. has

Elephant Words
🐘 was
🐘 want

Word Shapes   Write the Basic and Elephant Words that fit into these shapes. Color the boxes in which the letter **a** spells the short **a** sound.

1.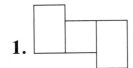

3.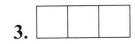

5.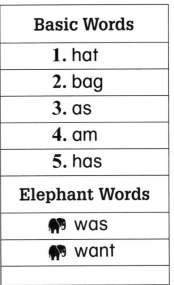

2.

4.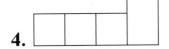

Puzzle Play   Write the missing Basic or Elephant Words. Use the letters in the boxes to answer the riddle below.

6. I ☐ __ busy getting ready for school.

7. All of my books are in my red ☐ __ __ .

8. I wave to my Dad ☐ __ I leave the house.

9. I __ __ __ ☐ to be early today.

10. My teacher ☐ __ __ a surprise for us.

Riddle: What did the dirty bird take?

Answer: __   __ __ __ __

Houghton Mifflin Spelling and Vocabulary. Copyright © Houghton Mifflin Company. All rights reserved.

Skill: Children will practice spelling words with the |ă| sound.

Home Use: Help your child practice the spelling words by having him or her complete the activities on this page. Check the completed page, and have your child practice saying and spelling any misspelled words.

Basic Words
1. hat
2. bag
3. as
4. am
5. has
6. sad
7. bat
8. ran
9. sat
10. bad

Elephant Words
🐘 was
🐘 want

PRACTICE B
Spelling the Short a Sound

Stairway to the Stars   Write the Basic or Elephant Word for each clue.

1. ➡ rested
2. ⬇ a cap
3. ➡ owns
4. ⬇ used to be
5. ➡ to wish
6. ⬇ a wooden stick
7. ➡ awful
8. ⬇ unhappy

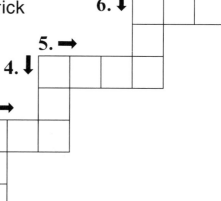

What Word Am I?   Write the letter for each clue to find a Basic Word. Then write the Basic Words.

9. My first letter is in **bed**, but not in **led**.   ___
   My second letter is in **cat**, but not in **cut**.   ___
   My third letter is in **peg**, but not in **pet**.   ___

10. My first letter is in **at**, but not in **it**.   ___
   My second letter is in **him**, but not in **hid**.   ___

11. My first letter is in **an**, but not in **on**.   ___
   My second letter is in **is**, but not in **it**.   ___

12. My first letter is in **red**, but not in **bed**.   ___
   My second letter is in **tan**, but not in **ten**.   ___
   My third letter is in **sun**, but not in **sum**.   ___

9. _____

10. _____

11. _____

12. _____

Skill: Children will practice spelling words with the |ă| sound.

Home Use: Help your child practice the spelling words by having him or her complete the activities on this page. Check the completed page, and have your child practice saying and spelling any misspelled words.

Houghton Mifflin Spelling and Vocabulary. Copyright © Houghton Mifflin Company. All rights reserved.

PRACTICE C
Spelling the Short a Sound

Word Towers   Start at the top of each tower. Add one letter to write the next word. Put the letters in the order that spells the word for each clue. The last word in each tower is a Challenge or Vocabulary Word.

Houghton Mifflin Spelling and Vocabulary. Copyright © Houghton Mifflin Company. All rights reserved.

Challenge Words
1. mask
2. fabric
Theme Vocabulary
3. cape
4. gown
5. vest
6. crown

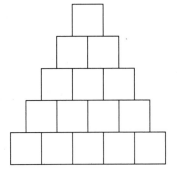

Clues

1.

the letter between **n** and **p**

rhymes with **for**

to move a boat

a big, black bird

a hat for a king

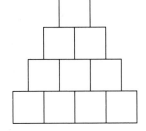

2.

the first letter

rhymes with **has**

to question

a cover for the face

The Latest Style   Write sentences that tell what the people in the picture are saying. Use the words **fabric**, **cape**, **gown**, and **vest**.

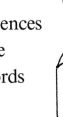

_____

- -

_____

- -

_____

_____

- -

Skill: Children will practice spelling words with the |ă| sound and words related to the theme of costumes.

Home Use: Help your child practice the spelling words by having him or her complete the activities on this page. Check the completed page, and have your child practice saying and spelling any misspelled words.

Unit **1** Test: Spelling the Short a Sound

Read each sentence. Is the underlined word spelled
right or wrong? Mark your answer.

	Right	**Wrong**
Sample: Throw away that <u>cann</u>.	○	●

		Right	Wrong
1.	Put the <u>bagg</u> of food on the table.	1. ○	○
2.	Sara <u>was</u> playing the game.	2. ○	○
3.	Theo <u>has</u> finished his book.	3. ○	○
4.	I <u>em</u> proud of you.	4. ○	○
5.	I <u>want</u> grapes after lunch.	5. ○	○
6.	Pedro could wear your <u>het</u>.	6. ○	○
7.	Is your bike the same <u>az</u> Dara's?	7. ○	○
8.	Last week there was a <u>bad</u> storm.	8. ○	○
9.	That clown looks <u>sed</u>.	9. ○	○
10.	Jimmy <u>ran</u> all the way home.	10. ○	○
11.	Meg <u>sat</u> in Grandma's chair.	11. ○	○
12.	That <u>batt</u> belongs to Gina.	12. ○	○

Houghton Mifflin Spelling and Vocabulary. Copyright © Houghton Mifflin Company. All rights reserved.

PRACTICE A
Spelling the Short e Sound

Summing Up

The vowel sound in **pet** and **leg** is called the short **e** sound. The short **e** sound may be spelled **e**.

Basic Words
1. pet
2. leg
3. ten
4. yes
5. bed
Elephant Words
🐘 any
🐘 said

Busy Bee Write the letter or letters that spell the short **e** sound to finish each Basic or Elephant Word. Color the two words in which the short **e** sound is not spelled **e**.

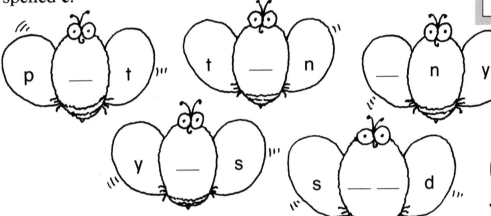

Now write the words in ABC order.

1. _____

2. _____

3. _____

4. _____

5. _____

6. _____

7. _____

8. _____

9. _____

Three of a Kind Write the Basic Word that finishes each group.

7. table, _____, chair

8. arm, _____, foot

9. five, _____, twenty

Houghton Mifflin Spelling and Vocabulary. Copyright © Houghton Mifflin Company. All rights reserved.

Skill: Children will practice spelling words with the |ĕ| sound.

Home Use: Help your child practice the spelling words by having him or her complete the activities on this page. Check the completed page, and have your child practice saying and spelling any misspelled words.

Basic Words
1. pet
2. leg
3. ten
4. yes
5. bed
6. help
7. set
8. went
9. pen
10. wet

Elephant Words
🐘 any
🐘 said

7. _____

8. _____

9. _____

10. _____

11. _____

12. _____

PRACTICE B
Spelling the Short e Sound

Hink Pink Write the Basic Word that answers the question and rhymes with the word in dark print.

1. What is a doctor for animals?   a _____ **vet**
2. What is a blushing cot?   a **red** _____
3. What does a chicken write with?   a **hen** _____
4. What is a damp plane?   a _____ **jet**
5. What do you need to lift a hippo?   _____ **men**
6. What is a ready fish trap?   a _____ **net**

1. _____   4. _____

2. _____   5. _____

3. _____   6. _____

Proofreading **7–12.** Find and cross out six Basic or Elephant Words that are spelled wrong in this story. Write each word correctly.

I needed a carrot costume for the school play. I asked Mom if she had eny ideas. Mom seid yas, she would hilp me. We wint and got ten boxes. We set some of them up. It was going to be a great costume! There was just one problem. There was only room for one laig!

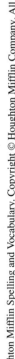

Houghton Mifflin Spelling and Vocabulary. Copyright © Houghton Mifflin Company. All rights reserved.

Skill: Children will practice spelling words with the |ĕ| sound.

Home Use: Help your child practice the spelling words by having him or her complete the activities on this page. Check the completed page, and have your child practice saying and spelling any misspelled words.

PRACTICE C
Spelling the Short e Sound

Welcome to the Zoo   Pretend you are a guide at a zoo.
Draw the path you would take to visit the animals in
ABC order.

Challenge Words
1. penguin
2. elk
Theme Vocabulary
3. snail
4. parrot
5. hamster
6. lizard

Houghton Mifflin Spelling and Vocabulary. Copyright © Houghton Mifflin Company. All rights reserved.

On a separate sheet of paper, write a sentence about each animal.
Use each Challenge and Vocabulary Word in your sentences.

Skill: Children will practice spelling words with the |ĕ| sound and words related to the theme of unusual pets.

Home Use: Help your child practice the spelling words by having him or her complete the activities on this page. Check the completed page, and have your child practice saying and spelling any misspelled words.

Unit 2 Test: Spelling the Short e Sound

Read each sentence. Is the underlined word spelled
right or wrong? Mark your answer.

	Right	Wrong
Sample: Do you want the <u>red</u> bike?	●	○

		Right	Wrong
1. Are there <u>eny</u> peanuts left?	1.	○	○
2. Can you hop on one <u>leg</u>?	2.	○	○
3. My birthday is in <u>ten</u> days.	3.	○	○
4. Did Mrs. Grey say <u>yas</u>?	4.	○	○
5. I have a worm for a <u>pet</u>.	5.	○	○
6. It is time to go to <u>bedd</u>.	6.	○	○
7. Did you hear what she <u>said</u>?	7.	○	○
8. Frank has a new green <u>penn</u>.	8.	○	○
9. Carlos will <u>set</u> the table.	9.	○	○
10. We <u>wint</u> to feed the ducks today.	10.	○	○
11. Adam was happy to <u>halp</u> Sara.	11.	○	○
12. My shoes got <u>wet</u> in the puddle.	12.	○	○

Houghton Mifflin Spelling and Vocabulary. Copyright © Houghton Mifflin Company. All rights reserved.

PRACTICE A
Spelling the Short i Sound

Summing Up

The vowel sound in **pig** and **is** is called the short **i** sound. The short **i** sound may be spelled **i**.

Basic Words
1. pig
2. win
3. is
4. six
5. his

Elephant Words
🐘 been
🐘 I

Shady Words   Color red each box that has a word in which the short **i** sound is spelled **i**. Color green the box that has the word in which the short **i** sound is not spelled **i**. Write the words.

six	his	win
cat	been	set
fun		hop
win	pig	is

1. _____

2. _____

3. _____

4. _____

5. _____

6. _____

7. _____

Look at the shape of the boxes you colored. Write the Elephant Word you see. _____

Silly Rhymes   Finish these silly sentences. Write a Basic Word to rhyme with the word in dark print.

8. My pet ____ ate a **fig**.

9. Can you **mix** ____ eggs with water?

10. How did you ____ a safety **pin**?

8. _____

9. _____

10. _____

Houghton Mifflin Spelling and Vocabulary. Copyright © Houghton Mifflin Company. All rights reserved.

Skill: Children will practice spelling words with the |ĭ| sound.

Home Use: Help your child practice the spelling words by having him or her complete the activities on this page. Check the completed page, and have your child practice saying and spelling any misspelled words.

Basic Words
1. pig
2. win
3. is
4. six
5. his
6. if
7. hit
8. fix
9. pin
10. dig

Elephant Words
🐘 been
🐘 I

PRACTICE B
Spelling the Short i Sound

Fill-In Fun   Write the missing Basic or Elephant Word.

1. needle and _____
2. _____ or lose
3. _____ and seven

4. Mike and _____
5. _____ or miss
6. _____ and hers

1. _____

2. _____

3. _____

4. _____

5. _____

6. _____

Tick-Tack-Code   Use the code below to write Basic or Elephant Words. Look at the letters and the shape of the lines around each letter.

b	d	g
f	i / e	n
p	s	x

Example: p | i⁄ | n = pin

7. _____

8. _____

9. _____

10. _____

11. _____

12. _____

7. ⅃ ⅂ ⌐

8. ◿ ⌐

9. ⌴ ⅂ L

10. ⅃ ◿ ◺ ⌐

11. ⌐ ◿ L

12. ◿ ⅂

Skill: Children will practice spelling words with the |ĭ| sound.

Home Use: Help your child practice the spelling words by having him or her complete the activities on this page. Check the completed page, and have your child practice saying and spelling any misspelled words.

Houghton Mifflin Spelling and Vocabulary. Copyright © Houghton Mifflin Company. All rights reserved.

PRACTICE C
Spelling the Short i Sound

Who's Who Rona is at a fair. She needs to find four people she has never met. Write the missing Challenge or Vocabulary Word for each clue.

1. Meg and Eve are standing on either side of the ticket _____.
2. Meg has a _____ in her hair.
3. Eve is carrying a _____ basket.
4. Ike and Meg are standing on a large _____ that they made.
5–6. Dave is holding a round _____ that a _____ gave him for winning a race.

Challenge Words
1. quilt
2. picnic
Theme Vocabulary
3. ribbon
4. booth
5. ring
6. judge

1. _____

2. _____

3. _____

4. _____

5. _____

6. _____

Then use the clues to write the name of each person.

_____ _____ _____ _____

Houghton Mifflin Spelling and Vocabulary. Copyright © Houghton Mifflin Company. All rights reserved.

Skill: Children will practice spelling words with the |ĭ| sound and words related to the theme of a country fair.

Home Use: Help your child practice the spelling words by having him or her complete the activities on this page. Check the completed page, and have your child practice saying and spelling any misspelled words.

Unit **3** Test: Spelling the Short i Sound

Read each sentence. Is the underlined word spelled right or wrong? Mark your answer.

	Right	**Wrong**
Sample: Sasha <u>did</u> her work.	●	○

	Right	Wrong
1. Who will <u>win</u> the new book?	1. ○	○
2. Jory has <u>benn</u> very busy.	2. ○	○
3. Tony gave the book to <u>hiz</u> sister.	3. ○	○
4. Aunt Brenda just fed the <u>pig</u>.	4. ○	○
5. This <u>iss</u> my teacher Mr. Taylor.	5. ○	○
6. Lou asked if <u>I</u> would go to the game.	6. ○	○
7. There are <u>sics</u> boys on my team.	7. ○	○
8. Will you <u>fix</u> my radio?	8. ○	○
9. I will be happy <u>iv</u> you visit.	9. ○	○
10. Andy can <u>deg</u> a hole in the sand.	10. ○	○
11. That <u>pin</u> is sharp.	11. ○	○
12. Chen was able to <u>hit</u> the ball.	12. ○	○

Houghton Mifflin Spelling and Vocabulary. Copyright © Houghton Mifflin Company. All rights reserved.

PRACTICE A
Spelling the Short o Sound

Basic Words
1. job
2. pot
3. nod
4. top
5. not
Elephant Word
🐘 of

Summing Up

The vowel sound in **job** and **pot** is called the short **o** sound. The short **o** sound may be spelled **o**.

Short o Nest   Use the consonant letters on the eggs and the letter **o** to write four Basic Words. Draw a line under the letter that spells the short **o** sound in each word.

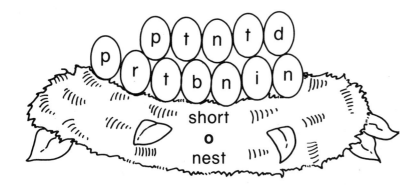

short
o
nest

Color the eight eggs you used. Find the answer to this riddle by writing the uncolored letters from the nest.

Riddle: What kind of bird is also a person's name?

Answer: ___ o ___ ___ ___

Into the Woods   Write the missing Basic or Elephant Words to finish the sentences in Cara's notebook.

My family went for a walk in the woods. It was my __(5)__ to find a bird's nest. At first I could __(6)__ see one. Then I looked up to the __(7)__ of the oak tree. There was a nest full __(8)__ eggs!

1. _____

2. _____

3. _____

4. _____

5. _____

6. _____

7. _____

8. _____

Houghton Mifflin Spelling and Vocabulary. Copyright © Houghton Mifflin Company. All rights reserved.

Skill: Children will practice spelling words with the |ŏ| sound.

Home Use: Help your child practice the spelling words by having him or her complete the activities on this page. Check the completed page, and have your child practice saying and spelling any misspelled words.

Basic Words
1. job
2. pot
3. nod
4. top
5. not
6. dot
7. fox
8. mop
9. spot
10. hop
Elephant Word
🐘 of

PRACTICE B
Spelling the Short o Sound

Buckle Up!   All of the seat belts need to be closed. Draw lines to match the parts of the seat belts to spell Basic or Elephant Words. Write the words.

1. _____   4. _____

2. _____   5. _____

3. _____   6. _____

Park the Car   Draw a line to match each meaning with a Basic Word. Write the Basic Words.

7. | a deep pan |

8. | a **no** word |

9. | jump |

10. | a cover |

11. | see |

hop
pot
top
spot
not

7. _____
8. _____
9. _____
10. _____
11. _____

Skill: Children will practice spelling words with the |ŏ| sound.

Home Use: Help your child practice the spelling words by having him or her complete the activities on this page. Check the completed page, and have your child practice saying and spelling any misspelled words.

18

Houghton Mifflin Spelling and Vocabulary. Copyright © Houghton Mifflin Company. All rights reserved.

PRACTICE C

Spelling the Short o Sound

Houghton Mifflin Spelling and Vocabulary. Copyright © Houghton Mifflin Company. All rights reserved.

Challenge Words
1. block
2. hospital
Theme Vocabulary
3. careful
4. injure
5. exit
6. alarm

Word Pairs   Write the words that complete each pair of sentences. Use a Challenge or Vocabulary Word in each pair.

1–2. A teacher works in a _____.
A doctor works in a _____.

1. _____   2. _____

3–4. You smell thick, black _____.
You hear the fire _____.

3. _____   4. _____

5–6. You can walk out an _____.
You can walk in an _____.

5. _____   6. _____

Best Sellers   Write the missing Challenge or Vocabulary Word for each book title. Use capital letters correctly.

7. Being _____ with Fire
   by Otto B. Safe

8. Never _____ a Stairway
   by Betsy Mae Trip

9. What to Do When You _____ Yourself
   by Iva Bandage

7. _____

8. _____

9. _____

Skill: Children will practice spelling words with the |ŏ| sound and words related to the theme of safety at home and at school.

Home Use: Help your child practice the spelling words by having him or her complete the activities on this page. Check the completed page, and have your child practice saying and spelling any misspelled words.

Unit 4 Test: Spelling the Short o Sound

Each item below gives three spellings of a word.
Choose the correct spelling. Mark the letter for that
word.

Sample:			**ANSWERS**
a. boks	**b.** bux	**c.** box	ⓐ ⓑ ●

1. **a.** not	**b.** nott	**c.** nat	1. ⓐ ⓑ ⓒ
2. **a.** top	**b.** topp	**c.** toop	2. ⓐ ⓑ ⓒ
3. **a.** ov	**b.** of	**c.** uf	3. ⓐ ⓑ ⓒ
4. **a.** pott	**b.** patt	**c.** pot	4. ⓐ ⓑ ⓒ
5. **a.** job	**b.** jub	**c.** jobb	5. ⓐ ⓑ ⓒ
6. **a.** nod	**b.** nodd	**c.** nud	6. ⓐ ⓑ ⓒ
7. **a.** hopp	**b.** hop	**c.** hup	7. ⓐ ⓑ ⓒ
8. **a.** dott	**b.** dat	**c.** dot	8. ⓐ ⓑ ⓒ
9. **a.** sput	**b.** spot	**c.** spott	9. ⓐ ⓑ ⓒ
10. **a.** mup	**b.** mopp	**c.** mop	10. ⓐ ⓑ ⓒ
11. **a.** foks	**b.** fex	**c.** fox	11. ⓐ ⓑ ⓒ

Houghton Mifflin Spelling and Vocabulary. Copyright © Houghton Mifflin Company. All rights reserved.

PRACTICE A
Spelling the Short u Sound

Summing Up

The vowel sound in **sun** and **mud** is called the short **u** sound. The short **u** sound may be spelled **u**.

Basic Words
1. sun
2. mud
3. bug
4. fun
5. but
Elephant Words
🐘 some
🐘 from

Picture This   Write the letter that begins each picture name. Make Basic Words.

1. + + =

2. + + =

3.  + + =

4.  + + + =

1. _____

2. _____

3. _____

4. _____

Riddles   Write a Basic or Elephant Word to finish each riddle. Then see if you can think of the answer to each riddle.

5. What fruit cannot lie in the hot _____?

6. When do _____ cars get angry?

7. What kind of music do dads have _____ singing?

8. How can you keep a skunk _____ smelling?

5. _____

6. _____

7. _____

8. _____

Riddle Answers: 5. a banana because it peels **6.** when they come to a crossroad **7.** pop music **8.** hold its nose

Houghton Mifflin Spelling and Vocabulary. Copyright © Houghton Mifflin Company. All rights reserved.

Skill: Children will practice spelling words with the |ŭ| sound.

Home Use: Help your child practice the spelling words by having him or her complete the activities on this page. Check the completed page, and have your child practice saying and spelling any misspelled words.

Basic Words
1. sun
2. mud
3. bug
4. fun
5. but
6. hug
7. bun
8. nut
9. bus
10. rug
Elephant Words
🐘 some
🐘 from

PRACTICE B
Spelling the Short u Sound

Word Search Write a word for each clue. Then circle each word in the puzzle. Look across and down.

1. a machine to drive
2. a good time
3. wet dirt
4. a kind of seed

5. a floor covering
6. an insect
7. a few
8. a bright star

1. _____

2. _____

3. _____

4. _____

5. _____

6. _____

7. _____

8. _____

x	a	s	o	m	e	r	b	u	s
p	n	u	t	u	i	r	u	g	l
f	u	n	v	d	w	o	g	u	b

Proofreading 9–12. Find and cross out four Basic or Elephant Words that are spelled wrong in Shirley's list. Write each word correctly.

- Eat a bunn for breakfast.
- Get some money frome Dad.
- Have fun at the park, bot do not stay late.
- Walk in the mud. Do not walk on the rug.
- Give Mom a heg.

9. _____

10. _____

11. _____

12. _____

Skill: Children will practice spelling words with the short |ŭ| sound.

Home Use: Help your child practice the spelling words by having him or her complete the activities on this page. Check the completed page, and have your child practice saying and spelling any misspelled words.

Houghton Mifflin Spelling and Vocabulary. Copyright © Houghton Mifflin Company. All rights reserved.

PRACTICE C
Spelling the Short u Sound

What Class Think how the words in each group are alike. Write the missing Challenge or Vocabulary Words. In the box below each group, write a Vocabulary Word that tells about all the things in the group.

Challenge Words
1. thunder
2. puddle
Theme Vocabulary
3. summer
4. winter
5. season
6. weather

spring
fall
1.
2.

lightning
rain
wind
4.

⬇

3.

⬇

5.

Double Trouble Write a word pair for each clue. Use one Challenge or Vocabulary Word in each word pair.

a small pool of water and dirt

6. __ __ __ __   __ __ __ __ __

a place to learn in July

7. __ __ __ __ __ __   __ __ __ __ __

skiing, sledding, and ice hockey

8. __ __ __ __ __ __   __ __ __ __ __

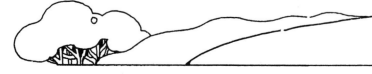

Houghton Mifflin Spelling and Vocabulary. Copyright © Houghton Mifflin Company. All rights reserved.

Skill: Children will practice spelling words with the |ŭ| sound and words related to the theme of seasons of the year.

Home Use: Help your child practice the spelling words by having him or her complete the activities on this page. Check the completed page, and have your child practice saying and spelling any misspelled words.

Unit 5 Test: Spelling the Short u Sound

Each item below gives three spellings of a word.
Choose the correct spelling. Mark the letter for that
word.

Sample:			ANSWERS
a. upp	**b.** up	**c.** op	ⓐ ● ⓒ

1. **a.** but **b.** bott **c.** buut   1. ⓐ ⓑ ⓒ

2. **a.** mudd **b.** med **c.** mud   2. ⓐ ⓑ ⓒ

3. **a.** frum **b.** from **c.** fromm   3. ⓐ ⓑ ⓒ

4. **a.** buug **b.** bug **c.** bugg   4. ⓐ ⓑ ⓒ

5. **a.** fun **b.** fen **c.** fonn   5. ⓐ ⓑ ⓒ

6. **a.** som **b.** sume **c.** some   6. ⓐ ⓑ ⓒ

7. **a.** sun **b.** sonn **c.** sunn   7. ⓐ ⓑ ⓒ

8. **a.** bon **b.** bun **c.** bund   8. ⓐ ⓑ ⓒ

9. **a.** heg **b.** hugg **c.** hug   9. ⓐ ⓑ ⓒ

10. **a.** nut **b.** nutt **c.** nott   10. ⓐ ⓑ ⓒ

11. **a.** rog **b.** ruug **c.** rug   11. ⓐ ⓑ ⓒ

12. **a.** bas **b.** bus **c.** bos   12. ⓐ ⓑ ⓒ

Houghton Mifflin Spelling and Vocabulary. Copyright © Houghton Mifflin Company. All rights reserved.

BULLETIN BOARD

SHORT STREET

Short a Sound

hat	sad	sat	ran	bad
bat	want	has	bag	am

I am home!

How to make: Make a sign that says "Short Street." Make a roof out of construction paper and attach it to the bulletin board. The lower edge of the roof should be the width of five sheets of construction paper. For Unit 1, write *Short a Sound* on a label and attach it to the roof. Change the label on the roof each week to match the spelling principle in the unit being studied. As an alternative, you may wish to allow room for five roofs, adding a new roof each week so that by the end of the cycle the students have created a neighborhood of five houses.

How to use: Have each student choose a Basic or Elephant Word to illustrate on a sheet of construction paper. Students should write their word on their paper and illustrate the word using a scene that could happen inside a house. A student illustrating the word *sat,* for example, might draw a scene of a family sitting at a kitchen table. Mount the illustrations under the roof to form the structure of the house.

Houghton Mifflin Spelling and Vocabulary. Copyright © Houghton Mifflin Company. All rights reserved.

Use: For use with Units 1-5.

SPELLING NEWSLETTER
for Students and Their Families

Getting Started

This year your child is using *Houghton Mifflin Spelling and Vocabulary*. The authors of this program have organized word lists according to spelling patterns and word parts common to English to help your child learn to spell the words in the weekly word lists and to provide skills that will help him or her spell many other words. The program also emphasizes vocabulary-building activities with words from the unit word lists and with theme-related word lists. Many opportunities are provided for your child to apply proofreading, dictionary, and thesaurus skills, to use writing skills, and to participate in an assortment of learning games.

Units 1 through 5 of your child's book have dealt with spelling patterns for the vowel sounds heard in *ran, bed, his, top,* and *fun.*

Word Lists

Your child has been studying the words below as well as others with similar patterns.

UNIT 1	UNIT 2	UNIT 3	UNIT 4	UNIT 5
bag	leg	pig	job	mud
am	yes	win	nod	fun
has	bed	his	top	but
sad	went	if	dot	hug
ran	pen	hit	fox	bus
sat	wet	fix	hop	rug

🏠 *Family Activity*

Fold 3 sheets of paper in half vertically to make a Word Wangler. Staple the sheets together across the top of the long side, and cut the booklet in 2 places to make 3 equal sections, as shown. Write *b, w, h, l,* or *r* on each of the left-hand pages. Write *g, t, s, d,* or *n* on each of the right-hand pages. Write *a, e, i, o,* or *u* on each of the middle pages.

Look at the first page, on which *b, a,* and *g* appear. Since this combination of letters makes a word, write *bag* on a piece of paper. Together, flip the pages on the right to make and write as many words as possible. Then flip the pages on the left, repeating the process. When you have tried all the combinations, look at your list of words and circle any words from Units 1 through 5.

Houghton Mifflin Spelling and Vocabulary. Copyright © Houghton Mifflin Company. All rights reserved.

Boletín de noticias de ortografía
para estudiantes y para sus familias

Para comenzar

Este año su hijo o hija está usando el libro *Houghton Mifflin Spelling and Vocabulary*. Los autores de este programa han preparado listas de palabras organizadas según patrones de ortografía y según partes de palabras que son comunes en inglés, para ayudar a su hijo o hija a aprender la ortografía de esas palabras y para darle conocimientos que le permitirán determinar la ortografía de muchas otras palabras. El programa también ofrece actividades para ampliar el vocabulario que contienen palabras de cada unidad y palabras relacionadas con un tema. Su hijo o hija podrá practicar corrección de pruebas y manejo de diccionarios y de libros de sinónimos, y participará en juegos de aprendizaje.

Listas de palabras

Su hijo o hija ha estado estudiando las siguientes palabras y otras palabras que siguen patrones similares en las Unidades 1 a 5 del libro *Houghton Mifflin Spelling and Vocabulary*.

UNIDAD 1	UNIDAD 2	UNIDAD 3	UNIDAD 4	UNIDAD 5
bag	leg	pig	job	mud
am	yes	win	nod	fun
has	bed	his	top	but
sad	went	if	dot	hug
ran	pen	hit	fox	bus
sat	wet	fix	hop	rug

👪 Actividad para la familia

Doblen tres hojas de papel por la mitad verticalmente para crear un librito. Engrapen las hojas por la parte de arriba del lado largo y corten el librito en dos lugares para hacer 3 secciones iguales, como se ve en la ilustración. Escriban *b, w, h, l* ó *r* en cada una de las páginas de la izquierda. Escriban *g, t, s, d* ó *n* en cada una de las páginas de la derecha. Escriban *a, e, i, o* ó *u* en cada una de las páginas del medio.

Como la combinación de letras *b, a* y *g* en la primera página forma una palabra, escriban *bag* en un papel. Pasen las páginas de la derecha para poder componer y escribir todas las palabras posibles. Después pasen las de la izquierda, repitiendo el proceso. Cuando tengan todas las combinaciones de palabras posibles, háganle un círculo alrededor de todas las que figuren en las Unidades 1 a 5.

Houghton Mifflin Spelling and Vocabulary. Copyright © Houghton Mifflin Company. All rights reserved.

SPELL IT!

SPELLING GAME

Players: 3 or more

You need: a copy of the game board for each player, pencils

How to play: One player is the caller. Each player uses a copy of the game board below and writes one vowel (**a, e, i, o,** or **u**) in the middle of each box. The caller calls out a Basic Word from Units 1, 2, 3, 4, or 5. The other players decide what vowel is used to spell that word. They find the vowel on their game boards and finish writing the word in the box. The caller calls out more words until one player has filled in the words in a row of boxes. The row can go across, down, or at a slant. The caller checks the words. If the words are correct, the player wins and becomes the next caller. Players use a new game board for each new game.

	SPELL IT!	

Houghton Mifflin Spelling and Vocabulary. Copyright © Houghton Mifflin Company. All rights reserved.

Use: For use with Units 1-5.

Unit 6 Review: Test A

Read each sentence. One of the underlined words in each
sentence is spelled wrong. Mark the letter for that word.

Sample:
My purple boot has mod on it.
    a   b

ANSWERS
ⓐ ●

1. Does Simon have a fon job?
              a   b

2. Della has a pig for a pett.
              a   b

3. If I nod, my het will fall off.
       a   b

4. Kay put som plums in the bag.
          a   b

5. The leg of the table es broken.
       a   b

6. I have bein playing in the sun.
          a   b

7. That bugg has six legs.
        a   b

8. Is there any soup in the pott?
          a   b

9. I sat up in bed az the alarm rang.
              a   b

10. I em not riding my bike today.
       a b

11. Reba ran but she did not wen.
            a   b

12. Paul's bus waz ten minutes late.
              a   b

1. ⓐ ⓑ
2. ⓐ ⓑ
3. ⓐ ⓑ
4. ⓐ ⓑ
5. ⓐ ⓑ
6. ⓐ ⓑ
7. ⓐ ⓑ
8. ⓐ ⓑ
9. ⓐ ⓑ
10. ⓐ ⓑ
11. ⓐ ⓑ
12. ⓐ ⓑ

Houghton Mifflin Spelling and Vocabulary. Copyright © Houghton Mifflin Company. All rights reserved.

Unit **6** Review: Test B

Read each sentence. One of the underlined words in each sentence is spelled wrong. Mark the letter for that word.

Sample: **ANSWERS**

Fran will <u>halp</u> me to <u>pin</u> the flower.   ● ⓑ
         a   **b**

1. Lin was <u>saad</u> when we <u>went</u> home.   1. ⓐ ⓑ
      a   **b**

2. Ella <u>ran</u> to give Grandma a <u>hugg</u>.   2. ⓐ ⓑ
     a   **b**

3. Jon will <u>hop</u> <u>ef</u> you ask him.   3. ⓐ ⓑ
       a **b**

4. Erin <u>het</u> the ball with the <u>bat</u>.   4. ⓐ ⓑ
      a   **b**

5. Tim <u>sat</u> in <u>wat</u> paint.   5. ⓐ ⓑ
      a   **b**

6. Did you <u>sett</u> my <u>pen</u> on the desk?   6. ⓐ ⓑ
        a   **b**

7. Can she <u>fix</u> the <u>sput</u>?   7. ⓐ ⓑ
       a   **b**

8. What <u>bus</u> does Kerry <u>wunt</u> to take?   8. ⓐ ⓑ
     a   **b**

9. Move the <u>rog</u> from Ivan's room.   9. ⓐ ⓑ
      a **b**

10. May <u>I</u> use any <u>mmop</u> or broom?   10. ⓐ ⓑ
    a   **b**

11. Vito <u>saed</u> he saw a <u>fox</u>.   11. ⓐ ⓑ
     a   **b**

12. Watch the animal <u>deg</u> for the <u>nut</u>.   12. ⓐ ⓑ
           a   **b**

Houghton Mifflin Spelling and Vocabulary. Copyright © Houghton Mifflin Company. All rights reserved.

Prewriting Ideas: Class Story

Choosing a Topic   Here is a list of ideas that one class made for writing a class story. What special times in class do these ideas make you think of?

On the lines below **My Three Ideas**, write three special things that your class has done together. Which idea do you like the best? Which one will a reader be interested in too? Which one do you remember most about? Circle the topic that you would like to write about.

Ideas for Writing

Pet Day at School	A Surprise for Our Teacher
Our Class Picnic	The Day Our Room Flooded

My Three Ideas

1. _____

2. _____

3. _____

Exploring Your Topic   You can make a bell cluster to help you think about your idea. Copy the bell cluster onto another sheet of paper. Make the bells large enough to write on. Write your topic in the bell in the middle. In the other bells, write words that tell about your topic.

Topic

Houghton Mifflin Spelling and Vocabulary. Copyright © Houghton Mifflin Company. All rights reserved.

Use: For use with Step 1: Prewriting on page 59.

PRACTICE A
Vowel-Consonant-e Spellings

Summing Up

The vowel sounds in **late** and **five** are called the long **a** and the long **i** sounds. These long vowel sounds may be spelled by the vowel-consonant-**e** pattern.

Basic Words
1. five
2. late
3. nine
4. made
5. side
Elephant Words
🐘 give
🐘 have

A Fine Bunch Help Mickie. Write the words from his bananas under the correct sounds.

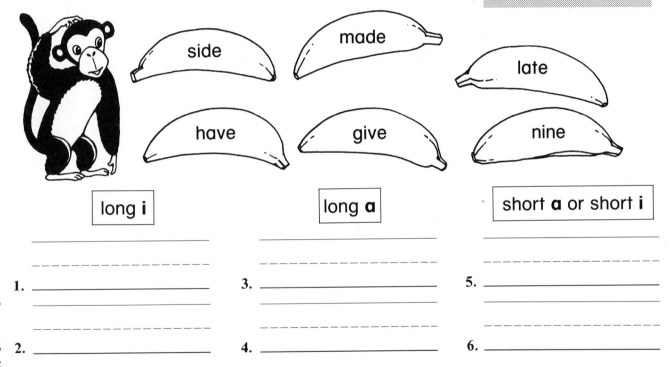

long i	long a	short a or short i

1. _____

2. _____

3. _____

4. _____

5. _____

6. _____

Monkey Rhymes Write the Basic Word for each set of clues.

7. It is a monkey that is not on time.
   It rhymes with **date**.

7. _____

8. It is one more than four monkeys.
   It rhymes with **dive**.

8. _____

9. It is not a monkey's front or back.
   It rhymes with **wide**.

9. _____

Houghton Mifflin Spelling and Vocabulary. Copyright © Houghton Mifflin Company. All rights reserved.

Skill: Children will practice spelling words with the |ā| and the |ī| sounds.

Home Use: Help your child practice the spelling words by having him or her complete the activities on this page. Check the completed page, and have your child practice saying and spelling any misspelled words.

33

Basic Words
1. five
2. late
3. nine
4. made
5. side
6. ate
7. fine
8. same
9. hide
10. line

Elephant Words
🐘 give
🐘 have

PRACTICE B
Vowel-Consonant-e Spellings

Crossword Clues   Write a Basic or Elephant Word for each clue.

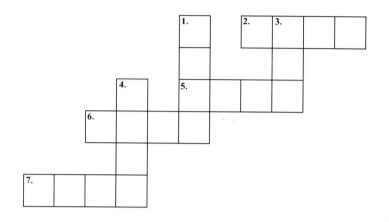

Across	**Down**
2. built	1. a long, thin mark
5. almost ten	3. rhymes with **late**
6. not the top or bottom	4. less than six
7. to own	

In the Family   Write the Basic or Elephant Word that is the opposite of the word in dark print.

8. Mr. Opposite is always **early**.
   Mrs. Opposite is always _____.

9. Mr. Opposite wears a **different** hat every day.
   Mrs. Opposite always wears the _____ one.

10. Mr. Opposite wants to **get** some new books.
    Mrs. Opposite wants to _____ away her old ones.

11. Mr. Opposite likes to **show** his paintings.
    Mrs. Opposite likes to _____ hers.

12. Mr. Opposite thinks the weather is **awful**.
    Mrs. Opposite thinks it is just _____.

8. _____

9. _____

10. _____

11. _____

12. _____

Skill: Children will practice spelling words with the |ā| and the |ī| sounds.

Home Use: Help your child practice the spelling words by having him or her complete the activities on this page. Check the completed page, and have your child practice saying and spelling any misspelled words.

Houghton Mifflin Spelling and Vocabulary. Copyright © Houghton Mifflin Company. All rights reserved.

PRACTICE C
Vowel-Consonant-e Spellings

School Books   Write the missing Challenge or
Vocabulary Word for each book title. Use capital letters.

1. How to Be a Smart _____   by Iva Brain
2. Games to Play in the _____   by P. E. Time
3. How to Correct a _____   by E. Raser

1. _____   3. _____

2. _____

Challenge Words
1. mistake
2. write
Theme Vocabulary
3. pupil
4. absent
5. locker
6. gym

Addagrams   Write a word for each clue. Then write
the correct letters in the numbered boxes. The letters
will spell a Challenge or Vocabulary Word.

4.

a rubber wheel = $\overline{}_{4} \, \overline{}_{3} \, \overline{}_{2} \, \overline{}_{5}$

a thin piece of metal = $\overline{}_{1} \, \overline{}_{3} \, \overline{}_{2} \, \overline{}_{5}$

1	2	3	4	5

5.

something a key fits = $\overline{}_{1} \, \overline{}_{2} \, \overline{}_{3} \, \overline{}_{4}$

the middle of an apple = $\overline{}_{3} \, \overline{}_{2} \, \overline{}_{6} \, \overline{}_{5}$

1	2	3	4	5	6

6.

an animal that flies = $\overline{}_{2} \, \overline{}_{1} \, \overline{}_{6}$

mailed = $\overline{}_{3} \, \overline{}_{4} \, \overline{}_{5} \, \overline{}_{6}$

1	2	3	4	5	6

Houghton Mifflin Spelling and Vocabulary. Copyright © Houghton Mifflin Company. All rights reserved.

Skill: Children will practice spelling words with the vowel-consonant-*e* pattern and words related to the theme of schools.

Home Use: Help your child practice the spelling words by having him or her complete the activities on this page. Check the completed page, and have your child practice saying and spelling any misspelled words.

Unit 7 Test: Vowel-Consonant-e Spellings

Read each sentence. Is the underlined word spelled right or wrong? Mark your answer.

	Right	Wrong
Sample: Freda <u>gave</u> me a funny hat.	●	○

		Right	Wrong
1.	Wave from the <u>sied</u> of the road.	○	○
2.	The library has <u>nine</u> new books.	○	○
3.	Bruno is never <u>late</u> for school.	○	○
4.	Edith <u>maed</u> a big mistake.	○	○
5.	I will <u>have</u> another muffin.	○	○
6.	They will leave in <u>five</u> minutes.	○	○
7.	Will Gabe <u>gife</u> you his skates?	○	○
8.	Draw a red <u>line</u> across the paper.	○	○
9.	Who will <u>hied</u> the gift?	○	○
10.	Nelson <u>ate</u> all of his dinner.	○	○
11.	Stan and Nina have the <u>saem</u> shoes.	○	○
12.	You did a <u>finn</u> job on the report.	○	○

Houghton Mifflin Spelling and Vocabulary. Copyright © Houghton Mifflin Company. All rights reserved.

PRACTICE A
More Vowel-Consonant-e Spellings

Basic Words
1. bone
2. nose
3. use
4. these
5. rope
Elephant Words
🐘 one
🐘 goes

Summing Up

The vowel sounds in **bone**, **use**, and **these** are called the long **o**, the long **u**, and the long **e** vowel sounds. These long vowel sounds may be spelled by the vowel-consonant-**e** pattern.

Puzzle Play Write the missing Basic or Elephant Words. Use the letters in the boxes to spell the name of a kind of bird.

1. My dog ☐ __ __ __ into the yard every day.

2. Fang digs ☐ __ __ hole in the dirt.

3. He puts his tasty __ ☐ __ __ inside.

4. He sniffs it with his __ __ ☐ __.

5. Fang never fills in __ __ __ __ ☐ holes.

Secret Word: __ __ __ __ __

Bingo! Color each box that has a word with the long **o**, the long **u**, or the long **e** vowel sound. Write the words that make a row.

fox	pot	bus	these	hug
these	rope	bone	goes	use
nose	some	sun	rope	from
fun	bone	hop	mud	these

Now circle the word you wrote that does not have the vowel-consonant-e pattern.

6. _____

7. _____

8. _____

9. _____

10. _____

Houghton Mifflin Spelling and Vocabulary. Copyright © Houghton Mifflin Company. All rights reserved.

Skill: Children will practice spelling words with the lōl, the lūl, and the lēl sounds.

Home Use: Help your child practice the spelling words by having him or her complete the activities on this page. Check the completed page, and have your child practice saying and spelling any misspelled words.

Basic Words
1. bone
2. nose
3. use
4. these
5. rope
6. home
7. cute
8. close
9. hope
10. those

Elephant Words
🐘 one
🐘 goes

PRACTICE B
More Vowel-Consonant-e Spellings

Letter Math   Add and take away letters to make Basic Words. Write the words.

1. the − e + ose = ?   **4.** hip − ip + ome = ?
2. cap − ap + ute = ?   **5.** hat − at + ope = ?
3. clay − ay + ose = ?   **6.** big − ig + one = ?

1. _____   4. _____

2. _____   5. _____

3. _____   6. _____

Proofreading   **7–12.** Find and cross out six Basic or Elephant Words that are spelled wrong in these airplane messages. Write each word correctly.

7. _____

8. _____

9. _____

10. _____

11. _____

12. _____

Do not let your noz burn.
Please yous Ray's sun cream.

We hope you will visit Dave's Store.
We sell ladders, paint, and rop!

Take home Mia's handmade hats for
two dollars! You can't beat theez prices.

Everyone gose to Patty's Pizza!
Buy two for the price of wun!

Skill: Children will practice spelling words with the |ō|, the |ū|, and the |ē| sounds.

Home Use: Help your child practice the spelling words by having him or her complete the activities on this page. Check the completed page, and have your child practice saying and spelling any misspelled words.

Houghton Mifflin Spelling and Vocabulary. Copyright © Houghton Mifflin Company. All rights reserved.

PRACTICE C
More Vowel-Consonant-e Spellings

Say It with Pictures   You can draw letters to show the meanings of the words they spell. Look at the example. Make a drawing for each Challenge and Vocabulary Word. Then write the word.

Challenge Words
1. globe
2. mule
Theme Vocabulary
3. huge
4. sharp
5. reptile
6. fossil

Example:

ate

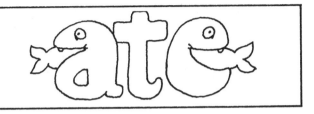

1. _____

2. _____

3. _____

4. _____

5. _____

6. _____

Houghton Mifflin Spelling and Vocabulary. Copyright © Houghton Mifflin Company. All rights reserved.

Skill: Children will practice spelling words with the vowel-consonant-*e* pattern and words related to the theme of dinosaurs.

Home Use: Help your child practice the spelling words by having him or her complete the activities on this page. Check the completed page, and have your child practice saying and spelling any misspelled words.

Unit 8 Test: More Vowel-Consonant-e Spellings

Each item below gives three spellings of a word. Choose the correct spelling. Mark the letter for that word.

Sample:			ANSWERS
a. ridde	**b.** ride	**c.** ried	ⓐ ● ⓒ

1. **a.** rope	**b.** rop	**c.** ropp	1. ⓐ ⓑ ⓒ
2. **a.** oon	**b.** une	**c.** one	2. ⓐ ⓑ ⓒ
3. **a.** thes	**b.** these	**c.** tese	3. ⓐ ⓑ ⓒ
4. **a.** bonn	**b.** bone	**c.** bon	4. ⓐ ⓑ ⓒ
5. **a.** uze	**b.** uss	**c.** use	5. ⓐ ⓑ ⓒ
6. **a.** goes	**b.** gos	**c.** gose	6. ⓐ ⓑ ⓒ
7. **a.** nos	**b.** noes	**c.** nose	7. ⓐ ⓑ ⓒ
8. **a.** close	**b.** clos	**c.** cloes	8. ⓐ ⓑ ⓒ
9. **a.** kute	**b.** cute	**c.** cutt	9. ⓐ ⓑ ⓒ
10. **a.** hup	**b.** hoep	**c.** hope	10. ⓐ ⓑ ⓒ
11. **a.** home	**b.** hom	**c.** homm	11. ⓐ ⓑ ⓒ
12. **a.** thos	**b.** those	**c.** tose	12. ⓐ ⓑ ⓒ

Houghton Mifflin Spelling and Vocabulary. Copyright © Houghton Mifflin Company. All rights reserved.

PRACTICE A
Words with Consonant Clusters

Summing Up

A **consonant cluster** is two consonant letters whose sounds are blended together. Some consonant clusters are **tr**, **sw**, **st**, **cl**, **xt**, **br**, and **gl**.

Basic Words
1. trip
2. swim
3. step
4. nest
5. club

Juggling Act   Color the balls with consonant clusters. Draw a line from each cluster to an ending to make a Basic Word. Then write the word.

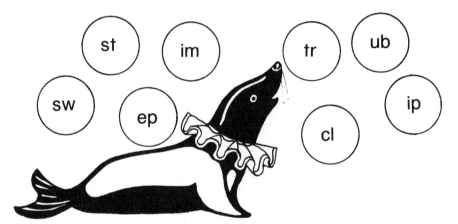

1. _____

2. _____

3. _____

4. _____

Word Search   Write a Basic Word for each clue. Then circle each word. Look across and down.

5. a bird's home
6. a way of walking
7. to move through water
8. a journey

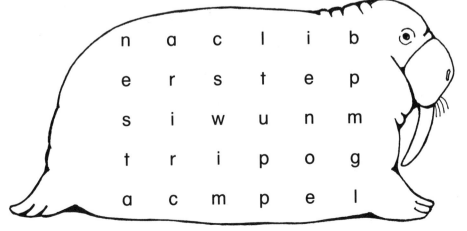

5. _____

6. _____

7. _____

8. _____

Houghton Mifflin Spelling and Vocabulary. Copyright © Houghton Mifflin Company. All rights reserved.

Skill: Children will practice spelling words with **consonant clusters.**

Home Use: Help your child practice the spelling words by having him or her complete the activities on this page. Check the completed page, and have your child practice saying and spelling any misspelled words.

Basic Words
1. trip
2. swim
3. step
4. nest
5. club
6. stone
7. next
8. brave
9. glad
10. lost

PRACTICE B
Words with Consonant Clusters

Puzzle Play Write a Basic Word for each clue. Use the letters in the boxes to spell two words that tell what the bee in the cartoon is.

1. a heavy stick of wood __ __ __ □
2. where birds live __ □ __ __
3. to float or move in water □ __ __ __
4. coming right after __ __ __ □
5. put a foot forward □ __ __ □
6. not afraid __ __ __ □
7. happy □ __ __
8. the opposite of **found** □ __ __ __
9. a piece of rock __ __ __ □
10. vacation __ □ __ __

Secret Words:

the __ __ __ __ __ __ __ __ __ __

EXTRA! Draw your own cartoon. Write a word pair to tell about it. Use at least one Basic Word.

Houghton Mifflin Spelling and Vocabulary. Copyright © Houghton Mifflin Company. All rights reserved.

Skill: Children will practice spelling words with **consonant clusters**.

Home Use: Help your child practice the spelling words by having him or her complete the activities on this page. Check the completed page, and have your child practice saying and spelling any misspelled words.

PRACTICE C
Words with Consonant Clusters

Who Did It?   Read the story and the clues. Write the missing Challenge and Vocabulary Words for the clues.

Four hikers stayed in a small hut in the woods. The last hiker to leave the next morning forgot to close the door. A raccoon got in and ate all the food. Who forgot to close the door?

Challenge Words
1. branches
2. storm
Theme Vocabulary
3. gear
4. cabin
5. clearing
6. camper

Clues

1. Jane put her camping ____ in her pack.
2. She went out the ____ door at seven o'clock.
3. Cleo, the oldest ____, left ten minutes after Jane did.
4. She crossed a ____ that had no trees.
5. Twenty minutes after Cleo left, Sue went off to gather twigs and ____.
6. Ten minutes before Sue left, Tina left to give everyone raincoats in case of a ____.

1. _____
2. _____
3. _____
4. _____
5. _____
6. _____

Now write the time each hiker left the hut.

Jane _____   Cleo _____   Sue _____   Tina _____

Who forgot to close the door? _____

Houghton Mifflin Spelling and Vocabulary. Copyright © Houghton Mifflin Company. All rights reserved.

Skill: Children will practice spelling words with consonant clusters and words related to the theme of camping and hiking.

Home Use: Help your child practice the spelling words by having him or her complete the activities on this page. Check the completed page, and have your child practice saying and spelling any misspelled words.

Unit 9 Test: Words with Consonant Clusters

Read each sentence. Find the correctly spelled word to complete each sentence. Mark the letter next to that word.

Sample: **ANSWERS**
Jack did not ___ on the ice.   ● slip   ⓑ slep   ⓒ slup

1. Al took one bag on his ___.   ⓐ trep   ⓑ tripp   ⓒ trip

2. Our ___ went to the park.   ⓐ club   ⓑ culb   ⓒ clubb

3. Do not ___ on a wet floor.   ⓐ stap   ⓑ step   ⓒ stip

4. Eva came to ___ in the pool.   ⓐ swem   ⓑ swom   ⓒ swim

5. I saw a robin's ___.   ⓐ nest   ⓑ nist   ⓒ nesst

6. Kyle threw the flat ___.   ⓐ ston   ⓑ stone   ⓒ stune

7. Lee ___ her new book.   ⓐ loct   ⓑ lostt   ⓒ lost

8. The ___ bus will come soon.   ⓐ next   ⓑ nixt   ⓒ naxt

9. I am ___ everyone had fun.   ⓐ gald   ⓑ glad   ⓒ gladd

10. The ___ girl saved Susan.   ⓐ brev   ⓑ brave   ⓒ berav

Houghton Mifflin Spelling and Vocabulary. Copyright © Houghton Mifflin Company. All rights reserved.

PRACTICE A
Words Spelled with k or ck

Summing Up

The words **lake** and **rock** end with the same consonant sound. This consonant sound may be spelled **k** or **ck**.

Basic Words
1. lake
2. rock
3. ask
4. pick
5. truck

Letter Load   Look at the spelling clue at the front of each truck. Then write the Basic Word for each picture.

k

1. _____

2. _____

ck

3. _____

4. _____

5. _____

Letter Drop   Write the Basic Word that rhymes with the word in dark print to finish each poem.

6. To hide my face, I wear a **mask**.
   If you want to see me, you must ____.

   6. _____

7. Snow is falling. I saw a **flake**.
   Is snow falling on the ____?

   7. _____

8. Thunder boomed and lightning **struck**.
   The rain splashed all around the ____.

   8. _____

Houghton Mifflin Spelling and Vocabulary. Copyright © Houghton Mifflin Company. All rights reserved.

Skill: Children will practice spelling words that end with **k** or **ck**.

Home Use: Help your child practice the spelling words by having him or her complete the activities on this page. Check the completed page, and have your child practice saying and spelling any misspelled words.

Basic Words
1. lake
2. rock
3. ask
4. pick
5. truck
6. black
7. back
8. bake
9. clock
10. kick

PRACTICE B
Words Spelled with k or ck

Riddles   Write a Basic Word to finish each riddle. Then see if you can think of the answer to each riddle.

1. What kind of trees grow near an ocean or a ____?

1. _____

2. What did the big hand on the ____ say to the little hand?

2. _____

3. What question did the little hand ____ the big hand?

3. _____

4. Why are cooks mean when they ____ a cake?

4. _____

5. What happens when you ____ a blue rock into the Red Sea?

5. _____

Proofreading   6–10. Find and cross out five Basic Words that are spelled wrong on these signs. Write each word correctly. Begin each word with a capital letter.

6. _____

7. _____

8. _____

9. _____

10. _____

6.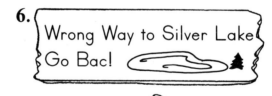
Wrong Way to Silver Lake
Go Bac!

9.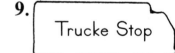
Trucke Stop

7. Blaak Hills

10.
Danger! Rok Slide

8.
Pic Your Own Blueberries!
Ask at Stand for Directions

Riddle Answers: 1. beech trees **2.** "I'll be back in an hour." **3.** "Got a minute?" **4.** because they beat eggs and whip cream **5.** It gets wet.

Houghton Mifflin Spelling and Vocabulary. Copyright © Houghton Mifflin Company. All rights reserved.

46

Skill: Children will practice spelling words that end with **k** or **ck**.

Home Use: Help your child practice the spelling words by having him or her complete the activities on this page. Check the completed page, and have your child practice saying and spelling any misspelled words.

Name _____ **Level 2 / Unit 10** ■

PRACTICE C
Words Spelled with k or ck

Crossword Clues Write the Challenge and Vocabulary
Words in the puzzle. Then write a clue for each
Across word and each **Down** word.

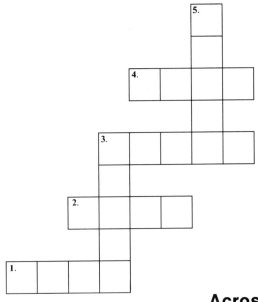

Challenge Words
1. dock
2. snake
Theme Vocabulary
3. wade
4. shore
5. brook
6. flow

Across

1. _____

2. _____

3. _____

4. _____

Down

3. _____

5. _____

Skill: Children will practice spelling words that
end with *k* or *ck* and words related to the theme
of rivers and lakes.

Home Use: Help your child practice the spelling words by having him
or her complete the activities on this page. Check the completed page,
and have your child practice saying and spelling any misspelled words.

Houghton Mifflin Spelling and Vocabulary. Copyright © Houghton Mifflin Company. All rights reserved.

Unit 10 Test: Words Spelled with k or ck

Read each sentence. Is the underlined word spelled
right or wrong? Mark your answer.

	Right	Wrong
Sample: Peter flew his new <u>kite</u>.	●	○

	Right	Wrong
1. Hans fed the ducks at the <u>lake</u>.	○	○
2. Which box would you <u>pik</u>?	○	○
3. Val has to <u>asck</u> her mother.	○	○
4. My brother drives a <u>truck</u>.	○	○
5. Troy found an interesting <u>rok</u>.	○	○
6. I often use my <u>black</u> pen.	○	○
7. Norma can <u>kik</u> the ball very far.	○	○
8. Read the <u>clock</u> on the wall.	○	○
9. What will you <u>bake</u> for the party?	○	○
10. Damon will be <u>bak</u> after lunch.	○	○

Houghton Mifflin Spelling and Vocabulary. Copyright © Houghton Mifflin Company. All rights reserved.

PRACTICE A
Words with Double Consonants

Basic Words
1. bell
2. off
3. dress
4. add
5. hill

Summing Up

In words like **bell**, **off**, and **dress**, the final consonant sound is spelled with two letters that are the same.

How Charming!   Write the missing final consonants. Then write the words in ABC order.

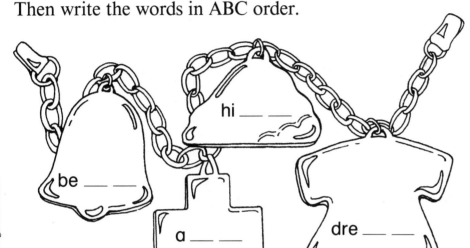

hi _ _

be _ _

a _ _

dre _ _

1. _____

2. _____

3. _____

4. _____

Silly Songs   Write a Basic Word to complete each song title. Begin each word with a capital letter.

5. I Would Climb Any _____ for Your Smile

6. Just Dance Until the Music Is Turned _____

7. I Hear a _____ Ringing in My Heart

8. Let's _____ Up for the Party

Houghton Mifflin Spelling and Vocabulary. Copyright © Houghton Mifflin Company. All rights reserved.

Skill: Children will practice spelling words that end with double consonants.

Home Use: Help your child practice the spelling words by having him or her complete the activities on this page. Check the completed page, and have your child practice saying and spelling any misspelled words.

Basic Words
1. bell
2. off
3. dress
4. add
5. hill
6. well
7. egg
8. will
9. grass
10. tell

PRACTICE B
Words with Double Consonants

Tick-Tack-Code Use the code below to write Basic Words. Look at the letters and the shape of the lines around each letter.

b	d	e
w		l
t	r	s

1. _____ 1. _____
2. _____ 2. _____
3. _____ 3. _____
4. _____ 4. _____

Mother Goose Times Write the missing Basic Words in these headlines. Begin each word with a capital letter.

Humpty Dumpty Falls __(5)__ Wall

Goose Lays Gold __(6)__ in Green __(7)__!

Jack and Jill Climb __(8)__! Jack Hurt in Fall!

Tommy Tucker __(9)__ Sing for His Supper

Snow White Can't Count!
Dwarfs Don't __(10)__ up to Seven

5. _____
6. _____
7. _____
8. _____
9. _____
10. _____

Houghton Mifflin Spelling and Vocabulary. Copyright © Houghton Mifflin Company. All rights reserved.

Skill: Children will practice words that end with double consonants.

Home Use: Help your child practice the spelling words by having him or her complete the activities on this page. Check the completed page, and have your child practice saying and spelling any misspelled words.

PRACTICE C
Words with Double Consonants

Mystery Music   Find out what instrument each boy plays. Use the clues and the chart. Mark an **X** in the boxes under the instruments each boy does not play. Draw a star in the box that shows the instrument each boy does play.

Challenge Words
1. brass
2. skill
Theme Vocabulary
3. tune
4. harp
5. tuba
6. pit

Clues

- Each boy plays a different instrument.
- No boy's name begins with the same letter as the instrument he plays.
- Ted does not play the violin.

	harp	tuba	violin
Hal			
Ted			
Vic			

Write each missing Challenge Word, Vocabulary Word, or boy's name to finish the story. Use the chart to help you.

   At two o'clock, the boys took their seats in the orchestra __(1)__ . Soon, __(2)__ began to __(3)__ his violin. Then Ted plucked at the strings of his __(4)__ . Finally, __(5)__ put the __(6)__ to his mouth and blew a few notes. He was proud of his shiny __(7)__ instrument. He hoped he had the __(8)__ to play it well.

1. _____

2. _____

3. _____

4. _____

5. _____

6. _____

7. _____

8. _____

Houghton Mifflin Spelling and Vocabulary. Copyright © Houghton Mifflin Company. All rights reserved.

Skill: Children will practice spelling words that end with double consonants and words related to the theme of songs and instruments.

Home Use: Help your child practice the spelling words by having him or her complete the activities on this page. Check the completed page, and have your child practice saying and spelling any misspelled words.

Unit **11** Test: Words with Double Consonants

Each item below gives three spellings of a word.
Choose the correct spelling. Mark the letter for that
word.

Sample: **ANSWERS**
a. fil   b. fill   c. fiil   ⓐ ● ⓒ

1. a. off   b. ofv   c. ovf   1. ⓐ ⓑ ⓒ

2. a. hil   b. holl   c. hill   2. ⓐ ⓑ ⓒ

3. a. ders   b. dress   c. dres   3. ⓐ ⓑ ⓒ

4. a. bel   b. behl   c. bell   4. ⓐ ⓑ ⓒ

5. a. add   b. adb   c. aad   5. ⓐ ⓑ ⓒ

6. a. wel   b. well   c. wehl   6. ⓐ ⓑ ⓒ

7. a. gras   b. gress   c. grass   7. ⓐ ⓑ ⓒ

8. a. egg   b. eg   c. igg   8. ⓐ ⓑ ⓒ

9. a. tel   b. tell   c. ttel   9. ⓐ ⓑ ⓒ

10. a. will   b. wwil   c. wil   10. ⓐ ⓑ ⓒ

Houghton Mifflin Spelling and Vocabulary. Copyright © Houghton Mifflin Company. All rights reserved.

Level 2 / Unit 12

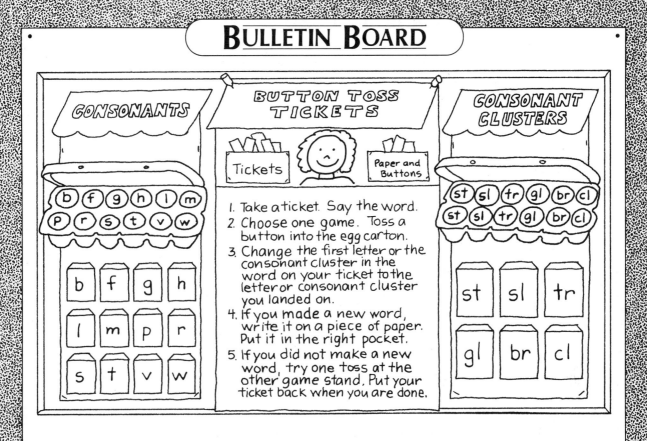

How to make: Turn your bulletin board into a school carnival to play the "Button Toss" game. From construction paper, make a ticket booth and two game stands with roofs. Make the roofs from folded paper so that they stand out from the board. On each stand attach tagboard pockets, labeling them with the single letters or consonant clusters shown. Above the pockets fasten the tops of two open cardboard egg cartons so that the cartons stand out from the board. In the compartments of each carton, print the same letters or consonant clusters, as shown.

   On the ticket booth, attach a pocket to hold "tickets." To make tickets, write Basic Words from the cycle on index cards. Underline the letter or the consonant cluster that begins each word. (See the list of suggested words below.) Attach an envelope of paper strips and buttons near the ticket pocket and label it as shown. Post the directions on the booth, as shown.

How to use: Introduce the game to the whole class. Read the directions aloud and demonstrate how to play the game. Students may play the game in pairs or individually as time permits.

<u>l</u>ate   <u>b</u>one   <u>h</u>ill   <u>gl</u>ad   <u>n</u>ine   <u>gr</u>ass   <u>p</u>ick   <u>t</u>ell   <u>tr</u>ip   <u>b</u>ack   <u>h</u>ide

Houghton Mifflin Spelling and Vocabulary. Copyright © Houghton Mifflin Company. All rights reserved.

Use: For use with Units 7 – 11.

53

SPELLING NEWSLETTER
for Students and Their Families

Moving Ahead

Units 7 through 11 in your child's level of *Houghton Mifflin Spelling and Vocabulary* have dealt with the spelling pattern for the vowel sounds heard in *five, made, bone, cute,* and *these* and with the consonant clusters *tr, sw, st,* and *cl.* These units also have presented words such as *ask* and *back* with *k* or *ck* spellings, and words such as *well, egg,* and *add* that have double consonants.

Word Lists

Your child has been studying the words below as well as other words with similar patterns.

UNIT 7	UNIT 8	UNIT 9	UNIT 10	UNIT 11
five	bone	trip	lake	off
made	nose	swim	ask	add
side	these	club	truck	hill
ate	home	stone	black	well
same	cute	next	back	egg
line	hope	glad	kick	grass

Family Activity

Play the game Make a Match with your child. Using at least two words from each unit above, make two duplicate sets of cards with a spelling word on one side of each card. Shuffle the cards, and scatter them face down on a table. With your child, take turns trying to find two matching cards. Turn over two cards, and say the word on each card. If the words on the cards do not match, turn the cards face down again and give up your turn. If the words do match, spell the word, keep the pair of cards, and take another turn. The player with the most cards after all matches have been made is the winner.

After the game, take turns with your child saying the words on the cards for the other to spell. Repeat the game, using the remaining words from Units 7–11.

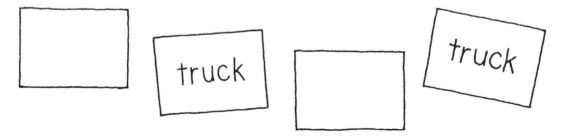

Houghton Mifflin Spelling and Vocabulary. Copyright © Houghton Mifflin Company. All rights reserved.

Boletín de noticias de ortografía
para estudiantes y para sus familias

Para continuar

Su hijo o hija ha estado estudiando las siguientes palabras y otras palabras que siguen patrones similares en las Unidades 7 a 11 del libro *Houghton Mifflin Spelling and Vocabulary.*

UNIDAD 7	UNIDAD 8	UNIDAD 9	UNIDAD 10	UNIDAD 11
five	bone	trip	lake	off
made	nose	swim	ask	add
side	these	club	truck	hill
ate	home	stone	black	well
same	cute	next	back	egg
line	hope	glad	kick	grass

Actividad para la familia

Jueguen a emparejar palabras con su hijo o hija. Usando por lo menos dos palabras de cada una de las unidades presentadas arriba, preparen dos grupos iguales de tarjetas con una de esas palabras en un lado de cada tarjeta. Mezclen las tarjetas y pónganlas esparcidas, boca abajo, sobre una mesa. Con su hijo o hija, túrnense para tratar de encontrar dos tarjetas iguales. El jugador o jugadora voltea dos tarjetas, y dice la palabra que está escrita en cada tarjeta. Si las palabras en las tarjetas no son iguales, pone las tarjetas boca abajo de nuevo y le pasa el turno a otro jugador o jugadora. Si las palabras son iguales, la persona que juega deletrea la palabra, se queda con el par de tarjetas, y se toma un nuevo turno. Gana la persona que tenga más tarjetas después de que se hayan emparejado todas.

Después del juego, túrnense con su hijo o hija para decir en voz alta las palabras que están en las tarjetas, para que la otra persona las deletree. Repitan el juego, usando las palabras restantes de las Unidades 7 a 11.

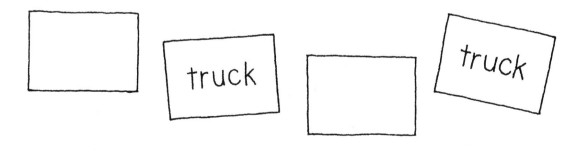

Houghton Mifflin Spelling and Vocabulary. Copyright © Houghton Mifflin Company. All rights reserved.

SPELLING TAG

SPELLING GAME

👥 **Players:**   4 or more

You need: a list of Basic and Elephant Words from a unit

How to play: All of the players sit in a circle. One player is the caller. The caller looks at the spelling list, calls out a word, and starts walking around the outside of the circle. When the caller stops behind another player and tags that player, that player must spell the caller's word. If the player spells the word correctly, he or she changes places with the caller and calls out a new word. If the word is spelled wrong, the caller taps another player, who has a chance to spell the word. Keep playing until all players have had a chance to be the caller.

Houghton Mifflin Spelling and Vocabulary. Copyright © Houghton Mifflin Company. All rights reserved.

Use: For use with Units 7 - 11.

Unit 12 Review: Test A

There are three words beside each number. One of the words is spelled wrong. Mark the letter next to that word.

Sample:
(a) kick
● tel
(c) lost

1. (a) truck
   (b) bone
   (c) tripp

2. (a) dres
   (b) nine
   (c) lake

3. (a) give
   (b) these
   (c) nestt

4. (a) rope
   (b) hil
   (c) late

5. (a) swem
   (b) ask
   (c) one

6. (a) five
   (b) uze
   (c) off

7. (a) rok
   (b) made
   (c) add

8. (a) side
   (b) nose
   (c) clubb

9. (a) step
   (b) bel
   (c) pick

Houghton Mifflin Spelling and Vocabulary. Copyright © Houghton Mifflin Company. All rights reserved.

Unit 12 Review: Test B

There are three words beside each number. One of the words is spelled wrong. Mark the letter next to that word.

Sample:
- (a) dress
- (b) swim
- ● truc

1.
- (a) brave
- (b) gras
- (c) cute

2.
- (a) bak
- (b) ate
- (c) kick

3.
- (a) hide
- (b) close
- (c) eg

4.
- (a) lost
- (b) wel
- (c) those

5.
- (a) black
- (b) tell
- (c) ston

6.
- (a) homm
- (b) glad
- (c) same

7.
- (a) bake
- (b) nixt
- (c) clock

8.
- (a) fien
- (b) have
- (c) hope

9.
- (a) line
- (b) goes
- (c) wil

Houghton Mifflin Spelling and Vocabulary. Copyright © Houghton Mifflin Company. All rights reserved.

Prewriting Ideas: A Story About Yourself

Choosing a Topic   Here is a list of ideas that one student thought of for writing a story. What special times of your own do these ideas make you think of?

On the lines below **My Three Ideas**, write three funny, scary, or happy things that have happened to you. Is each topic about only one idea? Which topic do you remember most about? Circle the topic that you would like to write about.

Ideas for Writing

| My First Swimming Lesson | My Magic Trick That Failed |
| The Day I Got Lost | How I Helped a Friend |

My Three Ideas

1. _____

2. _____

3. _____

Exploring Your Topic   You can use a map like this one to help you plan your story. Copy the map onto another sheet of paper. Make it large enough to write on. Write your topic in the box at the top. In the circles, write **who** the story is about, **what** happens, and **where** the story takes place.

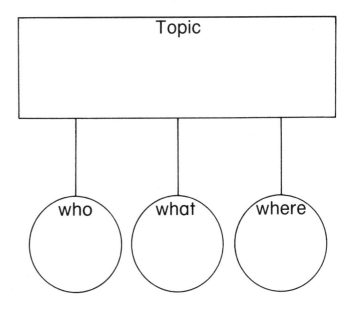

Houghton Mifflin Spelling and Vocabulary. Copyright © Houghton Mifflin Company. All rights reserved.

Use: For use with Step 1: Prewriting on page 95.

PRACTICE A
More Long a Spellings

Summing Up

The vowel sound in **way** and **train** is the long **a** sound. The long **a** sound may be spelled **ay** or **ai**.

Basic Words
1. train
2. way
3. mail
4. play
5. trail
Elephant Words
🐘 they
🐘 great

What a Place! Write the letters that spell the long **a** sound to finish each word. Color the two signs in which the long **a** sound is not spelled **ay** or **ai**.

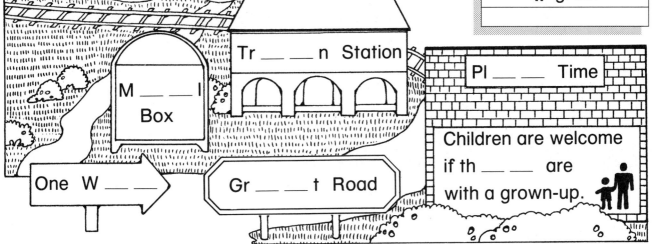

Now write the words you made.

1. _____

2. _____

3. _____

4. _____

5. _____

6. _____

Fine Rhymes Finish these sentences. Write a Basic Word to rhyme with the word in dark print.

7. If it starts to **rain** will you ride the _____?

8. It is fun to **sail** and to walk on the _____.

9. We **may** go this _____.

7. _____

8. _____

9. _____

Skill: Children will practice spelling words with the |ā| sound.

Home Use: Help your child practice the spelling words by having him or her complete the activities on this page. Check the completed page, and have your child practice saying and spelling any misspelled words.

61

Houghton Mifflin Spelling and Vocabulary. Copyright © Houghton Mifflin Company. All rights reserved.

Basic Words
1. train
2. way
3. mail
4. play
5. trail
6. pay
7. sail
8. hay
9. nail
10. rain
Elephant Words
🐘 they
🐘 great

PRACTICE B
More Long a Spellings

Puzzle Play   Write the Basic or Elephant Word for each clue. Use the letters in the boxes to spell a nice word to say.

1. give money □ __ __

2. have fun __ □ __ __

3. very large __ __ □ __ __

4. how to do something __ □ __

5. travel across water □ __ __ __

6. he and she __ __ □ __ __

Secret Word: __ __ __ __ __ __ __

Subtraction Facts   Take away one word from the letters in each box. Write the Basic Word that is left.

Example: Take away **toys**. Find fun.   ~~toplayys~~

7. Take away **stamp**. Find letters.   stamailmp

8. Take away **woods**. Find a path.   wotrailods

9. Take away **rose**. Find dried grass.   rohayse

10. Take away **track**. Find a railroad.   tratrainck

11. Take away **tool**. Find sharp metal.   tonailol

12. Take away **cloud**. Find water.   clorainud

EXTRA!   Make **Subtraction Facts** of your own, and have a classmate find the Basic Words that are left.

_____

7. _____

8. _____

9. _____

10. _____

11. _____

12. _____

Skill: Children will practice spelling words with the |ā| sound.

Home Use: Help your child practice the spelling words by having him or her complete the activities on this page. Check the completed page, and have your child practice saying and spelling any misspelled words.

Houghton Mifflin Spelling and Vocabulary. Copyright © Houghton Mifflin Company. All rights reserved.

PRACTICE C
More Long a Spellings

Word Sets   Write the missing words to complete each sentence. Use two Challenge Words in the first set and two Vocabulary Words in the second set.

Challenge Words
1. railroad
2. subway
Theme Vocabulary
3. caboose
4. engine
5. crossing
6. coach

1–2. Most ____ tracks run on top of the ground.
Most ____ tracks run under the ground.

_____   _____

_____   _____

1. _____   2. _____

3–4. The passengers in the ____ sit and read.
The crew in the ____ cook and sleep.

_____   _____

_____   _____

3. _____   4. _____

Words in Common   Write a word pair for each clue. Use a Challenge or Vocabulary Word in each pair. Write each word beside the correct number. The words in dark print will help you.

Example: mail that travels by **air**
a **carrier** who delivers **mail**

air	mail	carrier

5–6. the place where **deer cross** a street
6–7. a **guard** who helps children **cross** a street
8–9. a **train** that runs along **railroad** tracks
9–10. an **engine** that pulls a **train**

5.	6.	7.
8.	9.	10.

Houghton Mifflin Spelling and Vocabulary. Copyright © Houghton Mifflin Company. All rights reserved.

Skill: Children will practice spelling words with the |ā| sound and words related to the theme of trains.

Home Use: Help your child practice the spelling words by having him or her complete the activities on this page. Check the completed page, and have your child practice saying and spelling any misspelled words.

63

Unit **13** Test: More Long a Spellings

Read each sentence. Find the correctly spelled word to complete each sentence. Mark the letter next to that word.

Sample: ANSWERS
We spent the ____ at home. ⓐ dai ⓑ dae ● day

1. We ____ on the swings. ⓐ plae ⓑ play ⓒ plai

2. Henry sang on his ____ home. ⓐ way ⓑ wai ⓒ wey

3. My aunts said ____ like her. ⓐ thay ⓑ thaye ⓒ they

4. Jon will follow the ____. ⓐ tral ⓑ trail ⓒ trayl

5. Do you ride on the ____? ⓐ tran ⓑ trayn ⓒ train

6. Mr. Davis is a ____ teacher. ⓐ gret ⓑ great ⓒ grayt

7. I got a card in the ____. ⓐ mail ⓑ mal ⓒ mael

8. He ran quickly in the ____. ⓐ raen ⓑ rane ⓒ rain

9. Leon will ____ on the lake. ⓐ sail ⓑ sayl ⓒ sael

10. Do horses eat ____? ⓐ hae ⓑ hay ⓒ hai

11. I will ____ for your ticket. ⓐ pai ⓑ paiy ⓒ pay

12. Don't step on that ____! ⓐ nail ⓑ nayl ⓒ nale

Houghton Mifflin Spelling and Vocabulary. Copyright © Houghton Mifflin Company. All rights reserved.

PRACTICE A
More Long e Spellings

Summing Up

The vowel sound in **we**, **keep**, and **clean** is the long **e** sound. The long **e** sound may be spelled **e**, **ee**, or **ea**.

Basic Words
1. clean
2. keep
3. please
4. green
5. we
Elephant Words
🐘 the
🐘 people

Catch a Shooting Star Write each Basic Word under the star with the matching spelling for the long **e** sound.

1. _____

2. _____

3. _____

4. _____

5. _____

Falling Stars Write the missing Basic and Elephant Words.

Please ___(6)___ your eyes on ___(7)___ hat.

The ___(8)___ are watching! Where were you?

I took a carrot break! Can ___(9)___ start over?

6. _____

7. _____

8. _____

9. _____

Houghton Mifflin Spelling and Vocabulary. Copyright © Houghton Mifflin Company. All rights reserved.

Skill: Children will practice spelling words with the /ē/ sound.

Home Use: Help your child practice the spelling words by having him or her complete the activities on this page. Check the completed page, and have your child practice saying and spelling any misspelled words.

Basic Words
1. clean
2. keep
3. please
4. green
5. we
6. be
7. eat
8. tree
9. mean
10. read
Elephant Words
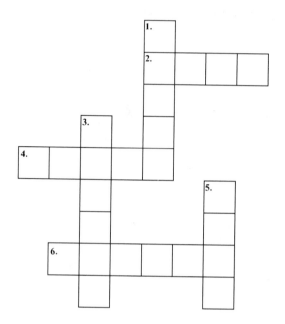 the
people

PRACTICE B
More Long e Spellings

Crossword Clues   Write a Basic or Elephant Word for each clue.

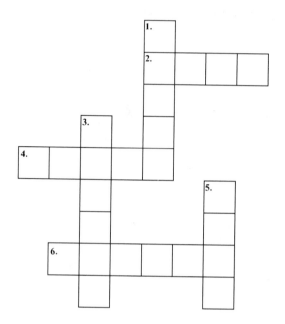

Across

2. _____ and write

4. opposite of **dirty**

6. _____ and thank you

Down

1. a color

3. men and women

5. a tall plant

Letter Math   Add and take away letters to make Basic or Elephant Words. Write each word.

7. win − in + e = **?**

8. b + he − h = **?**

9. e + bat − b = **?**

10. this − is + e = **?**

11. k + sheep − sh = **?**

12. m + clean − cl = **?**

7. _____

8. _____

9. _____

10. _____

11. _____

12. _____

Skill: Children will practice spelling words with the |ē| sound.

Home Use: Help your child practice the spelling words by having him or her complete the activities on this page. Check the completed page, and have your child practice saying and spelling any misspelled words.

Houghton Mifflin Spelling and Vocabulary. Copyright © Houghton Mifflin Company. All rights reserved.

PRACTICE C
More Long e Spellings

Signs of the Times Write what you think it says on each sign. Use a Challenge or Vocabulary Word for each sign. Use capital letters correctly.

Challenge Words
1. stream
2. street
Theme Vocabulary
3. trash
4. dump
5. collect
6. sewer

Example:

Street Cleaning

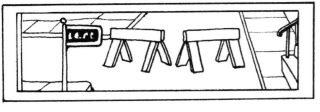

1. _____

2. _____

3. _____

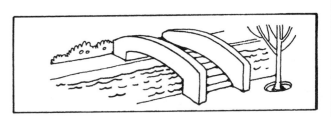

4. _____

5. _____

6. _____

Houghton Mifflin Spelling and Vocabulary. Copyright © Houghton Mifflin Company. All rights reserved.

Skill: Children will practice spelling words with the |ē| sound and words related to the theme of protecting our earth.

Home Use: Help your child practice the spelling words by having him or her complete the activities on this page. Check the completed page, and have your child practice saying and spelling any misspelled words.

Unit 14 Test: More Long e Spellings

Read each sentence. Is the underlined word spelled
right or wrong? Mark your answer.

	Right	**Wrong**
Sample: We put our <u>feet</u> in the water.	●	○

			Right	Wrong
1.	Tyler will try to <u>keap</u> quiet.	1.	○	○
2.	Is your house white or <u>grene</u>?	2.	○	○
3.	Rex asked for <u>the</u> answer.	3.	○	○
4.	Will you <u>please</u> do this?	4.	○	○
5.	Chris has to <u>cleen</u> his room.	5.	○	○
6.	Can <u>we</u> join you on the trip?	6.	○	○
7.	Some <u>peeple</u> work in the city.	7.	○	○
8.	Lou has a fruit <u>trea</u> in his yard.	8.	○	○
9.	What book did you <u>read</u> this week?	9.	○	○
10.	Kara will <u>be</u> home soon.	10.	○	○
11.	Ethan loves to <u>eet</u> corn.	11.	○	○
12.	That was a <u>mean</u> thing to do.	12.	○	○

Houghton Mifflin Spelling and Vocabulary. Copyright © Houghton Mifflin Company. All rights reserved.

PRACTICE A
The Vowel Sound in ball

Basic Words
1. dog
2. paw
3. call
4. saw
5. ball

Summing Up

The words **dog**, **paw**, and **call** have the same vowel sound. This vowel sound may be spelled **o**, **aw**, or **a** before **ll**.

Just Ducky   Write the missing letters to make Basic Words. Then write the words in the correct flower pots.

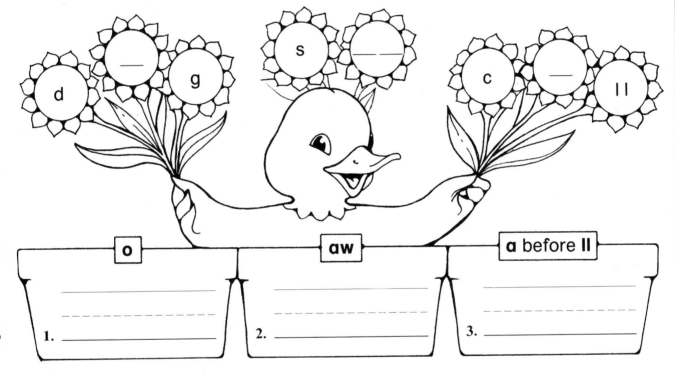

o	**aw**	**a before ll**
1. _____	2. _____	3. _____

Duck Prints   Each duck foot stands for a missing letter. Write the missing letters in each sentence to spell a Basic Word. Then write the Basic Words.

4. My 🦆et w🦆s dripping 🦆et.   _ _ _

5. Di🦆 y🦆u jump like a fro🦆?   _ _ _

6. The ba🦆y c🦆n p🦆ay a🦆l day.   _ _ _

4. _____

5. _____

6. _____

Skill: Children will practice spelling words with the same vowel sound as in **ball**.

Home Use: Help your child practice the spelling words by having him or her complete the activities on this page. Check the completed page, and have your child practice saying and spelling any misspelled words.

Houghton Mifflin Spelling and Vocabulary. Copyright © Houghton Mifflin Company. All rights reserved.

Basic Words
1. dog
2. paw
3. call
4. saw
5. ball
6. all
7. draw
8. small
9. log
10. fall

PRACTICE B
The Vowel Sound in ball

Proofreading   1–4. Find and cross out four Basic Words that are spelled wrong in this ad. Write each word correctly.

DOG FOR SALE
I have one white paww.
I am smol and cuddly.
You never sau a cuter dog!
Please call or come to see me at Jane's house.
(My owner did drau the frame,
but I made the picture!)

1. _____

2. _____

3. _____

4. _____

Riddles   Write a Basic Word to finish each riddle. Then see if you can think of the answer to each riddle.

5. What is black and white and red _____ over?

6. What do you _____ a bull when he is sleeping?

7. Why did Humpty Dumpty have a great _____?

8. How is a scrambled egg like a losing team?

9. Where does a fireplace _____ keep its money?

10. What kind of furry _____ keeps the best time?

5. _____

6. _____

7. _____

8. _____

9. _____

10. _____

Riddle Answers: 5. a zebra with a sunburn **6.** a bulldozer **7.** to make up for a bad summer **8.** Both are beaten. **9.** in a branch bank **10.** a watchdog

Houghton Mifflin Spelling and Vocabulary. Copyright © Houghton Mifflin Company. All rights reserved.

70

Skill: Children will practice spelling words with the same vowel sound as in **ball**.

Home Use: Help your child practice the spelling words by having him or her complete the activities on this page. Check the completed page, and have your child practice saying and spelling any misspelled words.

PRACTICE C
The Vowel Sound in ball

Word Towers   Start at the top of each tower. Add one letter to write the next word. Put the letters in the order that spells the word for each clue. The last word in each tower is a Challenge Word.

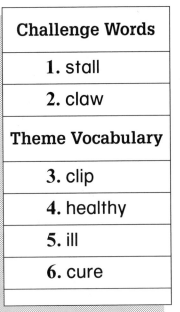

Challenge Words
1. stall
2. claw
Theme Vocabulary
3. clip
4. healthy
5. ill
6. cure

Clues

1.

the first letter of the alphabet

a musical note

everything

opposite of **short**

a place in a barn

2.

the first letter of the alphabet

a musical note

a rule

a nail of an animal's foot

Animal Helpers   Read each sign. Write a sentence telling what each person can do to help your pet. Use all of the Vocabulary Words in your sentences. Write your answers on a separate sheet of paper.

3. Haircuts for Dogs!
Ms. Chan

4. Help Your Pet Stay Well!
Dr. Veto

5. Animal Exercise Gym!
Mr. Mann

Houghton Mifflin Spelling and Vocabulary. Copyright © Houghton Mifflin Company. All rights reserved.

Skill: Children will practice spelling words with the vowel sound in **ball** and words related to the theme of animal doctor.

Home Use: Help your child practice the spelling words by having him or her complete the activities on this page. Check the completed page, and have your child practice saying and spelling any misspelled words.

Unit 15 Test: The Vowel Sound in ball

Each item below gives three spellings of a word.
Choose the correct spelling. Mark the letter for that
word.

Sample:			**ANSWERS**
a. wal	**b.** wawl	**c.** wall	(a) (b) ●

1. **a.** paw	**b.** po	**c.** pawe	1. (a) (b) (c)
2. **a.** cawl	**b.** cal	**c.** call	2. (a) (b) (c)
3. **a.** sawe	**b.** saw	**c.** sa	3. (a) (b) (c)
4. **a.** dolg	**b.** dawg	**c.** dog	4. (a) (b) (c)
5. **a.** ball	**b.** bal	**c.** bol	5. (a) (b) (c)
6. **a.** logg	**b.** log	**c.** lawg	6. (a) (b) (c)
7. **a.** droh	**b.** dro	**c.** draw	7. (a) (b) (c)
8. **a.** fawl	**b.** fall	**c.** fal	8. (a) (b) (c)
9. **a.** small	**b.** smal	**c.** smawl	9. (a) (b) (c)
10. **a.** oll	**b.** al	**c.** all	10. (a) (b) (c)

Houghton Mifflin Spelling and Vocabulary. Copyright © Houghton Mifflin Company. All rights reserved.

PRACTICE A
Words Spelled with sh or ch

Houghton Mifflin Spelling and Vocabulary. Copyright © Houghton Mifflin Company. All rights reserved.

Basic Words
1. sheep
2. chase
3. wish
4. much
5. chop

Elephant Words
catch
sure

Summing Up

The sound that begins **sheep** and ends **wish** may be spelled **sh**. The sound that begins **chase** and ends **much** may be spelled **ch**.

A Penny Saved   **1–6.** Write the letter or letters that spell the **sh** or the **ch** sound to finish each word. Draw a line from each coin to the correct bank. Color the two words in which the **sh** and **ch** sounds are not spelled **sh** or **ch**.

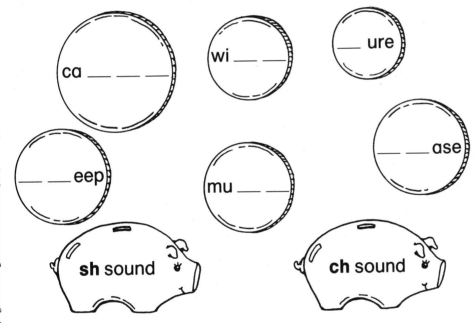

Now write the six words you made.

1. _____

2. _____

3. _____

4. _____

5. _____

6. _____

A Penny Earned   Write a Basic Word for each clue.

7. (a hope)

8. (to follow)

9. (to cut)

10. (an animal)

7. _____ 8. _____ 9. _____ 10. _____

Skill: Children will practice spelling words with the |sh| and the |ch| sounds.

Home Use: Help your child practice the spelling words by having him or her complete the activities on this page. Check the completed page, and have your child practice saying and spelling any misspelled words.

73

Basic Words

1.	sheep
2.	chase
3.	wish
4.	much
5.	chop
6.	each
7.	dish
8.	such
9.	wash
10.	ship

Elephant Words

🐘 catch

🐘 sure

PRACTICE B
Words Spelled with sh or ch

Dot-to-Dot   1–4. Find what race cars do. Connect the dots to spell Basic Words. Then write the words.

m•   •u   a•   •s   s•   •u   h•   •e

c•   •h   w•—•h   h•   •c   s•   •e   •p

1. _____

2. _____

3. _____

4. _____

Word Search   Write a Basic or Elephant Word for each clue. Then circle each word in the puzzle.

5. cut up   8. want   11. run after
6. a boat   9. every   12. get hold of
7. a plate   10. certain

5. _____

6. _____

7. _____

8. _____

9. _____

10. _____

11. _____

12. _____

s	u	r	e	m	b	w	s	y	i
e	t	d	a	s	v	i	l	m	z
v	g	i	c	h	a	s	e	s	h
e	e	s	h	i	o	h	b	w	j
h	c	h	o	p	c	a	t	c	h

Skill: Children will practice spelling words with the |sh| and the |ch| sounds.

Home Use: Help your child practice the spelling words by having him or her complete the activities on this page. Check the completed page, and have your child practice saying and spelling any misspelled words.

Houghton Mifflin Spelling and Vocabulary. Copyright © Houghton Mifflin Company. All rights reserved.

PRACTICE C
Words Spelled with sh or ch

Cattle Drive Write the name of each numbered cow. Use the clues in the story to help you.

At ten o'clock in the morning, Farmer Dell took his cows to the field. The cows walked in a single line. Lucky was ahead of Queen. Star was first in line. Lucky was behind Basil, and Basil was behind Star. The last cow kept stopping to nibble grass along the way. Finally, the farmer yelled at her to join the other cows.

Roundup Write the missing Challenge and Vocabulary Words. Use the information from the story above and your answers to numbers 1–4.

5. Lucky, Queen, Star, and Basil are _____.
6. A group of cows is called a _____.
7. Farmer Dell took the cows out before _____.
8. He took the cows to _____ on some grass.
9. Queen was a _____ cow.
10. Farmer Dell had to _____ at the last cow in line.

Challenge Words
1. shout
2. lunch
Theme Vocabulary
3. graze
4. cattle
5. herd
6. stray

1. _____
2. _____
3. _____
4. _____

5. _____
6. _____
7. _____
8. _____
9. _____
10. _____

Houghton Mifflin Spelling and Vocabulary. Copyright © Houghton Mifflin Company. All rights reserved.

Skill: Children will practice spelling words with the |sh| and the |ch| sounds and words related to the theme of ranching.

Home Use: Help your child practice the spelling words by having him or her complete the activities on this page. Check the completed page, and have your child practice saying and spelling any misspelled words.

75

Unit **16** Test: Words Spelled with sh or ch

Read each sentence. Find the correctly spelled word to complete each sentence. Mark the letter next to that word.

Sample:		**ANSWERS**	
Patti said _____ would be here.	ⓐ shee	ⓑ che	● she

1. I will count the _____.   ⓐ chepe   ⓑ sheep   ⓒ shep

2. Dina will _____ the wood.   ⓐ chop   ⓑ chope   ⓒ chob

3. How _____ did it cost?   ⓐ mushe ⓑ moch   ⓒ much

4. Scruffy likes to _____ cars.   ⓐ chas   ⓑ chaze   ⓒ chase

5. Are you _____ of that?   ⓐ sure   ⓑ shor   ⓒ chure

6. Joy made a _____.   ⓐ wich   ⓑ wish   ⓒ wesh

7. Doug tried to _____ the ball.   ⓐ cech   ⓑ catsh   ⓒ catch

8. That is _____ a great book!   ⓐ such   ⓑ sush   ⓒ soch

9. Give a horn to _____ child.   ⓐ ech   ⓑ each   ⓒ eech

10. Terry gave me a pretty _____.   ⓐ dish   ⓑ dich   ⓒ desh

11. A _____ took them home again.   ⓐ shup   ⓑ ship   ⓒ shipp

12. Carl had to _____ his hands.   ⓐ wach   ⓑ wosh   ⓒ wash

Houghton Mifflin Spelling and Vocabulary. Copyright © Houghton Mifflin Company. All rights reserved.

PRACTICE A
Words Spelled with th or wh

Houghton Mifflin Spelling and Vocabulary. Copyright © Houghton Mifflin Company. All rights reserved.

Basic Words
1. teeth
2. when
3. then
4. wheel
5. with

> **Summing Up**
>
> The sounds that begin **then** and end **teeth** may be spelled **th**. The sound that begins **when** may be spelled **wh**.

No Clues Puzzle   Complete each puzzle. Write the Basic Words that have the spelling shown in each bulb. Color the squares that have the letters **wh** or **th**.

Bright Ideas   Think how the words in each group are alike. Write the missing Basic Words.

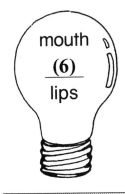

mouth
__(6)__
lips

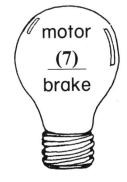

motor
__(7)__
brake

what
__(8)__
where

6. _____

7. _____

8. _____

Skill: Children will practice spelling words with the |hw|, the |th|, and the |th| sounds.

Home Use: Help your child practice the spelling words by having him or her complete the activities on this page. Check the completed page, and have your child practice saying and spelling any misspelled words.

77

Basic Words
1. teeth
2. when
3. then
4. wheel
5. with
6. what
7. than
8. while
9. them
10. which

PRACTICE B
Words Spelled with th or wh

Dots and Dashes   Use the Morse Code below to write Basic Words.

•—	= a	••••	= h	—	= t
•	= e	—•	= n	•——	= w

Example: — •••• •   = **the**

1.   — •••• • —•

3.   — •••• •— —•

2.   •—— •••• •— —

4.   — • • — ••••

1. _____

2. _____

3. _____

4. _____

Proofreading   **5–10.** Find and cross out six Basic Words that are spelled wrong in this note. Write each word correctly.

To: Billy   From: Mom

It's time to clean your room! It may take you less than an hour. Here is what I want you to do.
1. Please pick up your toys.
   Do not put tham in the bathtub!
2. Let me know whech toys need to be fixed.
3. Dust whit a clean rag!
4. Tell me wehn you finish. I will check your room wile you play.

P.S. The weel to your truck is in the sink.

5. _____

6. _____

7. _____

8. _____

9. _____

10. _____

Skill: Children will practice spelling words with the |hw|, the |th|, and the |th| sounds.

Home Use: Help your child practice the spelling words by having him or her complete the activities on this page. Check the completed page, and have your child practice saying and spelling any misspelled words.

Houghton Mifflin Spelling and Vocabulary. Copyright © Houghton Mifflin Company. All rights reserved.

PRACTICE C
Words Spelled with th **or** wh

Say It with Pictures You can draw letters to show
the meanings of the words they spell. Look at the
example. Make a drawing for each Challenge and
Vocabulary Word. Then write the words.

Houghton Mifflin Spelling and Vocabulary. Copyright © Houghton Mifflin Company. All rights reserved.

Challenge Words
1. mouth
2. whistle
Theme Vocabulary
3. toothbrush
4. rinse
5. roots
6. braces

Example:

wheel

1. _____

2. _____

3. _____

4. _____

5. _____

6. _____

Skill: Children will practice spelling words with the |hw|, the |th|, and the |*th*| sounds and words related to the theme of dentist.

Home Use: Help your child practice the spelling words by having him or her complete the activities on this page. Check the completed page, and have your child practice saying and spelling any misspelled words.

Unit **17** Test: Words Spelled with th or wh

Read each sentence. Is the underlined word spelled
right or wrong? Mark your answer.

Sample:	Right	Wrong
She used a can of <u>white</u> paint.	●	○

		Right	Wrong
1.	Kendi put a new <u>weel</u> on my bike.	○	○
2.	What did he say <u>then</u>?	○	○
3.	Mona went there <u>whith</u> us.	○	○
4.	The baby has two <u>teeth</u>.	○	○
5.	Dave left <u>wen</u> the movie ended.	○	○
6.	They waited <u>whil</u> I ran.	○	○
7.	I am taller <u>than</u> you are.	○	○
8.	Do you know <u>wich</u> hat is yours?	○	○
9.	Call <u>them</u> on the phone.	○	○
10.	Joshua knows <u>what</u> to buy.	○	○

Houghton Mifflin Spelling and Vocabulary. Copyright © Houghton Mifflin Company. All rights reserved.

Houghton Mifflin Spelling and Vocabulary. Copyright © Houghton Mifflin Company. All rights reserved.

BULLETIN BOARD

THE SPELLING EXPRESS

More Long **a** Spellings	More Long **e** Spellings	The Vowel Sound in **ball**	Words Spelled with **sh** or **ch**	Words Spelled with **th** or **wh**
	ee	**aw** **o**		
ay **ai**	**e** **ea**	**a before ll**	**sh** **ch**	**th** **wh**

Spelling Words

More Words

How to make: Turn the bulletin board into "The Spelling Express." Collect flat boxes and the lids from round plastic containers to use in creating five train cars as shown. (Forms can be made from construction paper as well.) Label each car with the title of a unit in the cycle. Attach pockets to the cars, and label each pocket with a spelling pattern studied in that unit. Make a train track from construction paper and tack the car for Unit 13 to the bulletin board. Write each Unit 13 Basic Word on an index card, and place the cards in an envelope, labeled as shown, at the bottom of the bulletin board. As students study each new unit, attach the other cars to the train with a paper chain. Add the new Basic Words to the envelope. As an alternative, you may wish to use the bulletin board for review of the cycle by putting up all of the train cars and words at once.

How to use: Have students sort the words into the pockets, showing the appropriate spelling pattern. You may want to include an envelope of blank cards for students to write and sort additional words that they come across in their reading.

Use: For use with Units 13–17.

SPELLING NEWSLETTER
for Students and Their Families

Moving Ahead

Units 13 through 17 in your child's level of *Houghton Mifflin Spelling and Vocabulary* have presented the spelling patterns *ai* and *ay* in words such as *mail* and *play* and the spelling patterns *ee, ea,* and *e* in words such as *green, clean,* and *be.* These units also present spelling patterns for the vowel sound heard in *draw, all,* and *log,* and the spellings *sh, ch, th,* and *wh* in words such as *ship, each, then, teeth,* and *while.*

Word Lists

Your child has been studying the words below as well as other words with similar patterns.

UNIT 13	UNIT 14	UNIT 15	UNIT 16	UNIT 17
train	clean	dog	sheep	teeth
mail	please	call	chase	then
play	green	saw	chop	wheel
pay	be	all	each	than
hay	tree	draw	dish	while
rain	read	log	ship	them

Family Activity

Play Spelling Signs with your child. Write each of the 30 words from the lists above on a separate slip of paper or index card. You may wish to have your child decorate each card as well. Together, think of places in your home where you could display these cards. Try to exhibit them in places that somehow illustrate the word. For example, the card with *read* on it could be placed on a bookshelf. Once all the cards have been displayed, the second part of the game begins. As the two of you come across the cards over the next few days, call out the word, spell it, and use it in a sentence. You may want to include other members of the family in the game as well.

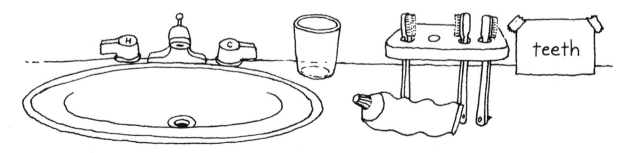

Houghton Mifflin Spelling and Vocabulary. Copyright © Houghton Mifflin Company. All rights reserved.

Houghton Mifflin Spelling and Vocabulary. Copyright © Houghton Mifflin Company. All rights reserved.

Boletín de noticias de ortografía
para estudiantes y para sus familias

Para continuar

Su hijo o hija ha estado estudiando las siguientes palabras y otras palabras que siguen patrones similares en las Unidades 13 a 17 del libro *Houghton Mifflin Spelling and Vocabulary.*

UNIDAD 13	UNIDAD 14	UNIDAD 15	UNIDAD 16	UNIDAD 17
train	clean	dog	sheep	teeth
mail	please	call	chase	then
play	green	saw	chop	wheel
pay	be	all	each	than
hay	tree	draw	dish	while
rain	read	log	ship	them

Actividad para la familia

Jueguen con anuncios para deletrear con su hijo o hija. Escriban cada una de las 30 palabras de las listas de arriba en un pedazo de papel o en una tarjeta aparte. Si lo desean, hagan que su hijo o hija decore las tarjetas. Piensen juntos en lugares de su casa donde puedan poner las tarjetas a la vista. Traten de ponerlas en lugares que de alguna forma ilustren la palabra. Por ejemplo, la tarjeta que tiene la palabra *read* puede colocarse en un estante de libros. Una vez que se hayan colocado a la vista todas las tarjetas, comienza la segunda parte del juego. Cuando ustedes encuentren las palabras durante los días siguientes, digan la palabra en voz alta, deletréenla y úsenla en una oración. Si lo desean, incluyan a otros miembros de la familia en el juego.

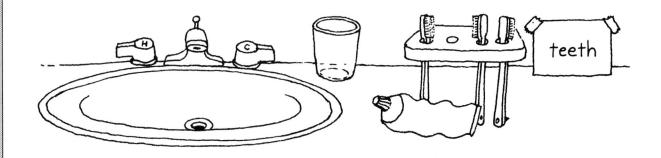

TOSS AND SPELL

SPELLING GAME

Players: 2 or more

You need: a copy of the game board on page 85, pencils, a tosser (a folded piece of paper), 15 cards with a Basic or Elephant Word on each one

How to play: Number each shape on the "Toss and Spell" game board from 1 to 15. Tape the board to a desk top or other flat surface.

Write one word from Units 13–17 on each card. Number each card from 1 to 15 on the other side. Place the cards in a pile. Each player throws a tosser onto the board. The player who lands on the highest number goes first.

Player 1 throws the tosser onto a number on the board. Another player picks the card with the same number and reads aloud the word on that card. Player 1 spells the word and uses it in a sentence. If the player is correct, he or she takes the card. If the spelling or sentence is wrong, the card is returned to the pile.

Players who land on a line may throw again. Players who land on a number that has already been used lose their turn. The game ends when all of the cards have been taken. The player with the most cards at the end of the game wins.

You may repeat the game with another set of cards with 15 different words from Units 13–17.

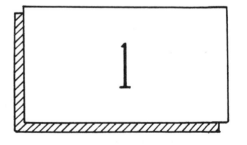

Houghton Mifflin Spelling and Vocabulary. Copyright © Houghton Mifflin Company. All rights reserved.

Use: For use with Units 13 - 17.

Houghton Mifflin Spelling and Vocabulary. Copyright © Houghton Mifflin Company. All rights reserved.

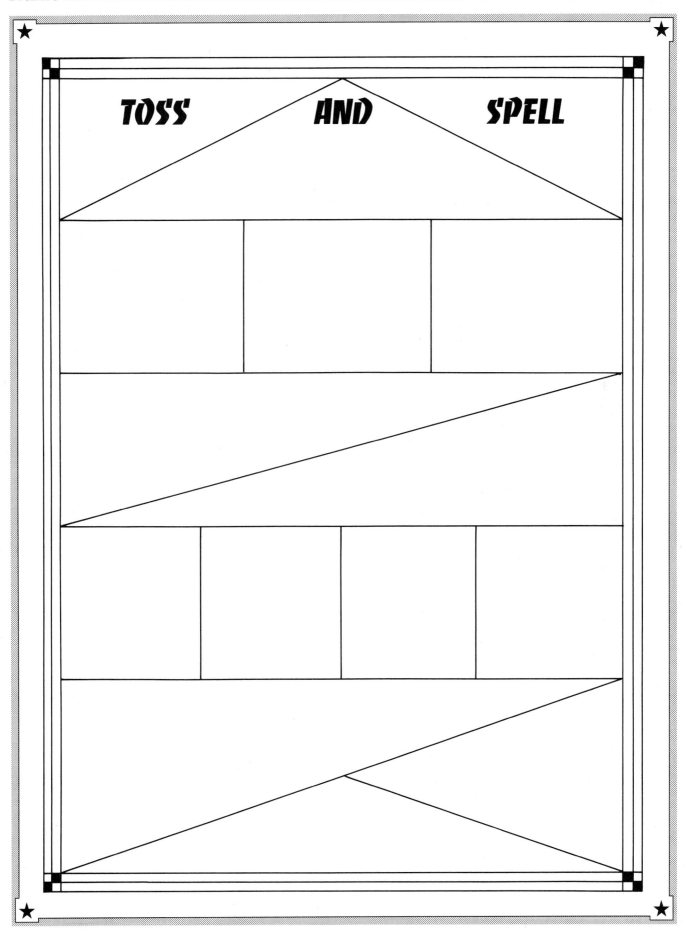

TOSS AND SPELL

Unit 18 Review: Test A

Read the three word groups. Find the underlined word that is spelled wrong. Mark the letter for that word.

Sample:
- ● will <u>stae</u> away
- (b) a new <u>day</u>
- (c) black and <u>white</u>

1. (a) wood to <u>chop</u>
   (b) a cat's <u>pau</u> print
   (c) to keep <u>quiet</u>

2. (a) a <u>traen</u> ticket
   (b) now and <u>then</u>
   (c) <u>green</u> grass

3. (a) to run and <u>play</u>
   (b) the big <u>dog</u>
   (c) too <u>mach</u>

4. (a) to throw or <u>cach</u>
   (b) two new <u>teeth</u>
   (c) a nature <u>trail</u>

5. (a) to be <u>sure</u>
   (b) <u>saw</u> the book
   (c) a car's <u>weel</u>

6. (a) the wrong <u>way</u>
   (b) a loud <u>caul</u>
   (c) with my <u>friends</u>

7. (a) to make a <u>wich</u>
   (b) where and <u>when</u>
   (c) in the <u>mail</u>

8. (a) the <u>answer</u>
   (b) a <u>greit</u> job
   (c) two <u>sheep</u>

9. (a) Sam and <u>they</u>
   (b) <u>please</u> and thank you
   (c) <u>cleen</u> dishes

10. (a) to <u>shase</u> away
    (b) a bat and a <u>ball</u>
    (c) you and <u>we</u>

Houghton Mifflin Spelling and Vocabulary. Copyright © Houghton Mifflin Company. All rights reserved.

Unit **18** Review: Test B

Read the three word groups. Find the underlined word that is spelled wrong. Mark the letter for that word.

Sample:
ⓐ she and he
● with both fe<u>it</u>
ⓒ a warm <u>bath</u>

1. ⓐ to <u>fall</u> off
   ⓑ food to <u>eat</u>
   ⓒ a <u>lawg</u> cabin

2. ⓐ for a <u>while</u>
   ⓑ to <u>wash</u> and dry
   ⓒ <u>al</u> in a row

3. ⓐ <u>rayn</u> and snow
   ⓑ more <u>than</u> that
   ⓒ <u>sure</u> enough

4. ⓐ a <u>sail</u> on a boat
   ⓑ <u>eash</u> and every
   ⓒ on a <u>ship</u>

5. ⓐ <u>tha</u> good news
   ⓑ a ball to <u>catch</u>
   ⓒ no <u>such</u> thing

6. ⓐ a bill to <u>pay</u>
   ⓑ <u>meen</u> and nasty
   ⓒ the tall <u>tree</u>

7. ⓐ a <u>nail</u> in the wall
   ⓑ to be <u>happy</u>
   ⓒ <u>smoll</u> wonder

8. ⓐ different <u>people</u>
   ⓑ <u>wat</u> to say
   ⓒ from <u>them</u>

9. ⓐ <u>hai</u> for horses
   ⓑ books to <u>read</u>
   ⓒ paper to <u>draw</u> on

10. ⓐ a <u>great</u> job
    ⓑ <u>which</u> way
    ⓒ a cup and a <u>dich</u>

Houghton Mifflin Spelling and Vocabulary. Copyright © Houghton Mifflin Company. All rights reserved.

Prewriting Ideas: Story

Choosing A Topic   Here is a list of ideas that one student made for writing a story. What story ideas of your own do these make you think of?

On the lines below **My Three Ideas**, write three ideas that you think would make a good make-believe story. Which idea do you like the best? Which one can you tell enough about? Which one will other people enjoy? Circle the topic that you would like to write about.

Ideas for Writing

The Dinosaur That Needed Help	The Magic Whistle
The Runaway Bicycle	The Secret Subway

My Three Ideas

1. _____

2. _____

3. _____

Exploring Your Topic   You can use a puzzle map to help you plan your story. Copy the map onto another sheet of paper. Make it large enough to write on. In each piece, write what will happen in the **beginning**, the **middle**, and the **end** of your story.

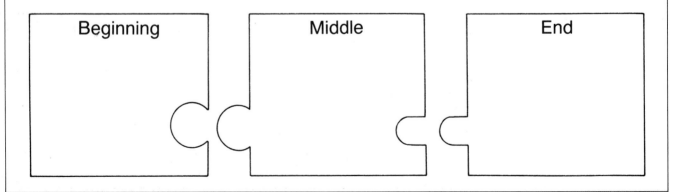

Beginning   Middle   End

Houghton Mifflin Spelling and Vocabulary. Copyright © Houghton Mifflin Company. All rights reserved.

Use: For use with Step 1: Prewriting on page 131.

Midyear Test

There are three words beside each number. One of the words is spelled wrong. Mark the letter next to that word.

Sample:
● pai
(b) read
(c) saw

1. (a) pau
   (b) truck
   (c) dress

2. (a) win
   (b) het
   (c) made

3. (a) train
   (b) chase
   (c) anny

4. (a) sunn
   (b) one
   (c) lake

5. (a) they
   (b) bal
   (c) then

6. (a) bell
   (b) bug
   (c) yuse

7. (a) bed
   (b) ov
   (c) trip

8. (a) cleen
   (b) has
   (c) his

9. (a) late
   (b) nest
   (c) waye

10. (a) green
    (b) sheap
    (c) catch

(continued)

Houghton Mifflin Spelling and Vocabulary. Copyright © Houghton Mifflin Company. All rights reserved.

Midyear Test (continued)

11. (a) the
    (b) pigg
    (c) side

12. (a) rock
    (b) we
    (c) teth

13. (a) sixx
    (b) nod
    (c) mail

14. (a) small
    (b) themm
    (c) dig

15. (a) line
    (b) black
    (c) al

16. (a) want
    (b) hop
    (c) clos

17. (a) hav
    (b) draw
    (c) will

18. (a) mop
    (b) brav
    (c) bad

19. (a) each
    (b) ran
    (c) gras

20. (a) those
    (b) spott
    (c) egg

21. (a) wett
    (b) from
    (c) next

22. (a) nail
    (b) shure
    (c) said

23. (a) bus
    (b) hope
    (c) backe

24. (a) whil
    (b) help
    (c) hug

25. (a) meen
    (b) stone
    (c) what

Houghton Mifflin Spelling and Vocabulary. Copyright © Houghton Mifflin Company. All rights reserved.

PRACTICE A
Words That End with nd, ng, or nk

Basic Words
1. king
2. thank
3. hand
4. sing
5. and

Summing Up

You hear the sounds of **n** and **d** in words that end with the consonant cluster **nd**.
You may not hear the sound of **n** in words that end with the consonants **ng** or **nk**.

Sing-along On each sign, write a Basic Word that has the letters that the singer is singing.

I can't hear you three in the back!

Who Is He? Write the missing Basic Words. Then see if you can think of the answer to the riddle.

Once upon a time, there lived a __(6)__. One day he was sitting at a table. In front of him were two cups filled with water __(7)__ one empty cup. He held a pitcher of water in his __(8)__. What was his name?

Riddle Answer: King Philip (fill up) the Third

6. _____

7. _____

8. _____

Houghton Mifflin Spelling and Vocabulary. Copyright © Houghton Mifflin Company. All rights reserved.

Skill: Children will practice spelling words that end with **nd**, **ng**, or **nk**.

Home Use: Help your child practice the spelling words by having him or her complete the activities on this page. Check the completed page, and have your child practice saying and spelling any misspelled words.

91

Basic Words
1. king
2. thank
3. hand
4. sing
5. and
6. think
7. bring
8. long
9. end
10. thing

PRACTICE B
Words That End with nd, ng, or nk

Silly Rhymes   Finish these silly sentences. Write a Basic Word to rhyme with the word in dark print.

1. The royal _____ ate a chicken **wing**.
2. Can you _____ your piggy **bank**?
3. I sang a **song** that was too _____!
4. I built a house of **sand** with one _____.
5. Why did you _____ your new gold **ring**?
6. Do you _____ this rock will **sink**?

1. _____   4. _____

2. _____   5. _____

3. _____   6. _____

Words in Words   Write the Basic Word you see in each of these longer words.

7. band   9. bend
8. singer   10. nothing

7. _____

8. _____

9. _____

10. _____

Skill: Children will practice spelling words that end with **nd**, **ng**, or **nk**.

Home Use: Help your child practice the spelling words by having him or her complete the activities on this page. Check the completed page, and have your child practice saying and spelling any misspelled words.

Houghton Mifflin Spelling and Vocabulary. Copyright © Houghton Mifflin Company. All rights reserved.

PRACTICE C
Words That End with nd, ng, or nk

What's Wrong?   Circle the four things that are
wrong in this picture.

Houghton Mifflin Spelling and Vocabulary. Copyright © Houghton Mifflin Company. All rights reserved.

Challenge Words
1. grand
2. young
Theme Vocabulary
3. throne
4. castle
5. page
6. feast

FEAST GRAND TODAY

Now write four sentences to tell what is wrong in the
picture above. Use all the Challenge and Vocabulary
Words in your sentences.

1. _____

2. _____

3. _____

4. _____

Skill: Children will practice spelling words that
end with **nd**, **ng**, or **nk** and words related to the
theme of castles and kings.

Home Use: Help your child practice the spelling words by having him
or her complete the activities on this page. Check the completed page,
and have your child practice saying and spelling any misspelled words.

Unit **19** Test: Words That End with nd, ng, **or** nk

Each item below gives three spellings of a word.
Choose the correct spelling. Mark the letter for that
word.

Sample:			**ANSWERS**
a. send	**b.** sen	**c.** seng	● ⓑ ⓒ

1. **a.** ank   **b.** and   **c.** ang   1. ⓐ ⓑ ⓒ

2. **a.** thangk   **b.** thang   **c.** thank   2. ⓐ ⓑ ⓒ

3. **a.** king   **b.** kig   **c.** kingg   3. ⓐ ⓑ ⓒ

4. **a.** sig   **b.** sing   **c.** sind   4. ⓐ ⓑ ⓒ

5. **a.** hend   **b.** hant   **c.** hand   5. ⓐ ⓑ ⓒ

6. **a.** think   **b.** thind   **c.** thinc   6. ⓐ ⓑ ⓒ

7. **a.** lonk   **b.** logn   **c.** long   7. ⓐ ⓑ ⓒ

8. **a.** enk   **b.** end   **c.** eng   8. ⓐ ⓑ ⓒ

9. **a.** birng   **b.** brind   **c.** bring   9. ⓐ ⓑ ⓒ

10. **a.** thing   **b.** thind   **c.** thign   10. ⓐ ⓑ ⓒ

Houghton Mifflin Spelling and Vocabulary. Copyright © Houghton Mifflin Company. All rights reserved.

PRACTICE A
Words That End with s or es

Summing Up

Add **s** to most words to name more than one.
Add **es** to words that end with **s**, **x**, **sh**, or **ch** to name more than one.

Basic Words
1. dishes
2. dresses
3. bells
4. boxes
5. beaches
Elephant Word
🐘 children

Addition Facts   Write the Basic or Elephant Word that names the things on each card. Circle the word that does not add **s** or **es**.

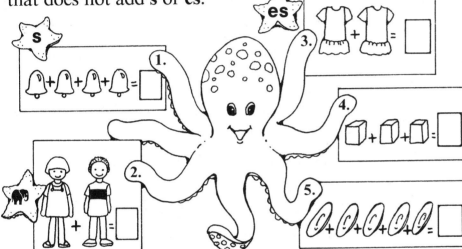

Find the sum of the things on each card. Write the total on the card.

1. _____

2. _____

3. _____

4. _____

5. _____

Subtraction Facts   Take away one word from the letters in each box. Write the Basic or Elephant Word that is left.

6. Take away **ocean**. Find sandy places.   `ocbeachesean`

7. Take away **cups**. Find plates.   `cudishesps`

8. Take away **animals**. Find boys and girls.   `animchildrenals`

6. _____   7. _____   8. _____

Houghton Mifflin Spelling and Vocabulary. Copyright © Houghton Mifflin Company. All rights reserved.

Skill: Children will practice spelling words that end with **s** or **es**.

Home Use: Help your child practice the spelling words by having him or her complete the activities on this page. Check the completed page, and have your child practice saying and spelling any misspelled words.

Basic Words
1. dishes
2. dresses
3. bells
4. boxes
5. beaches
6. days
7. bikes
8. wishes
9. things
10. names

Elephant Word

🐘 children

PRACTICE B
Words That End with s or es

Puzzle Play   Write the Basic or Elephant Word for each clue. Use the letters in the boxes to spell the names of two ways to measure time.

1. what people are called by ___ ___ □ ___ ___

2. cans, ____, and bags ___ □ ___ ___

3. boys and girls ___ ___ ___ ___ ___ ___ □

4. rhymes with **rings** □ ___ ___ ___ ___

5. strong hopes ___ ___ ___ □ ___

6. machines with two wheels ___ ___ ___ ___ □

7. opposite of **nights** ___ ___ □ ___

8. things that ring ___ □ ___ ___

9. places by the sea ___ □ ___ ___ ___

10. clothing for girls ___ □ ___ ___ ___

11. plates ___ ___ ___ ___ □

Secret Words:

___ ___ ___ ___ ___ ___ ___   and   ___ ___ ___ ___ ___

Houghton Mifflin Spelling and Vocabulary. Copyright © Houghton Mifflin Company. All rights reserved.

Skill: Children will practice spelling words that end with **s** or **es**.

Home Use: Help your child practice the spelling words by having him or her complete the activities on this page. Check the completed page, and have your child practice saying and spelling any misspelled words.

PRACTICE C
Words That End with s or es

Houghton Mifflin Spelling and Vocabulary. Copyright © Houghton Mifflin Company. All rights reserved.

Challenge Words
1. coins
2. classes
Theme Vocabulary
3. earn
4. sale
5. change
6. chores

Open Boxes   Write a Challenge or Vocabulary Word for the first clue in each row. Then write only the letters in the open boxes to make a new word. Make sure the new word matches its clue.

Example: water from clouds   raced

| r | a | i | n | → | r | a | █ | n |

coins   a walking stick

1. ⬜⬜⬜⬜⬜ → ⬜▓⬜▓⬜

groups of students   a large box

2. ⬜⬜⬜⬜⬜⬜⬜ → ⬜▓⬜▓⬜⬜▓

nickels and dimes   not **off**

3. ⬜⬜⬜⬜⬜ → ▓⬜▓⬜▓

Store Windows   The owner of a bike store needs help in his store during a big sale. Write a sentence for his sign. Use the words **earn**, **chores**, and **sale**.

$ HELP WANTED $

_____

_____

_____

_____

Skill: Children will practice spelling words that end with **s** or **es** and words related to the theme of earning money.

Home Use: Help your child practice the spelling words by having him or her complete the activities on this page. Check the completed page, and have your child practice saying and spelling any misspelled words.

97

Unit 20 Test: Words That End with s or es

Read each word group. Find the correctly spelled word to complete each group. Mark the letter next to that word.

Sample:

four _____ in a pond
(a) froges
(b) froggs
● frogs

1. little _____
   (a) childs
   (b) children
   (c) childern

2. in the _____
   (a) boxes
   (b) boxs
   (c) bocks

3. pretty, new _____
   (a) dresss
   (b) dreses
   (c) dresses

4. ringing _____
   (a) bels
   (b) bells
   (c) bellz

5. sandy _____
   (a) beachs
   (b) beacheys
   (c) beaches

6. two _____ of food
   (a) dishes
   (b) disses
   (c) dishs

7. their _____
   (a) namees
   (b) names
   (c) naems

8. many _____
   (a) tings
   (b) thinges
   (c) things

9. sunny _____
   (a) days
   (b) daes
   (c) dayes

10. dreams and _____
    (a) wishs
    (b) wishes
    (c) wishis

11. our _____
    (a) bikes
    (b) biks
    (c) bieks

Houghton Mifflin Spelling and Vocabulary. Copyright © Houghton Mifflin Company. All rights reserved.

PRACTICE A
More Long o Spellings

Summing Up

The vowel sound in **go**, **boat**, and **slow** is the long **o** sound. The long **o** sound may be spelled **o**, **oa**, or **ow**.

Basic Words
1. boat
2. cold
3. go
4. slow
5. no

Elephant Words
🐘 toe
🐘 do

Hop to It! Draw a line through all of the words with the long **o** sound to reach Mr. Frog. Then write the words with the long **o** sound on the correct lily pads.

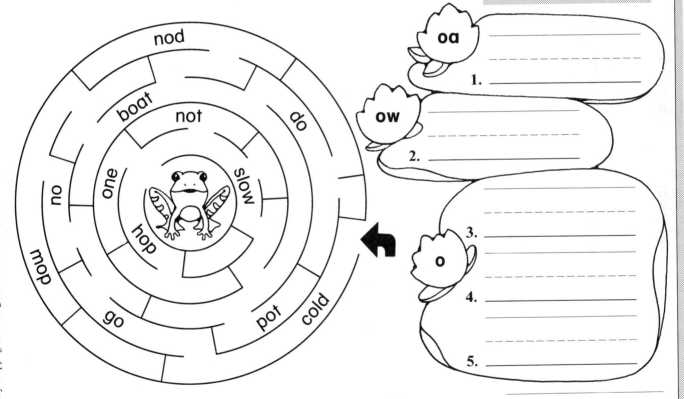

oa

1. _____

ow

2. _____

o

3. _____
4. _____
5. _____

Hink Pink Write the Basic or Elephant Word that answers the question and rhymes with the word in dark print.

6. What is another way to say "to carry out an act"? **to** __

7. What is a bird that does not fly fast? **a** __ **crow**

8. What is part of a deer's foot? **a doe** __

6. _____

7. _____

8. _____

Houghton Mifflin Spelling and Vocabulary. Copyright © Houghton Mifflin Company. All rights reserved.

Skill: Children will practice spelling words with the |ō| sound.

Home Use: Help your child practice the spelling words by having him or her complete the activities on this page. Check the completed page, and have your child practice saying and spelling any misspelled words.

Basic Words
1. boat
2. cold
3. go
4. slow
5. no
6. old
7. coat
8. grow
9. told
10. show

Elephant Words

🐘 toe

🐘 do

PRACTICE B
More Long o Spellings

What Word Am I?   Write a Basic or Elephant Word by writing a letter for each clue.

1. I am in **ten** but not in **den**.
I am in **lot** but not in **let**.
I am in **doe** but not in **dot**.   1. __ __ __

2. I am in **can** but not in **cap**.
I am in **of** but not in **if**.   2. __ __

3. I am in **dig** but not in **pig**.
I am in **fox** but not in **fix**.   3. __ __ __

4. I am in **on** but not in **an**.
I am in **sly** but not in **sky**.
I am in **cod** but not in **cot**.   4. __ __ __

5. I am in **cat** but not in **bat**.
I am in **fog** but not in **fig**.
I am in **beat** but not in **beet**.
I am in **lost** but not in **lose**.   5. __ __ __ __

6. I am in **got** but not in **dot**.
I am in **won** but not in **win**.   6. __ __

Proofreading   **7–12.** Find and cross out six Basic Words that are spelled wrong on these bumper stickers. Write each word correctly.

7. _____

8. _____

9. _____

10. _____

11. _____

12. _____

I Love My Old Bot!

Have I Toald You About My Cat?

Help a
Tree Groe!

Go Slo!

Cowld Driver on Board!
Honk if You Can Shoa Me
How to Fix My Heater.

Houghton Mifflin Spelling and Vocabulary. Copyright © Houghton Mifflin Company. All rights reserved.

Skill: Children will practice spelling words with the |ō| sound.

Home Use: Help your child practice the spelling words by having him or her complete the activities on this page. Check the completed page, and have your child practice saying and spelling any misspelled words.

PRACTICE C
More Long o Spellings

Something Is Fishy   Help Hugo finish making a sign for Seaside Park. Write the Challenge and Vocabulary Words in the correct places. Then write a sentence for the sign.

Challenge Words
1. coast
2. rainbow
Theme Vocabulary
3. ocean
4. jellyfish
5. shrimp
6. crab

1. _____

2. _____

3. _____

4. _____

5. _____

6. _____

_____

_____

_____

Houghton Mifflin Spelling and Vocabulary. Copyright © Houghton Mifflin Company. All rights reserved.

Skill: Children will practice spelling words with the |ō| sound and words related to the theme of the seashore.

Home Use: Help your child practice the spelling words by having him or her complete the activities on this page. Check the completed page, and have your child practice saying and spelling any misspelled words.

Unit 21 Test: More Long o Spellings

Each item below gives three spellings of a word.
Choose the correct spelling. Mark the letter for that
word.

Sample:			ANSWERS
a. so	**b.** soa	**c.** soe	● ⓑ ⓒ

1. **a.** toa	**b.** toe	**c.** towe	1. ⓐ ⓑ ⓒ
2. **a.** noe	**b.** noa	**c.** no	2. ⓐ ⓑ ⓒ
3. **a.** cold	**b.** coald	**c.** cowld	3. ⓐ ⓑ ⓒ
4. **a.** sloa	**b.** slow	**c.** slo	4. ⓐ ⓑ ⓒ
5. **a.** boat	**b.** bowt	**c.** bot	5. ⓐ ⓑ ⓒ
6. **a.** goe	**b.** gow	**c.** go	6. ⓐ ⓑ ⓒ
7. **a.** dow	**b.** doh	**c.** do	7. ⓐ ⓑ ⓒ
8. **a.** old	**b.** oald	**c.** owld	8. ⓐ ⓑ ⓒ
9. **a.** cowt	**b.** coat	**c.** cote	9. ⓐ ⓑ ⓒ
10. **a.** sho	**b.** showe	**c.** show	10. ⓐ ⓑ ⓒ
11. **a.** gro	**b.** grow	**c.** groe	11. ⓐ ⓑ ⓒ
12. **a.** told	**b.** towld	**c.** toald	12. ⓐ ⓑ ⓒ

Houghton Mifflin Spelling and Vocabulary. Copyright © Houghton Mifflin Company. All rights reserved.

PRACTICE A
The Vowel Sounds in moon and book

Summing Up

The vowel sounds you hear in **moon** and **book** may be spelled **oo**.

Basic Words
1. zoo
2. food
3. look
4. moon
5. book

Elephant Words
🐘 you
🐘 who

Bookworm Fill in the missing letters to make Basic or Elephant Words. Color the books in which the vowel sound in **moon** is spelled **oo**. Circle the two books with a different spelling for this sound.

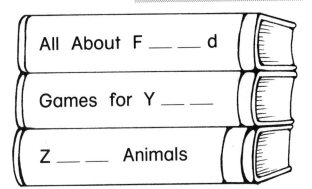

A B __ __ k of Facts

Wh __ Was There?

Take a L __ __ k

All About F __ __ d

Games for Y __ __

Z __ __ Animals

Now write the words you made.

1. _____

2. _____

3. _____

4. _____

5. _____

6. _____

7. _____

8. _____

9. _____

Three of a Kind Think how the words in each group are alike. Write the missing Basic Words.

7. sun, stars, _____

8. see, watch, _____

9. park, playground, _____

Houghton Mifflin Spelling and Vocabulary. Copyright © Houghton Mifflin Company. All rights reserved.

Skill: Children will practice spelling words with the |o͞o| and the |o͝o| sounds.

Home Use: Help your child practice the spelling words by having him or her complete the activities on this page. Check the completed page, and have your child practice saying and spelling any misspelled words.

Basic Words
1. zoo
2. food
3. look
4. moon
5. book
6. soon
7. took
8. good
9. room
10. foot

Elephant Words

🐘 you

🐘 who

PRACTICE B
The Vowel Sounds in moon **and** book

Hidden Words   Find and circle the hidden Basic Word in each box. Then write the word.

1. | o m i b o o k e t o u |

2. | b o u g o o d o o l u |

3. | t u l o o k e n y o o |

4. | r o o p u f o o d y |

5. | s t o o k o w o o n |

6. | z o u f o o t s o o |

1. _____

2. _____

3. _____

4. _____

5. _____

6. _____

Word Search   Write the missing Basic or Elephant Words. Then circle each word in the puzzle. Look across and down.

7. sun and ____   **10.** ____ keeper

8. ____ and I   **11.** lots of ____ to move

9. coming ____   **12.** ____ or what

r	b	t	s	f
o	w	h	o	z
o	y	z	o	o
m	o	o	n	m
o	u	b	t	g

7. _____

8. _____

9. _____

10. _____

11. _____

12. _____

Houghton Mifflin Spelling and Vocabulary. Copyright © Houghton Mifflin Company. All rights reserved.

Skill: Children will practice spelling words with the |o͞o| and the |o͝o| sounds.

Home Use: Help your child practice the spelling words by having him or her complete the activities on this page. Check the completed page, and have your child practice saying and spelling any misspelled words.

PRACTICE C
The Vowel Sounds in moon and book

Houghton Mifflin Spelling and Vocabulary. Copyright © Houghton Mifflin Company. All rights reserved.

Challenge Words
1. hoof
2. moose
Theme Vocabulary
3. tame
4. diet
5. groom
6. perch

Hink Pink   Write a Challenge or Vocabulary Word
and a word that rhymes with it to answer each question.

1. What is a large deer that is not tied up?

a _____   _____

2. What is food that does not make noise?

a _____   _____

3. What is a sport that is not wild?

a _____   _____

Change a Letter   Change one letter in each picture's
name to write a Challenge or Vocabulary Word.

4.    **4.** _____

5. _____

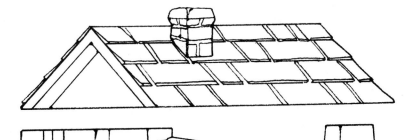

5.

6.   **6.** _____

Skill: Children will practice spelling words with the |oo| and the |o͝o| sounds and words related to the theme of zoos.

Home Use: Help your child practice the spelling words by having him or her complete the activities on this page. Check the completed page, and have your child practice saying and spelling any misspelled words.

105

Unit 22 Test: The Vowel Sounds in moon and book

Read each word group. Find the correctly spelled word to complete each group. Mark the letter next to that word.

Sample:

a ____ tooth
● loose
ⓑ looz
ⓒ luse

1. a new ____
   ⓐ bowk
   ⓑ bhok
   ⓒ book

2. at the ____
   ⓐ zoo
   ⓑ zew
   ⓒ zou

3. her favorite ____
   ⓐ fude
   ⓑ food
   ⓒ foud

4. why and ____
   ⓐ hoo
   ⓑ whoo
   ⓒ who

5. to ____ at
   ⓐ lewk
   ⓑ look
   ⓒ luk

6. the ____ and stars
   ⓐ moon
   ⓑ mune
   ⓒ mewn

7. for ____ and me
   ⓐ yeww
   ⓑ you
   ⓒ yoo

8. a ____ time
   ⓐ good
   ⓑ guud
   ⓒ goud

9. a ____ at home
   ⓐ roum
   ⓑ rume
   ⓒ room

10. on one ____
    ⓐ fut
    ⓑ foot
    ⓒ fout

11. ____ a long walk
    ⓐ took
    ⓑ tuk
    ⓒ tooc

12. one day ____
    ⓐ sune
    ⓑ suun
    ⓒ soon

Houghton Mifflin Spelling and Vocabulary. Copyright © Houghton Mifflin Company. All rights reserved.

PRACTICE A
Homophones

Houghton Mifflin Spelling and Vocabulary. Copyright © Houghton Mifflin Company. All rights reserved.

Basic Words
1. plane
2. plain
3. tail
4. tale

Elephant Words
🐘 to
🐘 too
🐘 two

> ### Summing Up
> **Homophones** are words that sound alike but do not have the same spelling or the same meaning.

Moo Clues   Write the missing Basic or Elephant Words to finish each set. The words in each set are homophones.

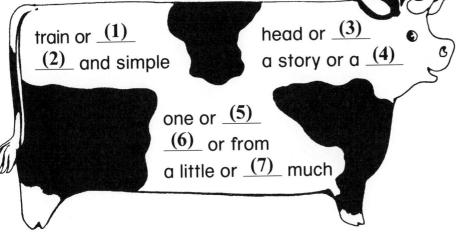

train or __(1)__
__(2)__ and simple

head or __(3)__
a story or a __(4)__

one or __(5)__
__(6)__ or from
a little or __(7)__ much

1. _____

2. _____

3. _____

4. _____

5. _____

6. _____

7. _____

Silly Poems   Write a Basic or Elephant word to finish each silly poem.

8. The sun was shining clear and bright.
   The wind tugged on the ____ of my kite.

9. We have plenty of time to sing your song,
   As long as it won't take ____ long!

10. I heard a ____ about a young bunny.
    It made me laugh because it was funny.

8. _____

9. _____

10. _____

Skill: Children will practice spelling words that are **homophones**.

Home Use: Help your child practice the spelling words by having him or her complete the activities on this page. Check the completed page, and have your child practice saying and spelling any misspelled words.

107

Basic Words
1. plane
2. plain
3. tail
4. tale
5. rode
6. road
7. hole
8. whole

Elephant Words
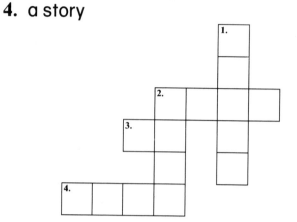 to
🐘 too
🐘 two

PRACTICE B
Homophones

Crossword Clues   Write a Basic or Elephant Word for each clue.

Across
2. a place for cars
3. the opposite of **from**
4. a story

Down
1. something that flies
2. drove in a car

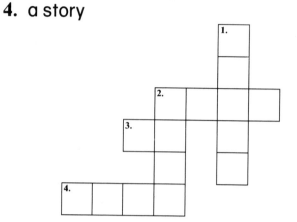

Proofreading   5–10. Find and cross out six Basic or Elephant Words that are spelled wrong on this menu. Write each word correctly.

Dom's Diner

Scrambled eggs with to muffins $2.50
A hole pizza $1.95
Lobster tale soup $3.25
Doughnut with or without a whole 45¢
Pudding
    plane 75¢
    with topping 90¢
Turkey (and the stuffing to) $3.75

5. _____

6. _____

7. _____

8. _____

9. _____

10. _____

Houghton Mifflin Spelling and Vocabulary. Copyright © Houghton Mifflin Company. All rights reserved.

Skill: Children will practice spelling words that are **homophones**.

Home Use: Help your child practice the spelling words by having him or her complete the activities on this page. Check the completed page, and have your child practice saying and spelling any misspelled words.

PRACTICE C
Homophones

Flying High Write the missing Challenge and Vocabulary Words. Find out about the pilots.

1. Eli and Ruby ____ over the ocean.

2. Nell and Ira ____ on the runway.

3. Eli is the only ____ wearing glasses.

4. Ruby just flew ____ a cloud.

5–6. Ira wears a pack that a ____ member ____ to him.

Challenge Words
1. threw
2. through
Theme Vocabulary
3. pilot
4. glide
5. land
6. crew

1. _____

2. _____

3. _____

4. _____

5. _____

6. _____

Now write the correct name of each pilot. Use the sentences above to help you.

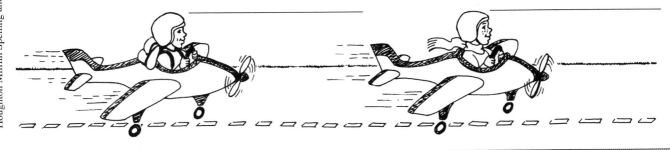

Houghton Mifflin Spelling and Vocabulary. Copyright © Houghton Mifflin Company. All rights reserved.

Skill: Children will practice spelling words that are **homophones** and words related to the theme of things that fly.

Home Use: Help your child practice the spelling words by having him or her complete the activities on this page. Check the completed page, and have your child practice saying and spelling any misspelled words.

109

Unit 23 Test: Homophones

Read each sentence. Is the underlined word spelled right or wrong? Mark your answer.

	Right	Wrong
Sample: I can <u>sea</u> a bird in the sky.	○	●

		Right	Wrong
1.	Angelo can sing well <u>two</u>.	1. ○	○
2.	We made a very <u>plane</u> dinner.	2. ○	○
3.	Rosie told us a funny <u>tale</u>.	3. ○	○
4.	Are you going <u>to</u> Sandra's party?	4. ○	○
5.	Fred watched the <u>plain</u> fly by.	5. ○	○
6.	My dog chases his own <u>tail</u>.	6. ○	○
7.	Would Irene like <u>too</u> go with us?	7. ○	○
8.	Carl <u>road</u> the horse to work.	8. ○	○
9.	The mask covered her <u>whole</u> face.	9. ○	○
10.	Vera and I live on the same <u>rode</u>.	10. ○	○
11.	There is a big <u>hole</u> in my shoe.	11. ○	○

Houghton Mifflin Spelling and Vocabulary. Copyright © Houghton Mifflin Company. All rights reserved.

BULLETIN BOARD

WORD BANK

COINS

CASH CARDS

WORD LIST

TOTAL
7 1 3 4

1 abc	2 def	3 ghi
4 jkl	5 mno	6 pqr
7 stu	8 vwx	9 yz

CARD SLOT
What boats do

How to make: Title the bulletin board "Word Bank." Make a cash register from construction paper. Label the "keys" with numbers and letters as shown. Label the register drawer *CARD SLOT*. In the TOTAL window, place seven small hooks or pushpins. Cut out nine tagboard circles to use as tags, and number them 1–9. (For Unit 20, make three number 7 tags. For Unit 22, make two number 5 tags.) Punch two holes in the tops of the circles and tie a loop of string through the holes.

Label two cardboard boxes *COINS* and *CASH CARDS*, and attach the boxes to the bulletin board. Place paper strips in the CASH CARD box. Hang a pencil next to this box. Attach an envelope for the list of Basic and Elephant Words from the unit being studied, or provide word lists for each unit in the cycle.

How to use: Have students work in pairs. One student takes a paper strip and a unit word list. The student writes a synonym or clue for one of the Basic or Elephant Words on the paper strip and tacks it onto the CARD SLOT space, as shown. The other student thinks of the list word that fits the clue and then uses the numbers and letters on the cash register to translate the word into a number code. For example, the word *sail* is 7–1–3–4 in code. The guesser finds the tags with the correct numbers and hangs them in the TOTAL window. Students switch roles each turn.

Houghton Mifflin Spelling and Vocabulary. Copyright © Houghton Mifflin Company. All rights reserved.

Use: For use with Units 19–23.

SPELLING NEWSLETTER
for Students and Their Families

Moving Ahead

Units 19 through 23 of your child's level of *Houghton Mifflin Spelling and Vocabulary* have discussed words that end with *nd, ng,* or *nk;* words that end with *s* or *es;* words such as *coat, go,* and *slow* that have the vowel spellings *oa, o,* and *ow;* and words such as *food* and *look* that have the *oo* spelling. Your child has also learned about homophones, words such as *tail* and *tale* that sound alike but have different spellings and meanings.

Word Lists

Your child has been studying the words below as well as other words with similar patterns.

UNIT 19	UNIT 20	UNIT 21	UNIT 22	UNIT 23
thank	dresses	boat	food	tail
sing	boxes	go	look	tale
and	beaches	slow	moon	rode
think	days	old	took	road
bring	bikes	coat	good	hole
end	wishes	told	room	whole

👪 Family Activity

Make a spelling-word jigsaw puzzle from cardboard. Cut a large sheet of cardboard into ten or more puzzle pieces. On each piece, write one word from the word lists above. Make sure that each puzzle piece contains one complete word and that each puzzle piece shape is different from the others. Place the pieces in a bag or other container.

Have your child select a puzzle piece from the bag, place the piece on a table, and say and spell the word on the piece. Next, have your child select a second piece, say and spell that word, and try to fit the piece correctly with the other piece. If the pieces do not fit together, leave both on the table. Take turns with your child choosing puzzle pieces, saying and spelling the words, and trying to solve the puzzle. Continue the procedure until you and your child have completed the puzzle.

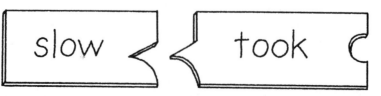

Houghton Mifflin Spelling and Vocabulary. Copyright © Houghton Mifflin Company. All rights reserved.

Boletín de noticias de ortografía
para estudiantes y para sus familias

Para continuar

Su hijo o hija ha estado estudiando las siguientes palabras y otras
palabras que siguen patrones similares en las Unidades 19 a 23 del libro
Houghton Mifflin Spelling and Vocabulary.

UNIDAD 19	UNIDAD 20	UNIDAD 21	UNIDAD 22	UNIDAD 23
thank	dresses	boat	food	tail
sing	boxes	go	look	tale
and	beaches	slow	moon	rode
think	days	old	took	road
bring	bikes	coat	good	hole
end	wishes	told	room	whole

♟ *Actividad para la familia*

Usando cartón, hagan un rompecabezas de palabras. Corten una hoja grande
de cartón en pedazos, hasta tener diez o más piezas de rompecabezas.
En cada pieza escriban una palabra de las listas que aparecen arriba. Asegúrense
de que cada pieza del rompecabezas contenga una palabra completa y de
que la forma de cada pieza del rompecabezas sea diferente de las otras
piezas. Coloquen las piezas en una bolsa o en algún otro recipiente.

Hagan que su hijo o hija saque una pieza del rompecabezas de la bolsa y
que ponga la pieza sobre una mesa. Pídanle que diga en voz alta la palabra
que está escrita en la pieza y que la deletree. Después hagan que su hijo o
hija saque otra pieza, que lea y deletree esa palabra y que trate de juntar la
pieza correctamente con la otra pieza. Si las piezas no encajan la una con la
otra, dejen ambas sobre la mesa. Túrnense con su hijo o hija para escoger
piezas del rompecabezas, para decir y deletrear las palabras y para tratar de
resolver el rompecabezas. Continúen el juego hasta completar el rompecabezas.

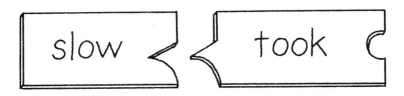

Houghton Mifflin Spelling and Vocabulary. Copyright © Houghton Mifflin Company. All rights reserved.

KING AND QUEEN'S CASTLE

SPELLING
GAME

Players: 2

You need: a copy of the game board on page 115, a spinner, 2 markers (small pieces of paper)

How to play: Write a Basic or Elephant Word in each space on the game board. Leave blanks for one, two, or three letters in each word. For example, the word **wishes** might look like this: **w__sh__s.**

Now help the king and queen get to their home in the castle. Cut out the spinner and the arrow below, and paste them to pieces of cardboard. Attach the arrow to the spinner so that it is loose enough to spin.

Take turns spinning the spinner. Move your marker the number of spaces the spinner shows. Spell each word that you land on, saying the missing letters. If you spell the word correctly, take another turn. The first player to land on the castle wins.

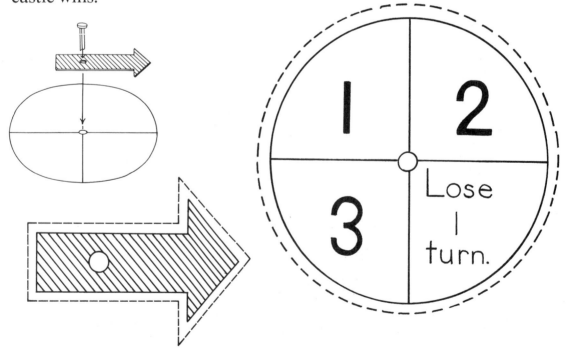

Houghton Mifflin Spelling and Vocabulary. Copyright © Houghton Mifflin Company. All rights reserved.

Use: For use with Units 19-23.

KING AND QUEEN'S CASTLE

Houghton Mifflin Spelling and Vocabulary. Copyright © Houghton Mifflin Company. All rights reserved.

Unit 24 Review: Test A

Read each sentence. One of the underlined words in each
sentence is spelled wrong. Mark the letter for that word.

Sample: **ANSWERS**

Mom wants <u>to</u> <u>lok</u> at my painting.   ⓐ ●
        a b

1. That <u>book</u> is in one of the <u>boxs</u>.   1. ⓐ ⓑ
      a   b

2. I will <u>thenk</u> the cook for this <u>food</u>.   2. ⓐ ⓑ
       a   b

3. Bev will tell <u>yoo</u> a funny <u>tale</u>.   3. ⓐ ⓑ
        a   b

4. Can I ride to the <u>moon</u> in a <u>boet</u>?   4. ⓐ ⓑ
         a   b

5. Did the <u>kign</u> fly in his <u>plane</u>?   5. ⓐ ⓑ
      a   b

6. It is very <u>coald</u> <u>and</u> windy today.   6. ⓐ ⓑ
       a   b

7. Touch your <u>toe</u> with your <u>hend</u>.   7. ⓐ ⓑ
       a   b

8. Will you <u>go</u> to buy new <u>dishs</u>?   8. ⓐ ⓑ
      a   b

9. There are <u>noe</u> <u>beaches</u> near here.   9. ⓐ ⓑ
      a   b

10. All of the <u>childran</u> went to the <u>zoo</u>.   10. ⓐ ⓑ
       a   b

11. I like to wear <u>plain</u> <u>dresss</u>.   11. ⓐ ⓑ
       a   b

12. My puppy's <u>tail</u> is not <u>tooo</u> long.   12. ⓐ ⓑ
      a   b

Houghton Mifflin Spelling and Vocabulary. Copyright © Houghton Mifflin Company. All rights reserved.

Unit **24** Review: Test B

Read each sentence. One of the underlined words in each sentence is spelled wrong. Mark the letter for that word.

Sample:	**ANSWERS**
How many <u>wishs</u> did <u>you</u> make? 　　　　　　a　　　　　b	

1. Will Maria <u>bring</u> her warm <u>cowt</u>?
   　　　　　　　a　　　　　　　　b

2. It took four <u>dayes</u> to get there.
   　　a　　　　b

3. Harvey <u>toald</u> me their <u>names</u>.
   　　　　a　　　　　　　b

4. Do you <u>thenk</u> <u>two</u> cars will fit?
   　　　　a　　b

5. The <u>whole</u> <u>rume</u> was painted green.
   　　　a　　b

6. They use their <u>biks</u> on the <u>road</u>.
   　　　　　a　　　　　　b

7. Betty should sew up that <u>hole</u> <u>sune</u>.
   　　　　　　　　　　a　　b

8. Please <u>sho</u> the note <u>to</u> Krisi.
   　　a　　　　　b

9. Do this <u>theng</u> by the <u>end</u> of the day.
   　　　a　　　　　b

10. What <u>do</u> you <u>grrow</u> in your garden?
    　　a　　　b

11. Ask them <u>whoe</u> <u>rode</u> on the bus.
    　　　　a　　b

12. Did you bring <u>good</u> <u>thinges</u> to eat?
    　　　　a　　b

1. ⓐ ⓑ
2. ⓐ ⓑ
3. ⓐ ⓑ
4. ⓐ ⓑ
5. ⓐ ⓑ
6. ⓐ ⓑ
7. ⓐ ⓑ
8. ⓐ ⓑ
9. ⓐ ⓑ
10. ⓐ ⓑ
11. ⓐ ⓑ
12. ⓐ ⓑ

Houghton Mifflin Spelling and Vocabulary. Copyright © Houghton Mifflin Company. All rights reserved.

Prewriting Ideas: Instructions

Choosing a Topic Here is a list of ideas that one student made for writing instructions. What things that you can do well do these ideas make you think of?

On the lines below **My Three Ideas**, write three things that you know how to do or make. Which idea do you know all the steps for? For which idea can you explain each step clearly? Circle the topic that you would like to write about.

Ideas for Writing

How to Make a Code	How to Eat Corn on the Cob
How to Whistle	How to Make a Mud Pie

My Three Ideas

1. _____

2. _____

3. _____

Exploring Your Topic You can use a picture like this one to help you plan your instructions. Copy the picture onto another sheet of paper. Make it large enough to write on. Write your topic on the big stone. Then write a few words about each step on the small stepping stones. Write the steps in order.

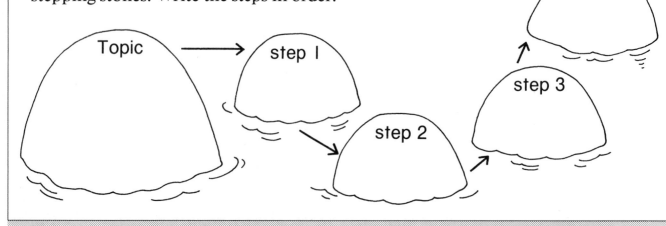

Houghton Mifflin Spelling and Vocabulary. Copyright © Houghton Mifflin Company. All rights reserved.

Use: For use with Step 1: Prewriting on page 167.

PRACTICE A
More Long i Spellings

Summing Up

The vowel sound in **sky**, **find**, and **night** is the long **i** sound. The long **i** sound may be spelled **y**, **i**, or **igh**.

Basic Words
1. sky
2. find
3. night
4. high
5. fly

Elephant Words
🐘 eye
🐘 buy

Catch a Fly   Help the bug make its web. Write the letter or letters that spell the long **i** sound to finish each Basic Word.

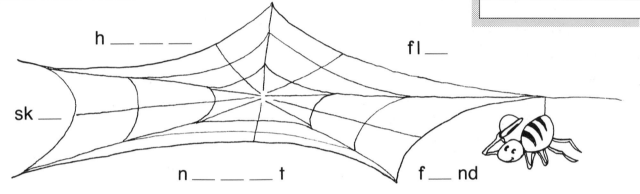

h _ _ _

fl _

sk _

n _ _ _ t

f _ nd

Now write each word from the web under the correct bug.

1. _____

2. _____

3. _____

4. _____

5. _____

Fill-In Fun   Write the missing Basic or Elephant Words.

6. ____ and ear   **7.** ____ a kite   **8.** ____ and sell

6. _____

7. _____

8. _____

Houghton Mifflin Spelling and Vocabulary. Copyright © Houghton Mifflin Company. All rights reserved.

Skill: Children will practice spelling words with the |ī| sound.

Home Use: Help your child practice the spelling words by having him or her complete the activities on this page. Check the completed page, and have your child practice saying and spelling any misspelled words.

Basic Words
1. sky
2. find
3. night
4. high
5. fly
6. try
7. light
8. dry
9. right
10. kind

Elephant Words
🐘 eye
🐘 buy

7. _____

8. _____

9. _____

10. _____

11. _____

12. _____

PRACTICE B
More Long i Spellings

Send a Message Use the code below to write Basic and Elephant Words.

1	2	3	4	5	6	7	8	9	10	11
d	e	f	i	k	l	n	r	s	t	y

1. 10 · 8 · 11   **3.** 3 · 6 · 11   **5.** 3 · 4 · 7 · 1

2. 2 · 11 · 2   **4.** 9 · 5 · 11   **6.** 1 · 8 · 11

1. _____   4. _____

2. _____   5. _____

3. _____   6. _____

In the Family Write the Basic or Elephant Word that is the opposite of the word in dark print.

7. Mr. Opposite has **dark** hair.
Mrs. Opposite's hair is _____.

8. Mr. Opposite writes with his **left** hand.
Mrs. Opposite writes with her _____ hand.

9. Mr. Opposite is sometimes **mean**.
Mrs. Opposite is often _____.

10. Mr. Opposite likes to walk during the **day**.
Mrs. Opposite likes to walk at _____.

11. Mr. Opposite has a **low** voice.
Mrs. Opposite's voice is _____.

12. Mr. Opposite wants to **sell** the old car.
Mrs. Opposite wants to _____ a new one.

Skill: Children will practice spelling words with the /ī/ sound.

Home Use: Help your child practice the spelling words by having him or her complete the activities on this page. Check the completed page, and have your child practice saying and spelling any misspelled words.

Houghton Mifflin Spelling and Vocabulary. Copyright © Houghton Mifflin Company. All rights reserved.

PRACTICE C
More Long i Spellings

Future Times   Write a headline for each news story. Use all the Challenge and Vocabulary Words. Use capital letters correctly.

Challenge Words
1. flight
2. behind
Theme Vocabulary
3. Mars
4. space
5. planet
6. Pluto

Future Times   Thursday March 23, 2050

_____

- - - - - - - - - - - - - - - - - -

_____

PALM SPRINGS—Buzz Smith, Gloria Tate, and Donna Carty are getting ready for a trip to the red planet. The trip will last several months.

_____

- - - - - - - - - - - - - - - - - -

_____

KENNEDY SPACE CENTER— Explorers have brought back several tiny plants from the planet farthest from the sun.

_____

- - - - - - - - - - - - - - - - - -

_____

The spaceship **Stardust** returned to Earth today after leaving a weather station among the stars.

Houghton Mifflin Spelling and Vocabulary. Copyright © Houghton Mifflin Company. All rights reserved.

Skill: Children will practice spelling words with the |ī| sound and words related to the theme of stars and planets.

Home Use: Help your child practice the spelling words by having him or her complete the activities on this page. Check the completed page, and have your child practice saying and spelling any misspelled words.

Unit **25** Test: More Long i Spellings

Each item below gives three spellings of a word. Choose the correct spelling. Mark the letter for that word.

Sample:

| a. cri | b. cry | c. crigh | **ANSWERS** ⓐ ● ⓒ |

1. **a.** fly   **b.** fli   **c.** fligh   1. ⓐ ⓑ ⓒ

2. **a.** nyt   **b.** night   **c.** nite   2. ⓐ ⓑ ⓒ

3. **a.** bigh   **b.** bi   **c.** buy   3. ⓐ ⓑ ⓒ

4. **a.** hy   **b.** hye   **c.** high   4. ⓐ ⓑ ⓒ

5. **a.** skie   **b.** sky   **c.** skigh   5. ⓐ ⓑ ⓒ

6. **a.** eigh   **b.** eie   **c.** eye   6. ⓐ ⓑ ⓒ

7. **a.** find   **b.** fynd   **c.** fighnd   7. ⓐ ⓑ ⓒ

8. **a.** ryt   **b.** right   **c.** rit   8. ⓐ ⓑ ⓒ

9. **a.** try   **b.** tri   **c.** trigh   9. ⓐ ⓑ ⓒ

10. **a.** drigh   **b.** dry   **c.** dri   10. ⓐ ⓑ ⓒ

11. **a.** lyt   **b.** liht   **c.** light   11. ⓐ ⓑ ⓒ

12. **a.** kind   **b.** kynd   **c.** kighnd   12. ⓐ ⓑ ⓒ

Houghton Mifflin Spelling and Vocabulary. Copyright © Houghton Mifflin Company. All rights reserved.

PRACTICE A
The Final Sound in puppy

Basic Words
1. puppy
2. baby
3. lucky
4. happy
5. very
Elephant Word
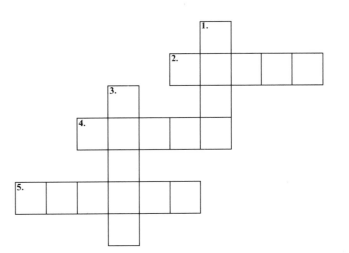 cookie

Summing Up

The words **puppy** and **baby** have two syllables. The long **e** sound at the end of a two-syllable word may be spelled **y**.

Crossword Fun   Write a Basic or Elephant Word for each clue.

Across

2. glad
4. a young dog
5. a small, sweet cake

Down

1. a very young child
3. having good luck

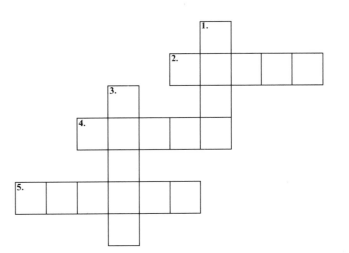

Chart-a-Word   Color the box under the letter or letters to finish each Basic Word. Write the words.

	y	py	by
6. hap			
7. luck			
8. ba			
9. ver			
10. pup			

6. _____

7. _____

8. _____

9. _____

10. _____

Circle the letter that spells the long **e** sound in each word you wrote.

Houghton Mifflin Spelling and Vocabulary. Copyright © Houghton Mifflin Company. All rights reserved.

Skill: Children will practice spelling two-syllable words with the final |ē| sound.

Home Use: Help your child practice the spelling words by having him or her complete the activities on this page. Check the completed page, and have your child practice saying and spelling any misspelled words.

123

Basic Words
1. puppy
2. baby
3. lucky
4. happy
5. very
6. lady
7. funny
8. silly
9. many
10. only
Elephant Word
cookie

PRACTICE B
The Final Sound in puppy

Rhyme Time   Help name the people in the play. Write the Basic Word that rhymes with the word in dark print. Begin each word with a capital letter.

1. _____ **Ducky**

2. _____ **Billy**

3. _____ **Bunny**

4. _____ **O'Grady**

5. _____ **Pappy**

Proofreading   6–11. Find and cross out six Basic or Elephant Words that are spelled wrong on these greeting cards. Write each word correctly.

Your silly pupy needs meny hugs!

How verry lucky he is to have you!

For your birthday, I'm giving you a cookee!

My other friends got onle cards!

A new babe boy will bring you great joy!

6. _____

7. _____

8. _____

9. _____

10. _____

11. _____

Skill: Children will practice spelling two-syllable words with the final |ē| sound.

124

Home Use: Help your child practice the spelling words by having him or her complete the activities on this page. Check the completed page, and have your child practice saying and spelling any misspelled words.

Houghton Mifflin Spelling and Vocabulary. Copyright © Houghton Mifflin Company. All rights reserved.

PRACTICE C
The Final Sound in puppy

Take a Close Look   Look at Pictures 1 and 2. Circle
five things in Picture 2 that are different from Picture 1.

Challenge Words
1. furry
2. noisy
Theme Vocabulary
3. piglet
4. kid
5. tadpole
6. hatch

Now write five sentences to tell how Picture 2 is different from
Picture 1. Use all the Challenge and Vocabulary Words.

1. _____

2. _____

3. _____

4. _____

5. _____

Houghton Mifflin Spelling and Vocabulary. Copyright © Houghton Mifflin Company. All rights reserved.

Skill: Children will practice spelling two-syllable words with the final |ē| sound and words related to the theme of baby animals.

Home Use: Help your child practice the spelling words by having him or her complete the activities on this page. Check the completed page, and have your child practice saying and spelling any misspelled words.

125

Unit **26** Test: The Final Sound in puppy

Read each word group. Find the correctly spelled word to complete each group. Mark the letter next to that word.

Sample:

a _____ picture

(ⓐ) prettie

(ⓑ) pritty

● pretty

1. a _____ ending
   ⓐ happy
   ⓑ happe
   ⓒ hapi

2. a crying _____
   ⓐ babie
   ⓑ baby
   ⓒ baybe

3. a _____ quiet day
   ⓐ veery
   ⓑ veree
   ⓒ very

4. from the _____ jar
   ⓐ cooki
   ⓑ kooke
   ⓒ cookie

5. your _____ day
   ⓐ lucki
   ⓑ lucky
   ⓒ luckiy

6. a playful _____
   ⓐ puppy
   ⓑ puppi
   ⓒ puppie

7. a _____ song
   ⓐ sillie
   ⓑ silly
   ⓒ sili

8. a _____ story
   ⓐ funny
   ⓑ fune
   ⓒ funni

9. in _____ one day
   ⓐ onle
   ⓑ ownly
   ⓒ only

10. few or _____
    ⓐ meny
    ⓑ many
    ⓒ manie

11. a young _____
    ⓐ lady
    ⓑ ladie
    ⓒ ladi

Houghton Mifflin Spelling and Vocabulary. Copyright © Houghton Mifflin Company. All rights reserved.

PRACTICE A
The Vowel Sound in cow

Summing Up

The words **town** and **house** have the same vowel sound. The vowel sound may be spelled **ow** or **ou**.

Basic Words
1. town
2. house
3. out
4. down
5. cow

Elephant Words
🐘 could
🐘 should

Queen of the Seas   Fill in the missing letters to finish each word. Then write the words that have the vowel sound in **town** and **house**.

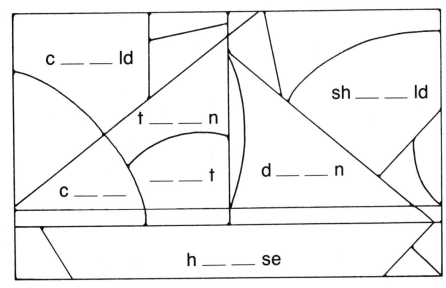

c __ __ ld

sh __ __ ld

t __ __ n

__ __ t

d __ __ n

c __ __

h __ __ se

1. _____

2. _____

3. _____

4. _____

5. _____

Now color the spaces for the words with the vowel sound in **town** and **house.** Find the hidden picture.

Scrambled Riddles   Unscramble the underlined Basic or Elephant Word in each riddle. Write the word. Then see if you can think of the answer to each riddle.

6. Why <u>holdus</u> dentists like potatoes?

7. What kind of <u>shoue</u> weighs the least?

8. How <u>locud</u> you make seven even?

6. _____

7. _____

8. _____

Riddle Answers: 6. They are always filling.   **7.** a lighthouse   **8.** Take away the s.

Houghton Mifflin Spelling and Vocabulary. Copyright © Houghton Mifflin Company. All rights reserved.

Skill: Children will practice spelling words with the |ou| sound.

Home Use: Help your child practice the spelling words by having him or her complete the activities on this page. Check the completed page, and have your child practice saying and spelling any misspelled words.

Basic Words
1. town
2. house
3. out
4. down
5. cow
6. now
7. found
8. how
9. mouse
10. brown

Elephant Words
🐘 could
🐘 should

PRACTICE B

The Vowel Sound in cow

Hink Pink   Write two Basic Words that rhyme to answer each question.

1–2. What is a home for a small animal?

_____   _____

a _____   _____

3–4. What is a village that is painted a dark color?

_____   _____

a _____   _____

Cow Catcher   Help Farmer Brown find her cow. Draw a line joining eight Basic and Elephant Words in ABC order. Then write those words in ABC order.

could

now

cow

how

down

cow

how

now

out

found

should

could

should

5. _____   8. _____   11. _____

6. _____   9. _____   12. _____

7. _____   10. _____

Skill: Children will practice spelling words with the |ou| sound.

Home Use: Help your child practice the spelling words by having him or her complete the activities on this page. Check the completed page, and have your child practice saying and spelling any misspelled words.

Houghton Mifflin Spelling and Vocabulary. Copyright © Houghton Mifflin Company. All rights reserved.

PRACTICE C
The Vowel Sound in COW

House for Sale   Write ads to help sell the homes below. Use all the Challenge and Vocabulary Words. Use a separate sheet of paper if you need more room.

Challenge Words
1. couch
2. crowded
Theme Vocabulary
3. cottage
4. igloo
5. trailer
6. palace

1.   For Sale

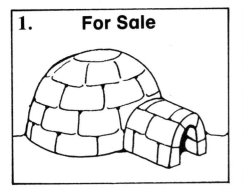

2.   For Sale

3.   For Sale

4.   For Sale

Houghton Mifflin Spelling and Vocabulary. Copyright © Houghton Mifflin Company. All rights reserved.

Skill: Children will practice spelling words with the |ou| sound and words related to the theme of places to live.

Home Use: Help your child practice the spelling words by having him or her complete the activities on this page. Check the completed page, and have your child practice saying and spelling any misspelled words.

Unit **27** Test: The Vowel Sound in cow

Each item below gives three spellings of a word.
Choose the correct spelling. Mark the letter for that
word.

Sample:			**ANSWERS**
a. cloun	**b.** clown	**c.** clouln	(a) ● (c)

1. **a.** owt   **b.** out   **c.** outt   1. (a) (b) (c)

2. **a.** cow   **b.** cou   **c.** kow   2. (a) (b) (c)

3. **a.** howse   **b.** hous   **c.** house   3. (a) (b) (c)

4. **a.** should   **b.** showd   **c.** shoud   4. (a) (b) (c)

5. **a.** toun   **b.** town   **c.** towen   5. (a) (b) (c)

6. **a.** cood   **b.** cuwd   **c.** could   6. (a) (b) (c)

7. **a.** doun   **b.** down   **c.** doown   7. (a) (b) (c)

8. **a.** brone   **b.** brounn   **c.** brown   8. (a) (b) (c)

9. **a.** how   **b.** hou   **c.** houe   9. (a) (b) (c)

10. **a.** fownd   **b.** found   **c.** fowend   10. (a) (b) (c)

11. **a.** nou   **b.** nawe   **c.** now   11. (a) (b) (c)

12. **a.** mouse   **b.** mowse   **c.** mawz   12. (a) (b) (c)

Houghton Mifflin Spelling and Vocabulary. Copyright © Houghton Mifflin Company. All rights reserved.

PRACTICE A
Compound Words

Summing Up

A **compound word** is a word that is made up of two shorter words.

Basic Words
1. bathtub
2. bedtime
3. myself
4. someone
5. maybe

Compound Maze Draw a line to join the two words that make up each Basic Word.

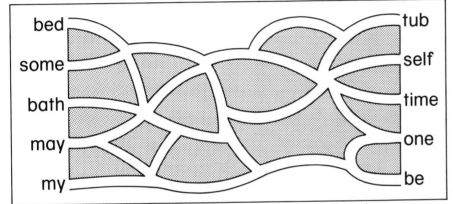

1. _____

2. _____

3. _____

4. _____

5. _____

Look at the Basic Words you made. Write a word for each clue.

1. another word for **perhaps**

2. a person

3. me, ____, and I

4. when you go to sleep

5. where you get clean

Dot-to-Dot What do you get whenever you sit in the bathtub? To find the answer, connect the dots to spell three Basic Words. Then write the words.

b •   • e   o •   • s   m •   y l   • f

e •   t •   • m   m   • e
                          o

d •   • i   n •   • e   s •   • e

6. _____

7. _____

8. _____

Houghton Mifflin Spelling and Vocabulary. Copyright © Houghton Mifflin Company. All rights reserved.

Skill: Children will practice spelling **compound words.**

Home Use: Help your child practice the spelling words by having him or her complete the activities on this page. Check the completed page, and have your child practice saying and spelling any misspelled words.

Basic Words
1. bathtub
2. bedtime
3. myself
4. someone
5. maybe
6. into
7. upon
8. anyone
9. without
10. cannot

PRACTICE B
Compound Words

Rhyme Time   Each word in dark print rhymes with the second part of a Basic Word. Write the Basic Words.

1. Can you get a bear **cub** to sit in the _____?
2. Give them a **dime** if they know when it's _____.
3. The books on the **shelf** are only for _____.
4. Tom _____ eat the food while it is **hot.**
5. Will Mom **shout** if I leave _____ my lunch?

1. _____

2. _____

3. _____

4. _____

5. _____

6. _____

7. _____

8. _____

9. _____

10. _____

Words in a Haystack   Circle five Basic Words hidden in the hay. Look across and down. Then write the words.

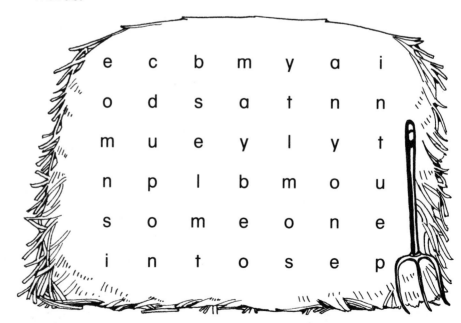

e	c	b	m	y	a	i
o	d	s	a	t	n	n
m	u	e	y	l	y	t
n	p	l	b	m	o	u
s	o	m	e	o	n	e
i	n	t	o	s	e	p

Houghton Mifflin Spelling and Vocabulary. Copyright © Houghton Mifflin Company. All rights reserved.

Skill: Children will practice spelling **compound words.**

Home Use: Help your child practice the spelling words by having him or her complete the activities on this page. Check the completed page, and have your child practice saying and spelling any misspelled words.

PRACTICE C
Compound Words

Staying in Shape   Draw a picture to finish this story. Then write sentences to tell what happens in each picture. Use all the Challenge and Vocabulary Words.

Challenge Words
1. playground
2. nobody
Theme Vocabulary
3. jog
4. fit
5. muscles
6. shape

1.

2.

3.

1. _____

2. _____

3. _____

Houghton Mifflin Spelling and Vocabulary. Copyright © Houghton Mifflin Company. All rights reserved.

Skill: Children will practice spelling **compound words** and words related to the theme of taking care of yourself.

Home Use: Help your child practice the spelling words by having him or her complete the activities on this page. Check the completed page, and have your child practice saying and spelling any misspelled words.

133

Unit **28** Test: Compound Words

Read each word group. Find the correctly spelled word to complete each group. Mark the letter next to that word.

Sample:
bright _____
(a) sunshin
(b) sonshine
● sunshine

1. yes, no, or _____
   (a) mabee
   (b) maybe
   (c) mayby

2. a story at _____
   (a) bettime
   (b) bedtim
   (c) bedtime

3. for _____ else
   (a) somone
   (b) someone
   (c) sumwun

4. me, _____, and I
   (a) myself
   (b) miself
   (c) mysself

5. out of the _____
   (a) bathub
   (b) battub
   (c) bathtub

6. once _____ a time
   (a) upon
   (b) oupon
   (c) uphon

7. _____ a word
   (a) witout
   (b) without
   (c) widthoud

8. to ask _____
   (a) anywun
   (b) enyone
   (c) anyone

9. _____ the room
   (a) into
   (b) intwo
   (c) entoo

10. _____ have one
    (a) canot
    (b) cannot
    (c) kenknot

Houghton Mifflin Spelling and Vocabulary. Copyright © Houghton Mifflin Company. All rights reserved.

PRACTICE A
Contractions

Summing Up

A **contraction** is a short way of writing two words. An **apostrophe** takes the place of the letter or letters that are left out.

Basic Words
1. I'll
2. we've
3. don't
4. you're
5. isn't
Elephant Word
🐘 can't

Contractions at Work   Help Ted's Sign Company fill six new orders. Write a contraction for the words on the brushes above each sign.

1.

You

_____

use this door.

2.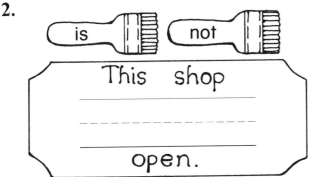

This   shop

_____

open.

3.

_____

vote!

4.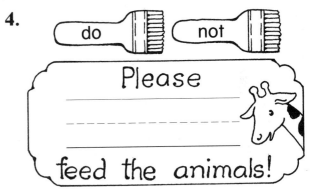

Please

_____

feed the animals!

5.

Sorry,

_____

gone to lunch.

6.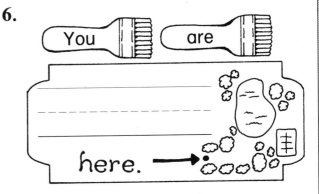

_____

here. ➡

Houghton Mifflin Spelling and Vocabulary. Copyright © Houghton Mifflin Company. All rights reserved.

Skill: Children will practice spelling words that are **contractions**.

Home Use: Help your child practice the spelling words by having him or her complete the activities on this page. Check the completed page, and have your child practice saying and spelling any misspelled words.

Basic Words
1. I'll
2. we've
3. don't
4. you're
5. isn't
6. didn't
7. you'll
8. I've
9. hasn't
10. we'll

Elephant Word
🐘 can't

PRACTICE B
Contractions

Letter Bugs   Write a contraction for each pair of words. Circle the letter or letters that you left out.

1.

_____

4.

_____

2.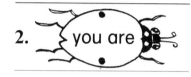

_____

5.

_____

3.

_____

6.

_____

What do the bugs say? In each space, write the letter or letters that you circled on the bug with the same number.

D ___ n ___ t hurt us! We ___ ll e ___ t the
⠀⠀6⠀⠀⠀3⠀⠀⠀⠀⠀⠀⠀⠀⠀⠀⠀⠀4⠀⠀⠀⠀2

bugs t ___ t hurt your fl ___ wers!
⠀⠀⠀⠀1⠀⠀⠀⠀⠀⠀⠀⠀⠀⠀⠀⠀⠀5

Proofreading   **7–11.** Find and cross out five Basic or Elephant Words that are spelled wrong in Ladybug's diary. Write each word correctly.

> Since our house burned, we've stayed with Aunt Bee. We didn't know where else to go. Her home isent like a ladybug's! Soon weill move to our new home. I cann't wait! Il'l be glad when Iv'e left this beehive!

7. _____

8. _____

9. _____

10. _____

11. _____

Skill: Children will practice spelling words that are **contractions.**

Home Use: Help your child practice the spelling words by having him or her complete the activities on this page. Check the completed page, and have your child practice saying and spelling any misspelled words.

Houghton Mifflin Spelling and Vocabulary. Copyright © Houghton Mifflin Company. All rights reserved.

PRACTICE C
Contractions

Groups of Three   Draw another thing that fits in each group. Write a sentence telling how the things in the group are alike. Use all the Vocabulary Words.

Houghton Mifflin Spelling and Vocabulary. Copyright © Houghton Mifflin Company. All rights reserved.

Challenge Words
1. they're
2. wouldn't
Theme Vocabulary
3. flea
4. moth
5. beetle
6. crawl

1.

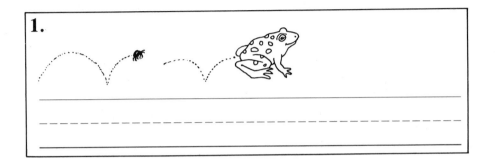

2.

3.

Riddle   Write the missing Challenge Words. Then write the answer to the riddle.

When _____ babies, they have gills so they can live in water. Then they grow lungs. Without lungs these green hoppers _____ be able to live on land. What are they?

Answer: __ __ __ __ __ __

4. _____

5. _____

Skill: Children will practice spelling words that are **contractions** and words related to the theme of insects.

Home Use: Help your child practice the spelling words by having him or her complete the activities on this page. Check the completed page, and have your child practice saying and spelling any misspelled words.

Unit 29 Test: Contractions

Each item below gives three spellings of a word. Choose the correct spelling. Mark the letter for that word.

Sample:			ANSWERS
a. letts	**b.** l'ets	**c.** let's	ⓐ ⓑ ●

1. **a.** isnt	**b.** izn't	**c.** isn't	1. ⓐ ⓑ ⓒ
2. **a.** don't	**b.** dowent	**c.** do'nt	2. ⓐ ⓑ ⓒ
3. **a.** weve	**b.** we've	**c.** w'eve	3. ⓐ ⓑ ⓒ
4. **a.** can'nt	**b.** ca'nt	**c.** can't	4. ⓐ ⓑ ⓒ
5. **a.** you're	**b.** yure	**c.** yo're	5. ⓐ ⓑ ⓒ
6. **a.** I'le	**b.** Il'l	**c.** I'll	6. ⓐ ⓑ ⓒ
7. **a.** hasent	**b.** hasn't	**c.** has'nt	7. ⓐ ⓑ ⓒ
8. **a.** yull	**b.** you'll	**c.** you'l	8. ⓐ ⓑ ⓒ
9. **a.** I've	**b.** Ive	**c.** Iv	9. ⓐ ⓑ ⓒ
10. **a.** di'dnt	**b.** didnt	**c.** didn't	10. ⓐ ⓑ ⓒ
11. **a.** weel	**b.** we'll	**c.** w'ell	11. ⓐ ⓑ ⓒ

Houghton Mifflin Spelling and Vocabulary. Copyright © Houghton Mifflin Company. All rights reserved.

Houghton Mifflin Spelling and Vocabulary. Copyright © Houghton Mifflin Company. All rights reserved.

BULLETIN BOARD

EGG MATCH

high / not low

fly / to use wings

Cracked Eggs Unit 25

Cracked Eggs Unit 26

Cracked Eggs Unit 27

Cracked Eggs Unit 29

Cracked Eggs Unit 28

Tacks

How to make: Make the title and a large hen from construction paper. Cut five bowl-shaped pockets out of tagboard, and label each with *Cracked Eggs* and a different unit number from the cycle. Attach the pockets to the board. Attach a box of thumbtacks to the bottom of the board.

How to use: Have students cut large eggs from construction paper or tagboard, and cut each egg into two equal parts. For Units 25–27, have students write a clue for a Basic or Elephant Word on one half of the egg and the matching word on the other half. For Unit 28, students may write one of the two words that make up the compound word on each half. For Unit 29, students may write the Elephant Word or a Basic Word on one half and the word or words that make up the contraction on the other half. Place the egg parts in the *Cracked Eggs* pocket for the unit.

Have students match the egg parts for the words in a unit and tack the matched parts onto the bulletin board.

Use: For use with Units 25 - 29.

139

SPELLING NEWSLETTER
for Students and Their Families

Moving Ahead

In your child's level of *Houghton Mifflin Spelling and Vocabulary*, Units 25 through 29 present words such as *high, fly,* and *kind* with the vowel spellings *igh, y,* and *i;* two-syllable words such as *baby* with the final sound spelled *y;* and words such as *found* and *now* that have the vowel spellings *ou* and *ow*. The units also discuss compound words such as *into* and contractions such as *don't.*

Word Lists

Your child has been studying the words below as well as other words with similar patterns.

UNIT 25	UNIT 26	UNIT 27	UNIT 28	UNIT 29
find	puppy	house	bathtub	we've
high	baby	out	myself	don't
fly	very	down	someone	you're
light	lady	now	into	didn't
dry	silly	found	upon	you'll
kind	only	brown	cannot	hasn't

👪 *Family Activity*

Play Spelling Steps with your child. Stand at one end of a room. Have your child stand at the other end of the room and face you. Call out a word from the word lists. If your child spells the word correctly, he or she takes two steps forward. If your child misspells the word, he or she takes one step backward. Repeat the procedure for other words. Tell your child to see how quickly he or she can reach you and become the new word caller.

Houghton Mifflin Spelling and Vocabulary. Copyright © Houghton Mifflin Company. All rights reserved.

140

Boletín de noticias de ortografía
para estudiantes y para sus familias

Para continuar

Su hijo o hija ha estado estudiando las siguientes palabras y otras
palabras que siguen patrones similares en las Unidades 25 a 29 del libro
Houghton Mifflin Spelling and Vocabulary.

UNIDAD 25	UNIDAD 26	UNIDAD 27	UNIDAD 28	UNIDAD 29
find	puppy	house	bathtub	we've
high	baby	out	myself	don't
fly	very	down	someone	you're
light	lady	now	into	didn't
dry	silly	found	upon	you'll
kind	only	brown	cannot	hasn't

Actividad para la familia

Con su hijo o hija, participen en un juego de pasos y deletreo. Párense
en un extremo de una habitación. Hagan que su hijo o hija se pare al otro
extremo de la habitación, de frente a ustedes. Digan en voz alta una palabra
de las listas de palabras. Si su hijo o hija deletrea la palabra correctamente,
él o ella da un paso hacia adelante. Si deletrea incorrectamente la palabra,
da un paso hacia atrás. Repitan ese procedimiento con otras palabras.
Pídanle a su hijo o hija que vea si puede avanzar rápidamente hasta llegar
donde están ustedes y pasar a ser así la persona que lee las palabras.

Houghton Mifflin Spelling and Vocabulary. Copyright © Houghton Mifflin Company. All rights reserved.

STAR SPELLER

Players: 2

You need: a copy of the game board on page 143, 2 markers, 25 cards with a Basic or Elephant Word and an instruction on each card

How to play: Write a Basic or Elephant Word on each card. Below the word, write an instruction, such as "Go ahead 3 spaces." Look at the examples at the bottom of the page.

Put the cards face down on the table. Player 1 picks a card and hands it to Player 2. Player 2 reads the word. If Player 1 spells the word correctly, he or she follows the instructions on the card and moves a marker from BLAST OFF. If Player 1 does not spell the word correctly, Player 2 takes a turn. Take turns picking cards and spelling the words for each other. The first player to reach FINISH wins.

Houghton Mifflin Spelling and Vocabulary. Copyright © Houghton Mifflin Company. All rights reserved.

Use: For use with Units 25 – 29.

STAR SPELLER

FINISH

BLAST OFF

Houghton Mifflin Spelling and Vocabulary. Copyright © Houghton Mifflin Company. All rights reserved.

Unit 30 Review: Test A

There are three words beside each number. One of the words is spelled wrong. Mark the letter next to that word.

Sample:
● funnie
ⓑ how
ⓒ I've

1. ⓐ can't
   ⓑ owt
   ⓒ buy

2. ⓐ coud
   ⓑ puppy
   ⓒ myself

3. ⓐ I'll
   ⓑ very
   ⓒ fligh

4. ⓐ town
   ⓑ isnt
   ⓒ bathtub

5. ⓐ high
   ⓑ cow
   ⓒ lucke

6. ⓐ howse
   ⓑ bedtime
   ⓒ we've

7. ⓐ sky
   ⓑ maebe
   ⓒ happy

8. ⓐ eye
   ⓑ baby
   ⓒ doun

9. ⓐ dont
   ⓑ someone
   ⓒ find

10. ⓐ you're
    ⓑ nyt
    ⓒ cookie

Houghton Mifflin Spelling and Vocabulary. Copyright © Houghton Mifflin Company. All rights reserved.

Unit 30 Review: Test B

There are three words beside each number. One of the words is spelled wrong. Mark the letter next to that word.

Sample:
ⓐ find
ⓑ baby
● mysself

1. ⓐ without
   ⓑ buy
   ⓒ onlie

2. ⓐ uppon
   ⓑ lady
   ⓒ we'll

3. ⓐ I've
   ⓑ fownd
   ⓒ light

4. ⓐ intoo
   ⓑ can't
   ⓒ cookie

5. ⓐ right
   ⓑ many
   ⓒ mowse

6. ⓐ bron
   ⓑ how
   ⓒ hasn't

7. ⓐ didn't
   ⓑ should
   ⓒ trigh

8. ⓐ dry
   ⓑ sillie
   ⓒ anyone

9. ⓐ kynd
   ⓑ funny
   ⓒ could

10. ⓐ now
    ⓑ yo'ull
    ⓒ cannot

Houghton Mifflin Spelling and Vocabulary. Copyright © Houghton Mifflin Company. All rights reserved.

Prewriting Ideas: Description

Choosing a Topic   Here is a list of ideas that one student made of things to describe. What people, places, or things do these ideas make you think of?

On the lines below **My Three Ideas**, write three interesting topics for a description. Which topic would someone else find most interesting? Can you remember how the topic looks, sounds, smells, feels, and tastes? Circle the topic that you would like to write about.

Ideas for Writing

My Favorite Place	A Strange Bug
My Favorite Teacher	A Thunderstorm

My Three Ideas

1. _____

2. _____

3. _____

Exploring Your Topic   You can use a flower cluster to help you plan your description. Copy the cluster onto another sheet of paper. Make it large enough to write on. Write your topic in the center. In the other flower parts, write exact words and details that describe how your topic looks, sounds, smells, tastes, and feels.

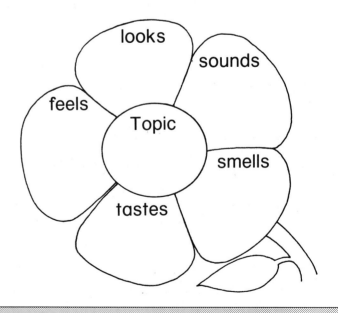

Houghton Mifflin Spelling and Vocabulary. Copyright © Houghton Mifflin Company. All rights reserved.

Use: For use with Step 1: Prewriting on page 203.

PRACTICE A
The Vowel + r Sound in car

Summing Up
You hear a vowel + r sound in **car** and **start**.
This sound is spelled **ar**.

All Aboard! Write the missing words. Find the words you wrote that have the vowel + **r** sound in **car**. Draw a line under the letters that spell that vowel sound.

Basic Words
1. car
2. start
3. arm
4. far
5. yard

Elephant Words
🐘 are
🐘 warm

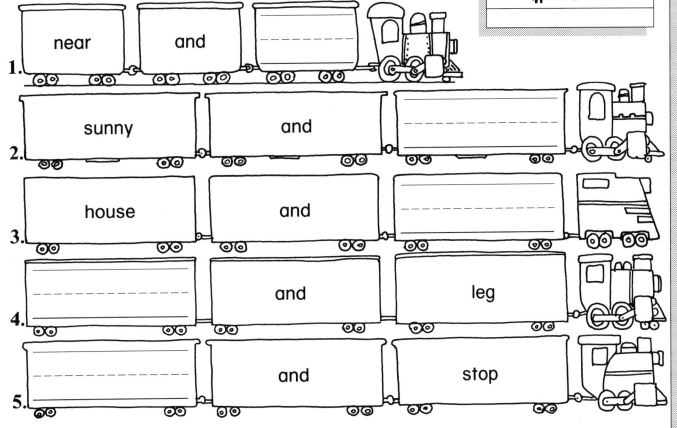

1. near / and / _____
2. sunny / and / _____
3. house / and / _____
4. _____ / and / leg
5. _____ / and / stop

Hidden Words Find and circle the hidden Basic or Elephant Word in each box. Then write the word.

6. | r a h t a r e m y |

7. | e n o v c a r u t |

8. | w o t h a r m i s |

6. _____

7. _____

8. _____

Houghton Mifflin Spelling and Vocabulary. Copyright © Houghton Mifflin Company. All rights reserved.

Skill: Children will practice spelling words with the vowel + |r| sound in **car**.

Home Use: Help your child practice the spelling words by having him or her complete the activities on this page. Check the completed page, and have your child practice saying and spelling any misspelled words.

147

Basic Words
1. car
2. start
3. arm
4. far
5. yard
6. part
7. barn
8. hard
9. party
10. farm

Elephant Words

🐘 are

🐘 warm

PRACTICE B

The Vowel + r Sound in car

Picture Math   Write the word for each clue.

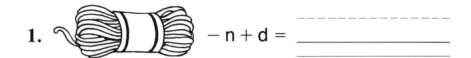

1.   − n + d = _____

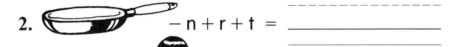

2.   − n + r + t = _____

3.   f + _____ = _____

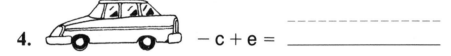

4.   − c + e = _____

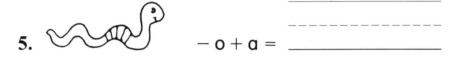

5.   − o + a = _____

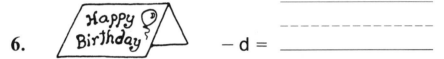

6.   − d = _____

Word Pairs   Write a Basic Word to finish the second sentence in each pair.

7. Your **foot** is part of your **leg**.
    Your **hand** is part of your ____.

8. **People** sleep in a **house**.
    Animals sleep in a ____.

9. A **pillow** is **soft**.
    A **rock** is ____.

10. At the **end**, you **stop**.
    At the **beginning**, you ____.

11. The opposite of **low** is **high**.
    The opposite of **near** is ____.

12. On the **Fourth of July**, you have a **parade**.
    On your **birthday**, you have a ____.

7. _____

8. _____

9. _____

10. _____

11. _____

12. _____

Houghton Mifflin Spelling and Vocabulary. Copyright © Houghton Mifflin Company. All rights reserved.

Skills: Children will practice spelling words with the vowel + |r| sound in **car**.

Home Use: Help your child practice the spelling words by having him or her complete the activities on this page. Check the completed page, and have your child practice saying and spelling any misspelled words.

PRACTICE C
The Vowel + r Sound in car

Crossword Clues   Write the Challenge and Vocabulary Words in the puzzle. Then write a clue for each **Across** word and each **Down** word.

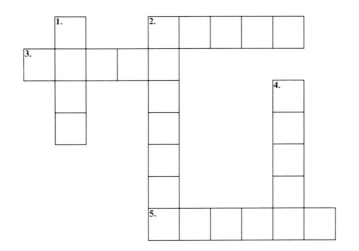

Challenge Words
1. large
2. carpet
Theme Vocabulary
3. hood
4. motor
5. trunk
6. traffic

Across

_____

2. _____

3. _____

5. _____

Down

1. _____

2. _____

4. _____

Houghton Mifflin Spelling and Vocabulary. Copyright © Houghton Mifflin Company. All rights reserved.

Skill: Children will practice spelling words with the vowel + |r| sound in **car** and words related to the theme of automobiles.

Home Use: Help your child practice the spelling words by having him or her complete the activities on this page. Check the completed page, and have your child practice saying and spelling any misspelled words.

Unit 31 Test: The Vowel + r Sound in car

Read each sentence. Find the correctly spelled word to complete each sentence. Mark the letter next to that word.

Sample:	ANSWERS
Fill the glass ____.	(a) jur ● jar (c) jer

1. May we ____ to play?   (a) stirt   (b) stert   (c) start

2. Bert travels near and ____.   (a) far   (b) fer   (c) furr

3. We ____ the winners!   (a) ar   (b) arr   (c) are

4. I like my old ____.   (a) kar   (b) car   (c) cor

5. Marty works in the ____.   (a) yard   (b) yarde   (c) yerd

6. Dora has a ____ blanket.   (a) warme   (b) warm   (c) wurm

7. Move your left ____.   (a) arme   (b) arn   (c) arm

8. Is that ____ or soft?   (a) haad   (b) hard   (c) hird

9. Come to my birthday ____.   (a) party   (b) parti   (c) pardy

10. The cow is in the red ____.   (a) bern   (b) barrn   (c) barn

11. Paul has a ____ in the play.   (a) pard   (b) part   (c) parte

12. My class will visit a ____.   (a) farm   (b) farn   (c) ferm

Houghton Mifflin Spelling and Vocabulary. Copyright © Houghton Mifflin Company. All rights reserved.

PRACTICE A
The Vowel + r **Sound in** store

Summing Up
You hear a vowel + **r** sound in **corn** and **store**.
This sound is spelled **or** or **ore**.

Basic Words

1. store
2. corn
3. for
4. more
5. or

Elephant Words

🐘 four

🐘 your

Good Knight! Write the missing letters to finish each Basic Word. Then write the words on the correct flags.

c ___ ___ n

m ___ ___ ___

f ___ ___

st ___ ___ ___

or
1. _____
2. _____

ore
3. _____
4. _____

Crossword Clues Write a Basic or Elephant Word for each clue.

Across
7. one more than three
9. a shop
10. something you eat

Down
5. the opposite of **less**
6. one ___ the other
8. belonging to you

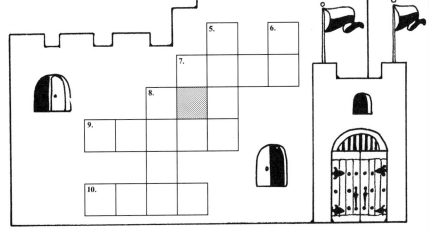

Houghton Mifflin Spelling and Vocabulary. Copyright © Houghton Mifflin Company. All rights reserved.

Skill: Children will practice spelling words with the vowel + |r| sound in **store**.

Home Use: Help your child practice the spelling words by having him or her complete the activities on this page. Check the completed page, and have your child practice saying and spelling any misspelled words.

Basic Words
1. store
2. corn
3. for
4. more
5. or
6. morning
7. short
8. born
9. story
10. horn
Elephant Words
🐘 four
🐘 your

PRACTICE B
The Vowel + r **Sound in** store

Letter Swap Change the letters in dark print to make Basic Words. Write the words.

1. bu**rn**   3. **c**ord   5. s**to**ve
2. **m**are   4. **s**tony   6. **sh**irt

1. _____   4. _____

2. _____   5. _____

3. _____   6. _____

Proofreading **7–12.** Find and cross out six Basic or Elephant Words that are spelled wrong on these boxes. Write each word correctly.

7. _____

8. _____

9. _____

10. _____

11. _____

12. _____

Now it's made with more corn! Eat a bowl every moring fer breakfast!

Each flake is shaped like a hourn to make yor mouth sing! Eat a bowl three ore fore times a week.

Houghton Mifflin Spelling and Vocabulary. Copyright © Houghton Mifflin Company. All rights reserved.

Skill: Children will practice spelling words with the vowel +|r| sound in **store**.

Home Use: Help your child practice the spelling words by having him or her complete the activities on this page. Check the completed page, and have your child practice saying and spelling any misspelled words.

PRACTICE C

The Vowel + r **Sound in** store

Mixed-up Market   Circle the four things that are
wrong in this picture.

Challenge Words
1. afford
2. before
Theme Vocabulary
3. dairy
4. counter
5. price
6. cart

Now write sentences to tell what is wrong in the picture above. Use
all the Challenge and Vocabulary Words in your sentences.

_____

_____

_____

_____

_____

_____

_____

_____

Houghton Mifflin Spelling and Vocabulary. Copyright © Houghton Mifflin Company. All rights reserved.

Skill: Children will practice spelling words with
the vowel + |r| sound in **store** and words
related to the theme of supermarkets.

Home Use: Help your child practice the spelling words by having him
or her complete the activities on this page. Check the completed page,
and have your child practice saying and spelling any misspelled words.

Unit **32** Test: The Vowel + r **Sound in** store

Each item below gives three spellings of a word.
Choose the correct spelling. Mark the letter for that
word.

Sample:			**ANSWERS**
a. befor	**b.** before	**c.** befour	ⓐ ● ⓒ

1. **a.** or	**b.** orr	**c.** oure	1. ⓐ ⓑ ⓒ
2. **a.** mor	**b.** mour	**c.** more	2. ⓐ ⓑ ⓒ
3. **a.** corne	**b.** corn	**c.** korn	3. ⓐ ⓑ ⓒ
4. **a.** fer	**b.** for	**c.** forr	4. ⓐ ⓑ ⓒ
5. **a.** yor	**b.** youre	**c.** your	5. ⓐ ⓑ ⓒ
6. **a.** store	**b.** stour	**c.** stor	6. ⓐ ⓑ ⓒ
7. **a.** forr	**b.** foure	**c.** four	7. ⓐ ⓑ ⓒ
8. **a.** horne	**b.** horn	**c.** honn	8. ⓐ ⓑ ⓒ
9. **a.** morning	**b.** moring	**c.** morening	9. ⓐ ⓑ ⓒ
10. **a.** short	**b.** shorte	**c.** chort	10. ⓐ ⓑ ⓒ
11. **a.** stori	**b.** stary	**c.** story	11. ⓐ ⓑ ⓒ
12. **a.** bron	**b.** born	**c.** boren	12. ⓐ ⓑ ⓒ

Houghton Mifflin Spelling and Vocabulary. Copyright © Houghton Mifflin Company. All rights reserved.

PRACTICE A
Words That End with er

Summing Up

The sound at the end of **flower** and **water** is a vowel + **r** sound. This sound is spelled **er**.

Basic Words
1. flower
2. water
3. under
4. over
5. better

Word Maze   Draw a line to join the two syllables that make up each Basic Word. Use a different colored crayon for each word.

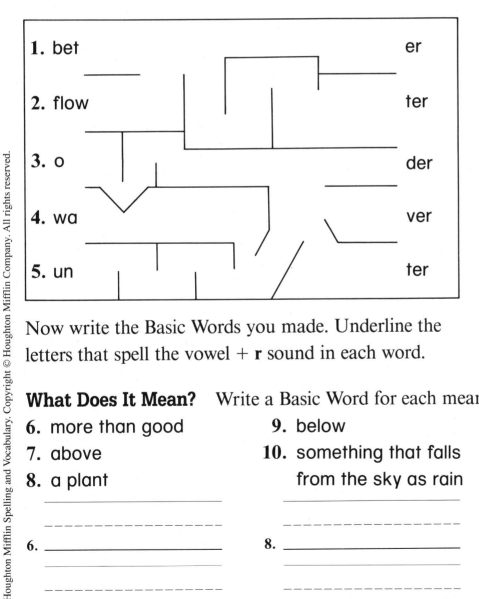

1. bet   er

2. flow   ter

3. o   der

4. wa   ver

5. un   ter

1. _____
2. _____
3. _____
4. _____
5. _____

Now write the Basic Words you made. Underline the letters that spell the vowel + **r** sound in each word.

What Does It Mean?   Write a Basic Word for each meaning.

6. more than good
7. above
8. a plant

9. below
10. something that falls
      from the sky as rain

6. _____

7. _____

8. _____

9. _____

10. _____

Houghton Mifflin Spelling and Vocabulary. Copyright © Houghton Mifflin Company. All rights reserved.

Skill: Children will practice spelling words that end with the |ər| sounds.

Home Use: Help your child practice the spelling words by having him or her complete the activities on this page. Check the completed page, and have your child practice saying and spelling any misspelled words.

Basic Words
1. flower
2. water
3. under
4. over
5. better
6. sister
7. brother
8. mother
9. father
10. after

PRACTICE B
Words That End with er

Billy Goat Books Write the missing Basic Word for each book title. Begin each word with a capital letter.

My Home in the Water __(1)__ a Bridge
  by J. Troll

Greener Grass Tastes __(2)__
  by the Gruff Brothers

My Life __(3)__ I Met the Troll
  by Little Willie Gruff

New Ways to Cross __(4)__ a Stream
  by Big Bill Gruff

1. _____

2. _____

3. _____

4. _____

Family Picture Write the Basic Words that name the people and things in this picture.

5. _____

6. _____

7. _____

8. _____

9. _____

10. _____

Skill: Children will practice spelling words that end with the |ər| sounds.

Home Use: Help your child practice the spelling words by having him or her complete the activities on this page. Check the completed page, and have your child practice saying and spelling any misspelled words.

Houghton Mifflin Spelling and Vocabulary. Copyright © Houghton Mifflin Company. All rights reserved.

PRACTICE C
Words That End with er

Word Change Write the Challenge or Vocabulary Word for each clue. Then follow the directions to change that word to another word.

Challenge Words
1. gather
2. center
Theme Vocabulary
3. soil
4. petals
5. shoot
6. hoe

1. Write a Vocabulary Word that means **a plant that has just begun to grow**.
2. Change the second vowel to a consonant to write a word that means the opposite of **tall**.

1. _____ 2. _____

3. Write a Challenge Word that means **to bring together**.
4. Change one consonant to write a word that means **a male parent**.

3. _____ 4. _____

What Class Think how the words in each group are alike. Write the missing Challenge or Vocabulary Word. In the box next to each group, write a word or words that tell about all the things in the group.

5.	rake	shovel		➡	
6.	side	top		➡	
7.	earth	dirt		➡	
8.	stem	leaf		➡	

Houghton Mifflin Spelling and Vocabulary. Copyright © Houghton Mifflin Company. All rights reserved.

Skill: Children will practice spelling words that end with the |ər| sound and words related to the theme of gardening.

Home Use: Help your child practice the spelling words by having him or her complete the activities on this page. Check the completed page, and have your child practice saying and spelling any misspelled words.

Unit **33** Test: Words That End with er

Read each word group. Find the correctly spelled word to complete each group. Mark the letter next to that word.

Sample:

a very hot _____

(a) sommer

(b) sumer

● summer

1. up and _____
   (a) ower
   (b) over
   (c) ovver

2. cool, fresh _____
   (a) water
   (b) watter
   (c) warter

3. for _____ or worse
   (a) beter
   (b) better
   (c) battur

4. a pretty red _____
   (a) floer
   (b) flowr
   (c) flower

5. down and _____
   (a) under
   (b) ander
   (c) undr

6. father and _____
   (a) mothr
   (b) muther
   (c) mother

7. sister or _____
   (a) bruther
   (b) brother
   (c) brouther

8. before and _____
   (a) after
   (b) aftar
   (c) aftr

9. my little _____
   (a) sistr
   (b) sester
   (c) sister

10. son and _____
    (a) fawther
    (b) father
    (c) fathar

Houghton Mifflin Spelling and Vocabulary. Copyright © Houghton Mifflin Company. All rights reserved.

PRACTICE A
Words That End with ed or ing

Summing Up

Some words end with a short vowel sound followed by one consonant. The final consonant in these words is usually doubled before **ed** or **ing** is added.

Basic Words
1. batted
2. running
3. clapped
4. stopped
5. getting

Elephant Words
🐘 missed
🐘 telling

Spelling Blocks Finish each Basic Word by writing a letter in the empty block. Then write the words.

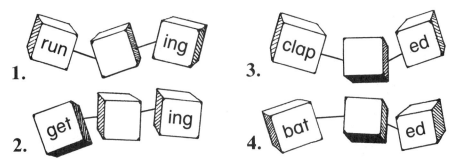

1. run ☐ ing

2. get ☐ ing

3. clap ☐ ed

4. bat ☐ ed

City Scene Sentences Look at the picture. Write a Basic or Elephant Word to finish each sentence.

5. Todd just _____ the bus.

6. Mrs. Wong is _____ a story to her friend.

7. Officer Cole _____ the cars.

8. Penny is _____ something to eat.

1. _____

2. _____

3. _____

4. _____

5. _____

6. _____

7. 🐘 _____

8. _____

Skill: Children will practice spelling words that double the final consonant before **ed** or **ing** is added.

Home Use: Help your child practice the spelling words by having him or her complete the activities on this page. Check the completed page, and have your child practice saying and spelling any misspelled words.

159

Houghton Mifflin Spelling and Vocabulary. Copyright © Houghton Mifflin Company. All rights reserved.

Basic Words
1. batted
2. running
3. clapped
4. stopped
5. getting
6. shopping
7. stepped
8. hugging
9. pinned
10. sitting

Elephant Words

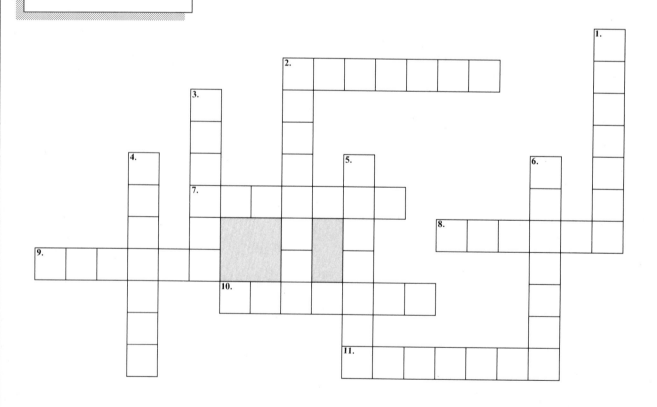 missed

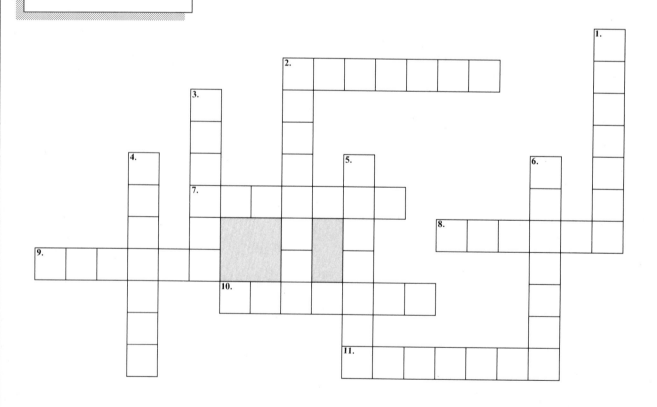 telling

PRACTICE B
Words That End with ed or ing

Crossword Fun   Write a Basic or Elephant Word for each clue.

Across
2. ended
7. walked
8. hit a ball
9. held with a pin
10. putting your arms around someone
11. becoming

Down
1. slapped hands together
2. visiting stores
3. did not hit
4. moving quickly
5. saying in words
6. resting on the lower part of your body

Houghton Mifflin Spelling and Vocabulary. Copyright © Houghton Mifflin Company. All rights reserved.

Skill: Children will practice spelling words that double the final consonant before **ed** or **ing** is added.

Home Use: Help your child practice the spelling words by having him or her complete the activities on this page. Check the completed page, and have your child practice saying and spelling any misspelled words.

PRACTICE C
Words That End with *ed* or *ing*

The Name of the Game   Write the missing Challenge
or Vocabulary Word for each clue.

1. Maria said, "I was ____ when I hurt my foot."
2. Suki said, "The ____ was six to five when I
   hit a home run."
3–4. Abby said, "I ____ the puck into the net and
   scored a ____."
5–6. Pat said, "The ____ between my friend and
   me ended in a ____."

Challenge Words
1. jogging
2. flipped
Theme Vocabulary
3. score
4. tie
5. goal
6. match

1. _____   3. _____   5. _____

2. _____   4. _____   6. _____

Now use the clues to write the correct name under
each girl. Then write the name of the sport she plays.

Sports	
baseball	hockey
tennis	running

_____   _____   _____   _____

Houghton Mifflin Spelling and Vocabulary. Copyright © Houghton Mifflin Company. All rights reserved.

Skill: Children will practice spelling words that
double the final consonant before **ed** or **ing** is
added and words related to the theme of sports.

Home Use: Help your child practice the spelling words by having him
or her complete the activities on this page. Check the completed page,
and have your child practice saying and spelling any misspelled words.

161

Unit 34 Test: Words That End with *ed* or *ing*

Each item below gives three spellings of a word.
Choose the correct spelling. Mark the letter for that
word.

Sample:			**ANSWERS**
a. wening	**b.** winning	**c.** wineng	ⓐ ● ⓒ

1. **a.** mised	**b.** mesed	**c.** missed	1. ⓐ ⓑ ⓒ
2. **a.** getting	**b.** gitting	**c.** geting	2. ⓐ ⓑ ⓒ
3. **a.** beted	**b.** batted	**c.** battad	3. ⓐ ⓑ ⓒ
4. **a.** ranning	**b.** runink	**c.** running	4. ⓐ ⓑ ⓒ
5. **a.** clapped	**b.** klapped	**c.** claped	5. ⓐ ⓑ ⓒ
6. **a.** telind	**b.** telling	**c.** teeling	6. ⓐ ⓑ ⓒ
7. **a.** stoped	**b.** stopped	**c.** staped	7. ⓐ ⓑ ⓒ
8. **a.** hugging	**b.** hugeing	**c.** huging	8. ⓐ ⓑ ⓒ
9. **a.** steped	**b.** stapped	**c.** stepped	9. ⓐ ⓑ ⓒ
10. **a.** sitting	**b.** siting	**c.** seting	10. ⓐ ⓑ ⓒ
11. **a.** pinnd	**b.** pened	**c.** pinned	11. ⓐ ⓑ ⓒ
12. **a.** shoping	**b.** shopping	**c.** choping	12. ⓐ ⓑ ⓒ

Houghton Mifflin Spelling and Vocabulary. Copyright © Houghton Mifflin Company. All rights reserved.

PRACTICE A
More Words with ed or ing

Houghton Mifflin Spelling and Vocabulary. Copyright © Houghton Mifflin Company. All rights reserved.

Basic Words
1. liked
2. hoping
3. baked
4. using
5. chased

Summing Up

Some words end with the vowel-consonant-e pattern. The final **e** in these words is dropped before **ed** or **ing** is added.

Odd One Out Cross out the shape that is different from the others in the row. Write a Basic Word with the letters that are left.

1. b a k (e) + e d

2. △l △i △k e + △e △d

3. (u) (s) e + (i) (n) (g)

4. h o p △e + i n g

1. _____

2. _____

3. _____

4. _____

A Better Letter Write the missing Basic Words to finish this letter.

January 16, 1991

Dear Mitch,

I went to the circus last night! It was funny when the clowns ran and __(5)__ each other. An elephant picked one clown up by __(6)__ its trunk! I __(7)__ it so much that I want to go again. I was __(8)__ you could come with me next time.

Your friend,

Liz

5. _____

6. _____

7. _____

8. _____

Skill: Children will practice spelling words that drop the final **e** before **ed** or **ing** is added.

Home Use: Help your child practice the spelling words by having him or her complete the activities on this page. Check the completed page, and have your child practice saying and spelling any misspelled words.

163

Basic Words
1. liked
2. hoping
3. baked
4. using
5. chased
6. making
7. closed
8. hiding
9. named
10. riding

PRACTICE B
More Words with ed or ing

Proofreading 1–4. Find and cross out four Basic Words that are spelled wrong in this news story. Write each word correctly.

Chip Baker was namd Cook of the Year. He baked 1000 cookies in two hours. Everyone liked the cookies. Next year he will be makeing a new kind of cookie, useing nuts. He is hopeing the new cookies will be even better.

1. _____   3. _____

2. _____   4. _____

Word Search   Write a Basic Word for each clue. Then find the word in the puzzle and circle it.

5. cooked   8. shut
6. covering up   9. moving on a bike
7. enjoyed   10. followed

k	e	l	c	l	o	s	e	d	v
v	p	u	r	i	d	i	n	g	q
l	e	b	a	k	e	d	r	n	c
c	h	a	s	e	d	t	w	i	e
o	b	h	i	d	i	n	g	f	s

5. _____

6. _____

7. _____

8. _____

9. _____

10. _____

Houghton Mifflin Spelling and Vocabulary. Copyright © Houghton Mifflin Company. All rights reserved.

Skill: Children will practice spelling words that drop the final **e** before **ed** or **ing** is added.

Home Use: Help your child practice the spelling words by having him or her complete the activities on this page. Check the completed page, and have your child practice saying and spelling any misspelled words.

PRACTICE C
More Words with ed or ing

Eddie's Decisions   Read each problem. Write what you think Eddie decided to do to be a good friend. Use all the Challenge and Vocabulary Words.

Challenge Words
1. teasing
2. decided
Theme Vocabulary
3. neighbor
4. share
5. welcome
6. invite

1. A new child moved into a house near Eddie. What did Eddie decide to do?

    _____

    - - - - - - - - - - - - - - - - -

    1. _____

    _____

    - - - - - - - - - - - - - - - - -

    _____

2. Eddie's friend forgot her lunch. What did Eddie decide to do?

    _____

    - - - - - - - - - - - - - - - - -

    2. _____

    _____

    - - - - - - - - - - - - - - - - -

    _____

3. Eddie's friend Sam was crying because Eddie made fun of him. What did Eddie decide to do?

    _____

    - - - - - - - - - - - - - - - - -

    3. _____

    _____

    - - - - - - - - - - - - - - - - -

    _____

4. A friend was left out of a game that Eddie was playing. What did Eddie decide to do?

    _____

    - - - - - - - - - - - - - - - - -

    4. _____

    _____

    - - - - - - - - - - - - - - - - -

    _____

Houghton Mifflin Spelling and Vocabulary. Copyright © Houghton Mifflin Company. All rights reserved.

Skill: Children will practice spelling words that drop the final **e** before **ed** or **ing** is added and words related to the theme of friendship.

Home Use: Help your child practice the spelling words by having him or her complete the activities on this page. Check the completed page, and have your child practice saying and spelling any misspelled words.

Unit 35 Test: More Words with ed or ing

Read each word group. Find the correctly spelled word to complete each group. Mark the letter next to that word.

Sample:

_____ a trip
- (a) tacing
- ● taking
- (c) takeng

1. boiled or _____
   - (a) bakked
   - (b) backeg
   - (c) baked

2. _____ your head
   - (a) using
   - (b) ussig
   - (c) uzing

3. _____ that book
   - (a) likked
   - (b) liked
   - (c) liket

4. wishing and _____
   - (a) hoping
   - (b) hopeink
   - (c) hopeng

5. _____ up a tree
   - (a) chasd
   - (b) chassed
   - (c) chased

6. _____ and seeking
   - (a) hideing
   - (b) hiding
   - (c) hidding

7. a dog _____ Frank
   - (a) namd
   - (b) nammed
   - (c) named

8. _____ a mud pie
   - (a) making
   - (b) macking
   - (c) makeind

9. _____ the door
   - (a) closd
   - (b) clozed
   - (c) closed

10. _____ a horse
    - (a) riddign
    - (b) riding
    - (c) rideig

Houghton Mifflin Spelling and Vocabulary. Copyright © Houghton Mifflin Company. All rights reserved.

BULLETIN BOARD

Feed the Bunnies

flower

Mr. MacGregor's Basket

Tacks

How to make: Make the title and two large rabbits out of construction paper. Make carrots out of orange construction paper. Write a Basic or Elephant Word on one side of each carrot. Label a box *Mr. MacGregor's Basket*, staple the box to the board, and place the carrots face down in the box. Attach a box of thumbtacks to the bottom of the board.

How to use: Students work in pairs. Each student chooses a rabbit. One student picks a carrot from the basket and, without looking at the word, hands it to the other student. The other student says the word aloud. The first student spells the word aloud. If the student spells the word correctly, he or she tacks the carrot next to his or her rabbit. If the student spells the word incorrectly, the carrot goes back into the basket. Students take turns spelling words. When all the words have been spelled, the student whose rabbit has the most carrots wins. Use the game to review words from one unit at a time or from all five units in the cycle.

Use: For use with Units 31–35.

Houghton Mifflin Spelling and Vocabulary. Copyright © Houghton Mifflin Company. All rights reserved.

SPELLING NEWSLETTER
for Students and Their Families

Wrapping Up

In Units 31 through 35 of *Houghton Mifflin Spelling and Vocabulary,* your child has studied words such as *far, barn, or,* and *story,* and two-syllable words that end with *er,* such as *sister.* These units have also dealt with words that end with *ing* or *ed,* such as *shopping, pinned, making,* and *named.*

Word Lists

Your child has been studying the words below as well as other words with similar patterns.

UNIT 31	UNIT 32	UNIT 33	UNIT 34	UNIT 35
start	store	flower	running	liked
arm	corn	water	clapped	hoping
far	or	better	getting	chased
barn	morning	sister	shopping	making
hard	short	father	stepped	named
party	story	after	pinned	riding

👪 *Family Activity*

Play Spelling Sack with your child. Have your child copy the words from the lists on small cards or pieces of paper. Put all of the word cards in a paper bag. Fold over the top of the bag and shake it gently to mix up the cards. Take turns with your child picking a card from the bag, spelling the word aloud, and using it in a sentence. If you both agree that the word has been spelled correctly and used correctly in the sentence, put the word card aside. Otherwise, return the word card to the bag. Repeat the procedure until all the word cards have been removed from the bag.

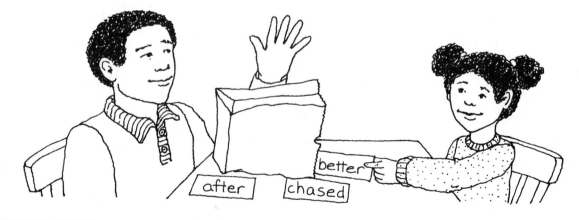

Houghton Mifflin Spelling and Vocabulary. Copyright © Houghton Mifflin Company. All rights reserved.

168

Boletín de noticias de ortografía
para estudiantes y para sus familias

Para terminar

Su hijo o hija ha estado estudiando las siguientes palabras y otras palabras que siguen patrones similares en las Unidades 31 a 35 del libro *Houghton Mifflin Spelling and Vocabulary*.

UNIDAD 31	UNIDAD 32	UNIDAD 33	UNIDAD 34	UNIDAD 35
start	store	flower	running	liked
arm	corn	water	clapped	hoping
far	or	better	getting	chased
barn	morning	sister	shopping	making
hard	short	father	stepped	named
party	story	after	pinned	riding

Actividad para la familia

Jueguen al "saco de deletrear" con su hijo o hija. Hagan que su hijo o hija copie las palabras de las listas en tarjetas pequeñas o en pedazos de papel. Pongan todas las tarjetas con palabras en una bolsa de papel. Doblen la parte de arriba de la bolsa y sacúdanla suavemente para mezclar las tarjetas. Túrnense con su hijo o hija para escoger una tarjeta de la bolsa, para deletrearla en voz alta y luego usarla en una oración. Si están de acuerdo en que la palabra ha sido deletreada correctamente y usada correctamente en una oración, pongan la tarjeta que tiene esa palabra a un lado. Si no ha sido así, vuelvan a poner la tarjeta en la bolsa. Repitan el procedimiento hasta que ya no queden tarjetas con palabras en la bolsa.

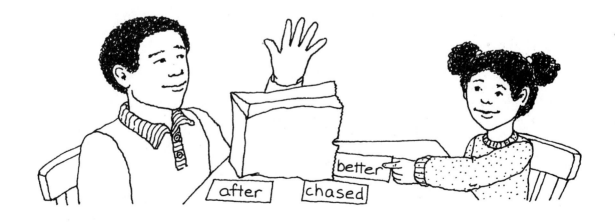

Houghton Mifflin Spelling and Vocabulary. Copyright © Houghton Mifflin Company. All rights reserved.

SPELLING BASEBALL

SPELLING
GAME

Players: 2 teams of 2 or more

You need: a copy of the game board on page 171, 20 cards with a Basic or Elephant Word on each card

How to play: Paste the game board onto a large sheet of cardboard. Place the cards face down in a pile on the pitcher's mound. One team bats and one team pitches. The pitching team chooses a pitcher. That player picks a card and says the word to a batter from the other team. If the batter spells the word correctly, he or she puts the card on first base. The pitcher picks another card and says the word to the next batter. If that batter spells the word correctly, the batter puts that card on first base and moves the other card to second base.

As batters spell words, move the word cards around the bases. Each card that reaches home plate makes 1 point for the team at bat, and the card is put back into the pile. If a word is not spelled correctly, the batter is out, and the pitcher reads the word to the next batter. After 2 outs, the other team is at bat. The team with the most points after both teams have batted 6 times wins.

Hold cards with words that batters spelled wrong for review after the game.

Use: For use with Units 31 – 35.

Houghton Mifflin Spelling and Vocabulary. Copyright © Houghton Mifflin Company. All rights reserved.

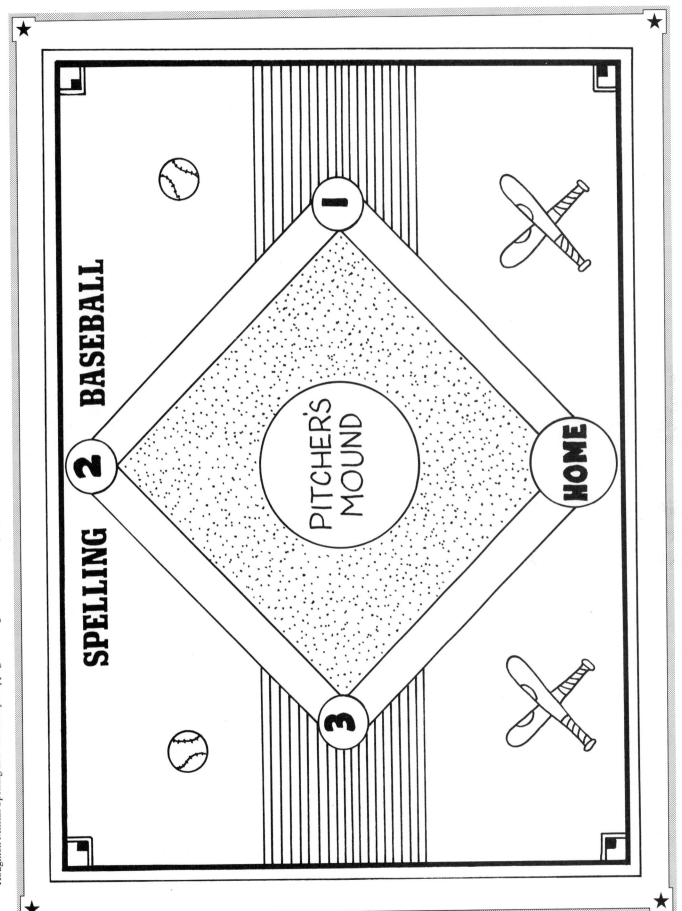

Houghton Mifflin Spelling and Vocabulary. Copyright © Houghton Mifflin Company. All rights reserved.

Unit **36** Review: Test A

Read the three word groups. Find the underlined word
that is spelled wrong. Mark the letter for that word.

Sample:
- ● the silly <u>storry</u>
- (b) at the <u>farm</u>
- (c) <u>making</u> bread

1. (a) <u>corne</u> on the cob
   (b) are at <u>home</u>
   (c) <u>clapped</u> their hands

2. (a) <u>baked</u> beans
   (b) a pretty <u>flowar</u>
   (c) <u>over</u> the top

3. (a) feeling <u>better</u>
   (b) a strong <u>arm</u>
   (c) <u>runing</u> the race

4. (a) <u>mor</u> careful
   (b) <u>getting</u> ready
   (c) <u>using</u> my pen

5. (a) under the <u>table</u>
   (b) a gift <u>for</u> you
   (c) <u>batid</u> the ball

6. (a) <u>missed</u> the bus
   (b) in our <u>yared</u>
   (c) four <u>years</u> old

7. (a) yes <u>or</u> no
   (b) <u>hopeing</u> for
   (c) from the <u>start</u>

8. (a) <u>telling</u> the truth
   (b) a blue <u>car</u>
   (c) at the <u>stour</u>

9. (a) cool <u>watir</u>
   (b) <u>chased</u> the ball
   (c) <u>stopped</u> the car

10. (a) too <u>farr</u> away
    (b) <u>liked</u> the book
    (c) on a <u>warm</u> day

Houghton Mifflin Spelling and Vocabulary. Copyright © Houghton Mifflin Company. All rights reserved.

Unit **36** Review: Test B

Read the three word groups. Find the underlined word
that is spelled wrong. Mark the letter for that word.

Sample:
- ● his old <u>cor</u>
- (b) <u>more</u> or less
- (c) wishing and <u>hoping</u>

---

1. (a) <u>after</u> dinner
   (b) a better <u>part</u>
   (c) <u>yur</u> turn

2. (a) my big <u>brothir</u>
   (b) <u>four</u> new friends
   (c) <u>hugging</u> my doll

3. (a) early in the <u>morning</u>
   (b) <u>makeing</u> my lunch
   (c) <u>farm</u> animals

4. (a) <u>siting</u> on the grass
   (b) a <u>horn</u> to blow
   (c) <u>hard</u> to do

5. (a) from my <u>fathe</u>
   (b) a good <u>hiding</u> place
   (c) <u>pinned</u> the sleeve

6. (a) <u>riding</u> my bike
   (b) with your <u>mother</u>
   (c) a <u>storry</u> to tell

7. (a) at the <u>party</u>
   (b) <u>teling</u> time
   (c) <u>closed</u> the door

8. (a) <u>shourt</u> or tall
   (b) in the <u>barn</u>
   (c) her older <u>sister</u>

9. (a) <u>shopping</u> for food
   (b) <u>warrm</u> clothing
   (c) <u>born</u> today

10. (a) <u>missed</u> the bus
    (b) a boy <u>named</u> Fred
    (c) <u>steped</u> on the rug

Houghton Mifflin Spelling and Vocabulary. Copyright © Houghton Mifflin Company. All rights reserved.

Prewriting Ideas: Letters

Choosing a Topic   Here is a list of ideas that one student made for writing a letter. What ideas of your own do they give you?

On the lines below **My Three Ideas**, write three ideas that you would like to tell someone about in a letter. Which idea do you like the best? Will it interest the person that you are writing to? Circle the idea that you would like to write about.

Ideas for Writing

My Trip to the Zoo   Why I Like Camp
My New Baby Brother   My Long Plane Ride

My Three Ideas

1. _____

2. _____

3. _____

Exploring Your Topic   You can use a stamp cluster to help you plan whom you will write to and what you want to say. Copy the cluster onto another sheet of paper. Make it large enough to write on. Write your topic in the big stamp. Use the smaller stamps to write some details about your idea and to tell who will get your letter.

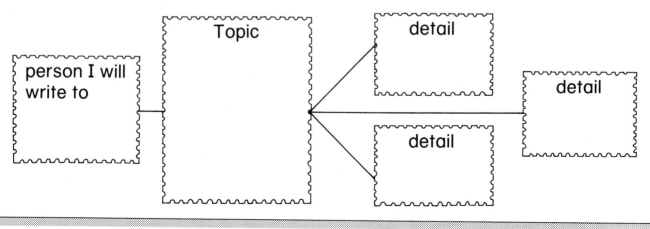

Houghton Mifflin Spelling and Vocabulary. Copyright © Houghton Mifflin Company. All rights reserved.

Use: For use with Step 1: Prewriting on page 239.

End-of-Year Test

There are three words beside each number. One of the words is spelled wrong. Mark the letter next to that word.

Sample:
● carr
ⓑ baked
ⓒ brown

1. ⓐ king
   ⓑ tayle
   ⓒ boat

2. ⓐ very
   ⓑ myself
   ⓒ ar

3. ⓐ better
   ⓑ hoping
   ⓒ childran

4. ⓐ ey
   ⓑ but
   ⓒ of

5. ⓐ club
   ⓑ trale
   ⓒ please

6. ⓐ boxes
   ⓑ moon
   ⓒ howse

7. ⓐ fly
   ⓑ you'r
   ⓒ store

8. ⓐ mised
   ⓑ as
   ⓒ pet

9. ⓐ is
   ⓑ nine
   ⓒ noze

10. ⓐ adde
    ⓑ pick
    ⓒ saw

(continued)

Houghton Mifflin Spelling and Vocabulary. Copyright © Houghton Mifflin Company. All rights reserved.

End-of-Year Test (continued)

11. (a) chop
    (b) louk
    (c) plane

12. (a) town
    (b) can't
    (c) cookey

13. (a) whith
    (b) made
    (c) swim

14. (a) great
    (b) sutch
    (c) should

15. (a) rideng
    (b) toe
    (c) hugging

16. (a) while
    (b) grow
    (c) ryte

17. (a) canot
    (b) party
    (c) bat

18. (a) fix
    (b) dott
    (c) kick

19. (a) people
    (b) who
    (c) brothar

20. (a) anyone
    (b) clossed
    (c) stepped

21. (a) longe
    (b) which
    (c) funny

22. (a) you'll
    (b) storry
    (c) said

23. (a) rug
    (b) cute
    (c) tel

24. (a) fal
    (b) two
    (c) short

25. (a) father
    (b) farm
    (c) naems

Houghton Mifflin Spelling and Vocabulary. Copyright © Houghton Mifflin Company. All rights reserved.

Additional Resources

Individual Progress Chart
Class Progress Chart
Scoring Chart
Proofreading Marks
Proofreading Checklist
Handwriting Models

Additional Resources

★ Individual Progress Chart ★

Prebook Test (TRB)	Midyear Test (TRB)	End-of-Year Test (TRB)

	Pretest (TE)	Unit Evaluation (TE)	Unit Test (TRB)			Pretest (TE)	Unit Evaluation (TE)	Unit Test (TRB)	
Unit 1					Unit 19				
Unit 2					Unit 20				
Unit 3					Unit 21				
Unit 4					Unit 22				
Unit 5					Unit 23				
Unit 6 Review			A	B	Unit 24 Review			A	B
Unit 7					Unit 25				
Unit 8					Unit 26				
Unit 9					Unit 27				
Unit 10					Unit 28				
Unit 11					Unit 29				
Unit 12 Review			A	B	Unit 30 Review			A	B
Unit 13					Unit 31				
Unit 14					Unit 32				
Unit 15					Unit 33				
Unit 16					Unit 34				
Unit 17					Unit 35				
Unit 18 Review			A	B	Unit 36 Review			A	B

Houghton Mifflin Spelling and Vocabulary. Copyright © Houghton Mifflin Company. All rights reserved.

Class Progress Chart

Name	Extra Test	Unit ___			Unit ___			Unit ___			Unit ___			Unit ___			Review Unit ___				Extra Tests	
	Prebook Test (TRB)	Pretest (TE)	Unit Evaluation (TE)	Unit Test (TRB)	Pretest (TE)	Unit Evaluation (TE)	Unit Test (TRB)	Pretest (TE)	Unit Evaluation (TE)	Unit Test (TRB)	Pretest (TE)	Unit Evaluation (TE)	Unit Test (TRB)	Pretest (TE)	Unit Evaluation (TE)	Unit Test (TRB)	Pretest (TE)	Unit Evaluation (TE)	Review Test A (TRB)	Review Test B (TRB)	Midyear Test (TRB)	End-of-Year Test (TRB)
1.																						
2.																						
3.																						
4.																						
5.																						
6.																						
7.																						
8.																						
9.																						
10.																						
11.																						
12.																						
13.																						
14.																						
15.																						
16.																						
17.																						
18.																						
19.																						
20.																						
21.																						
22.																						
23.																						
24.																						
25.																						
26.																						
27.																						
28.																						
29.																						
30.																						
31.																						
32.																						
33.																						
34.																						
35.																						

Houghton Mifflin Spelling and Vocabulary. Copyright © Houghton Mifflin Company. All rights reserved.

Scoring Chart

Use the scoring bars below to convert the raw score for each test to a percentage.

For 5-item tests, number and percent correct:

Number	3	4	5
Percent	60	80	100

For 9-item tests, number and percent correct:

Number	5	6	7	8	9
Percent	56	67	78	89	100

For 10-item tests, number and percent correct:

Number	5	6	7	8	9	10
Percent	50	60	70	80	90	100

For 11-item tests, number and percent correct:

Number	6	7	8	9	10	11
Percent	55	64	73	82	91	100

For 12-item tests, number and percent correct:

Number	6	7	8	9	10	11	12
Percent	50	58	67	75	83	92	100

For 13-item tests, number and percent correct:

Number	7	8	9	10	11	12	13
Percent	54	62	69	77	85	92	100

For 14-item tests, number and percent correct:

Number	7	8	9	10	11	12	13	14
Percent	50	57	64	71	79	86	93	100

For 15-item tests, number and percent correct:

Number	8	9	10	11	12	13	14	15
Percent	53	60	67	73	80	87	93	100

For 16-item tests, number and percent correct:

Number	8	9	10	11	12	13	14	15	16
Percent	50	56	63	69	75	81	88	94	100

For 20-item tests, number and percent correct:

Number	10	11	12	13	14	15	16	17	18	19	20
Percent	50	55	60	65	70	75	80	85	90	95	100

For use with Levels 2–8

Houghton Mifflin Spelling and Vocabulary. Copyright © Houghton Mifflin Company. All rights reserved.

Scoring Chart (continued)

For 24-item tests, number and percent correct:

Number	12	13	14	15	16	17	18	19	20	21	22	23	24
Percent	50	54	58	63	67	71	75	79	83	88	92	96	100

For 25-item tests, number and percent correct:

Number	13	14	15	16	17	18	19	20	21	22	23	24	25
Percent	52	56	60	64	68	72	76	80	84	88	92	96	100

For 26-item tests, number and percent correct:

Number	13	14	15	16	17	18	19	20	21	22	23	24	25	26
Percent	50	54	58	62	65	69	73	77	81	85	88	92	96	100

For 28-item tests, number and percent correct:

Number	14	15	16	17	18	19	20	21	22	23	24	25	26	27	28
Percent	50	54	57	61	64	68	71	75	79	82	86	89	93	96	100

For 29-item tests, number and percent correct:

Number	15	16	17	18	19	20	21	22	23	24	25	26	27	28	29
Percent	52	55	59	62	66	69	72	76	79	83	86	90	93	97	100

For 30-item tests, number and percent correct:

Number	15	16	17	18	19	20	21	22	23	24	25	26	27	28	29	30
Percent	50	53	57	60	63	67	70	73	77	80	83	87	90	93	97	100

For 34-item tests, number and percent correct:

Number	17	18	19	20	21	22	23	24	25	26	27	28	29	30	31	32	33	34
Percent	50	53	56	59	62	65	68	71	74	76	79	82	85	88	91	94	97	100

For 35-item tests, number and percent correct:

Number	18	19	20	21	22	23	24	25	26	27	28	29	30	31	32	33	34	35
Percent	51	54	57	60	63	66	69	71	74	77	80	83	86	89	91	94	97	100

For 36-item tests, number and percent correct:

Number	18	19	20	21	22	23	24	25	26	27	28	29	30	31	32	33	34	35	36
Percent	50	53	56	58	61	64	67	69	72	75	78	81	83	86	89	92	94	97	100

For 50-item tests, number and percent correct:

Number	25	26	27	28	29	30	31	32	33	34	35	36	37	38	39	40	41	42	43	44
Percent	50	52	54	56	58	60	62	64	66	68	70	72	74	76	78	80	82	84	86	88

Number	45	46	47	48	49	50
Percent	90	92	94	96	98	100

For use with Levels 2–8.

182

Houghton Mifflin Spelling and Vocabulary. Copyright © Houghton Mifflin Company. All rights reserved.

★ Proofreading Marks ★

Mark	Meaning	Example
∧	Add one or more words.	I ∧ seen the play. (have)
———	Take out one or more words. Change the spelling.	Kate ~~has~~ went home. The ~~baloon~~ popped. (balloon)
≡	Make a small letter a capital letter.	My birthday is in june.
/	Make a capital letter a small letter.	My Dog is brown.

Houghton Mifflin Spelling and Vocabulary. Copyright © Houghton Mifflin Company. All rights reserved.

★ Proofreading Checklist ★

Read each question. Check your paper for each kind of mistake. Correct any mistakes you find. Put a check in each box when you have looked for that kind of mistake.

☐ **1.** Did I begin each sentence with a capital letter?

☐ **2.** Did I use correct end marks?

☐ **3.** Did I spell each word correctly?

☐ **4.** Did I indent each paragraph?

☐ **5.** Did I use commas correctly?

Is there anything else you should look for? Do you make the same kind of mistake many times? Make your own proofreading list.

☐ _____

☐ _____

☐ _____

☐ _____

☐ _____

☐ _____

Houghton Mifflin Spelling and Vocabulary. Copyright © Houghton Mifflin Company. All rights reserved.

★ Handwriting Models ★

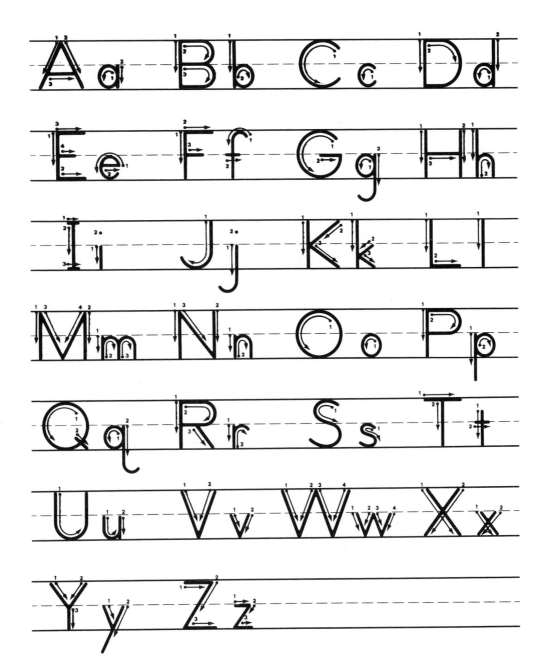

The Zaner-Bloser alphabet is reprinted from *Handwriting: Basic Skills and Application*. Copyright © 1989. Reprinted with permission of Zaner-Bloser, Inc., Columbus, OH.

Houghton Mifflin Spelling and Vocabulary. Copyright © Houghton Mifflin Company. All rights reserved.

★ Handwriting Models ★

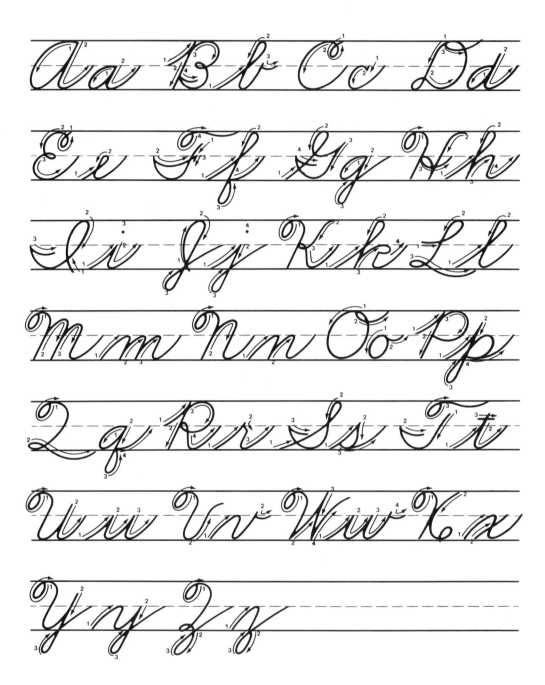

The Zaner-Bloser alphabet is reprinted from *Handwriting: Basic Skills and Application*. Copyright © 1989. Reprinted with permission of Zaner-Bloser, Inc., Columbus, OH.

Houghton Mifflin Spelling and Vocabulary. Copyright © Houghton Mifflin Company. All rights reserved.

★ Handwriting Models ★

Handwriting style reprinted from HBJ HANDWRITING, copyright © 1987 by Harcourt Brace Jovanovich, Inc. Reproduced by permission of the publisher.

Houghton Mifflin Spelling and Vocabulary. Copyright © Houghton Mifflin Company. All rights reserved.

★ # Handwriting Models ★

Aa Bb Cc Dd

Ee Ff Gg Hh

Ii Jj Kk Ll

Mm Nn Oo Pp

Qq Rr Ss Tt

Uu Vv Ww Xx

Yy Zz

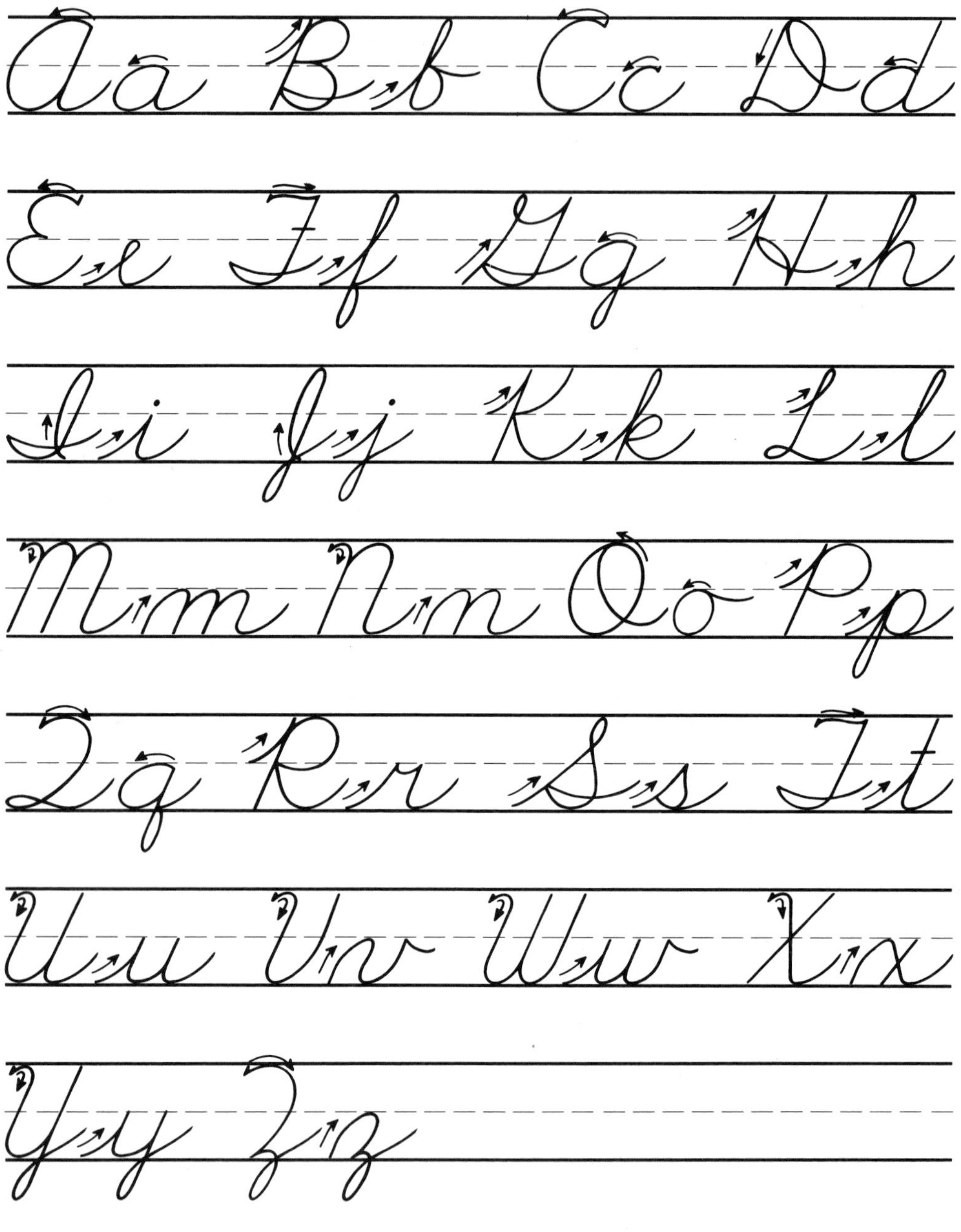

Handwriting style reprinted from HBJ HANDWRITING, copyright © 1987 by Harcourt Brace Jovanovich, Inc. Reproduced by permission of the publisher.

Houghton Mifflin Spelling and Vocabulary. Copyright © Houghton Mifflin Company. All rights reserved.

★ Handwriting Models ★

The McDougal, Littell alphabet is used with permission from *McDougal, Littell Handwriting*. Copyright © 1990 by McDougal, Littell and Company, Evanston, Illinois.

Houghton Mifflin Spelling and Vocabulary. Copyright © Houghton Mifflin Company. All rights reserved.

★ Handwriting Models ★

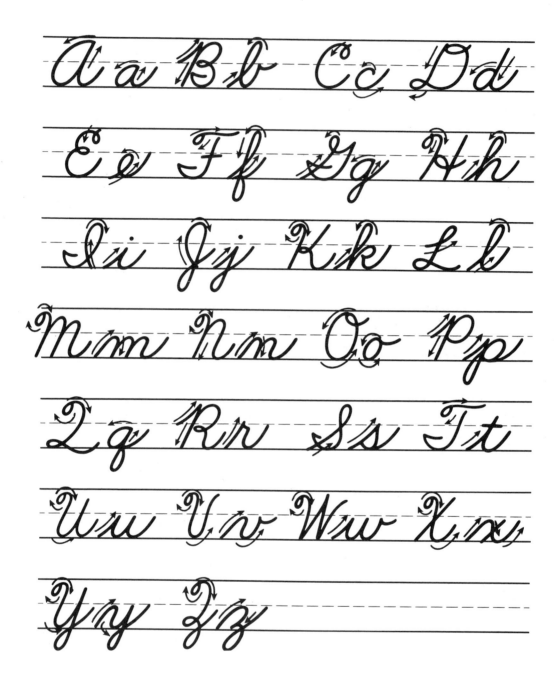

The McDougal, Littell alphabet is used with permission from *McDougal, Littell Handwriting*. Copyright © 1990 by McDougal, Littell and Company, Evanston, Illinois.

Houghton Mifflin Spelling and Vocabulary. Copyright © Houghton Mifflin Company. All rights reserved.

★ Handwriting Models ★

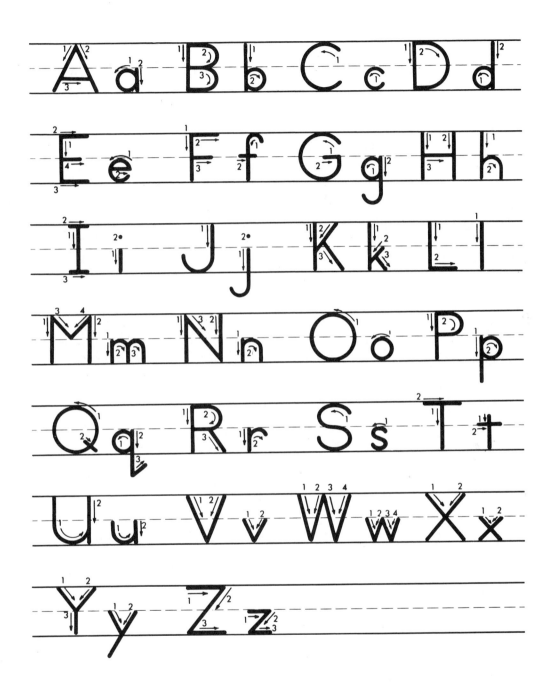

The Palmer alphabet is reprinted with permission of Macmillan/McGraw-Hill School Publishing Company from *Palmer Method Handwriting*, Centennial Edition. Copyright © 1987 by Macmillan Publishing Company.

Houghton Mifflin Spelling and Vocabulary. Copyright © Houghton Mifflin Company. All rights reserved.

★ # Handwriting Models ★

Aa Bb Cc Dd

Ee Ff Gg

Hh Ii Jj Kk

Ll Mm Nn Oo

Pp Qq Rr

Ss Tt Uu Vv

Ww Xx Yy Zz

The Palmer alphabet is reprinted with permission of Macmillan/McGraw-Hill
School Publishing Company from *Palmer Method Handwriting*, Centennial
Edition. Copyright © 1987 by Macmillan Publishing Company.

Houghton Mifflin Spelling and Vocabulary. Copyright © Houghton Mifflin Company. All rights reserved.

Practice Master and Test Answers

Prebook Test (continued)

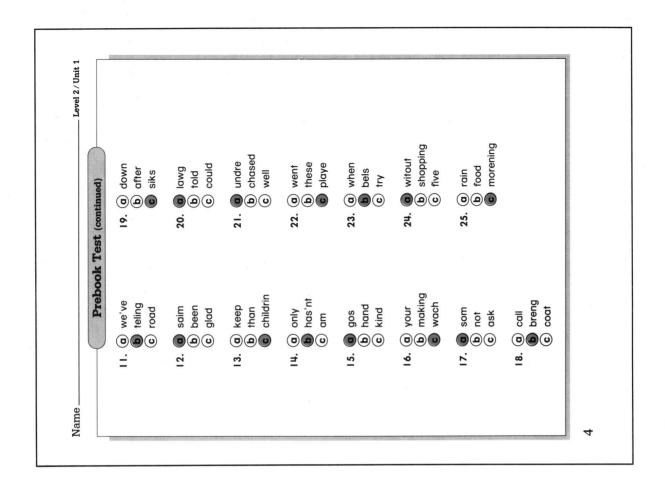

11. (a) we've (b) teling (c) road
12. (a) saim (b) been (c) glad
13. (a) keep (b) than (c) childrin
14. (a) only (b) has'nt (c) am
15. (a) gos (b) hand (c) kind
16. (a) your (b) making (c) wach
17. (a) som (b) not (c) ask
18. (a) call (b) breng (c) coat

19. (a) down (b) after (c) siks
20. (a) lawg (b) told (c) could
21. (a) undre (b) chased (c) well
22. (a) went (b) these (c) playe
23. (a) when (b) bels (c) try
24. (a) witout (b) shopping (c) five
25. (a) rain (b) food (c) morening

Prebook Test

There are three words beside each number. One of the words is spelled wrong. Mark the letter next to that word.

Sample:
(a) bat ● digg (c) job

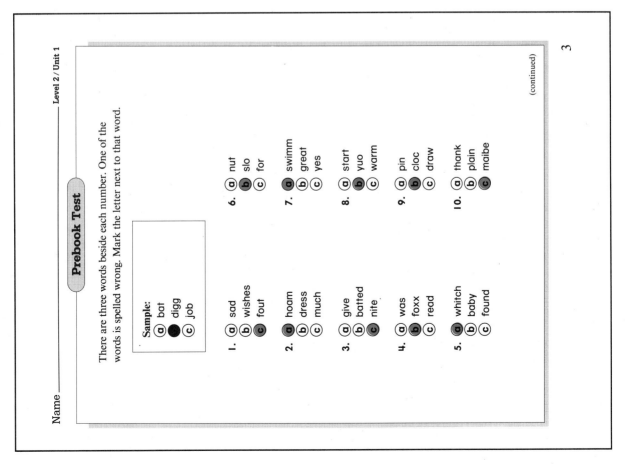

1. (a) sad (b) wishes (c) fout
2. (a) hoam (b) dress (c) much
3. (a) give (b) batted (c) nite
4. (a) was (b) foxx (c) read
5. (a) whitch (b) baby (c) found

6. (a) nut (b) slo (c) for
7. (a) swimm (b) great (c) yes
8. (a) start (b) yuo (c) warm
9. (a) pin (b) cloc (c) draw
10. (a) thank (b) plain (c) maibe

(continued)

Practice Master and Test Answers

195

PRACTICE B
Spelling the Short a Sound

Basic Words
1. hat
2. bag
3. as
4. am
5. has
6. sad
7. bat
8. ran
9. sat
10. bad

Elephant Words
🐘 was
🐘 want

Stairway to the Stars   Write the Basic or Elephant
Word for each clue.

1. → rested
2. → a cap
3. → owns
4. → used to be
5. → to wish
6. → a wooden stick
7. → awful
8. → unhappy

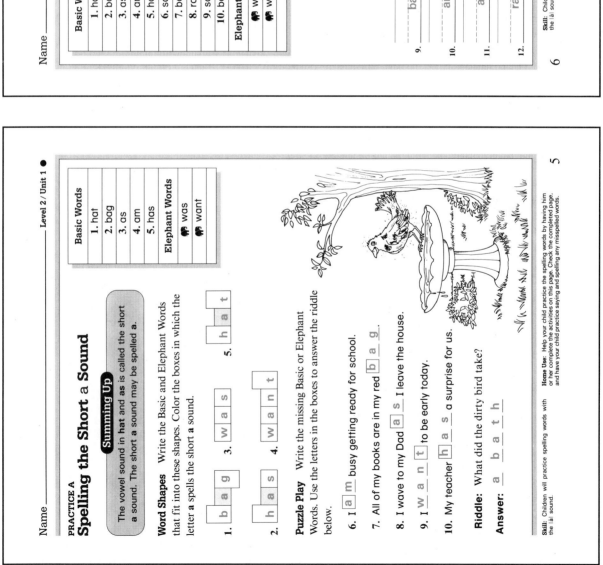

What Word Am I?   Write the letter for each clue to
find a Basic Word. Then write the Basic Words.

9. My first letter is in **bed**, but not in **led**.   b
My second letter is in **cat**, but not in **cut**.   a
My third letter is in **peg**, but not in **pet**.   g

10. My first letter is in **at**, but not in **it**.   a
My second letter is in **him**, but not in **hid**.   m

11. My first letter is in **an**, but not in **on**.   a
My second letter is in **is**, but not in **it**.   s

12. My first letter is in **red**, but not in **bed**.   r
My second letter is in **ran**, but not in **ten**.   a
My third letter is in **sun**, but not in **sum**.   n

9. _bag_
10. _am_
11. _as_
12. _ran_

Skill: Children will practice spelling words with the /a/ sound.   **Home Use**: Help your child practice spelling the spelling words by having him or her complete the activities on this page. Check the completed page, and have your child practice saying and spelling any misspelled words.

PRACTICE A
Spelling the Short a Sound

Basic Words
1. hat
2. bag
3. as
4. am
5. has

Elephant Words
🐘 was
🐘 want

> ### Summing Up
> The vowel sound in **hat** and **as** is called the short
> a sound. The short a sound may be spelled **a**.

Word Shapes   Write the Basic and Elephant Words
that fit into these shapes. Color boxes in which the
letter **a** spells the short a sound.

1. | b | a | g | 3. | w | a | s | 5. | h | a | t |

2. | h | a | s | 4. | w | a | n | t |

Puzzle Play   Write the missing Basic or Elephant
Words. Use the letters in the boxes to answer the riddle
below.

6. I | a | m | busy getting ready for school.

7. All of my books are in my red | b | a | g |.

8. I wave to my Dad | a | s | I leave the house.

9. I | w | a | n | t | to be early today.

10. My teacher | h | a | s | a surprise for us.

Riddle: What did the dirty bird take?

Answer: a   b a t h

Skill: Children will practice spelling words with the /a/ sound.   **Home Use**: Help your child practice the spelling words by having him or her complete the activities on this page. Check the completed page, and have your child practice saying and spelling any misspelled words.

196

Unit 1 Test: Spelling the Short a Sound

Read each sentence. Is the underlined word spelled right or wrong? Mark your answer.

	Right	Wrong
Sample: Throw away that cann.	○	●

Items 1–7 test Basic Words 1–5 and the Elephant Words.
Items 8–12 test Basic Words 6–10.

		Right	Wrong
1.	Put the bagg of food on the table.	○	●
2.	Sara was playing the game.	●	○
3.	Theo has finished his book.	●	○
4.	I em proud of you.	○	●
5.	I want grapes after lunch.	●	○
6.	Pedro could wear your het.	○	●
7.	Is your bike the same az Dara's?	○	●
8.	Last week there was a bad storm.	●	○
9.	That clown looks sed.	○	●
10.	Jimmy ran all the way home.	●	○
11.	Meg sat in Grandma's chair.	●	○
12.	That batt belongs to Gina.	○	●

8

PRACTICE C
Spelling the Short a Sound

Word Towers Start at the top of each tower. Add one letter to write the next word. Put the letters in the order that spells the word for each clue. The last word in each tower is a Challenge or Vocabulary Word.

Challenge Words
1. mask
2. fabric
Theme Vocabulary
3. cape
4. gown
5. vest
6. crown

Clues

1.
| o |
| o r |
| r o w |
| c r o w |
| c r o w n |

the letter between **n** and **p**
rhymes with **for**
to move a boat
a big, black bird
a hat for a king

2.
| a |
| a s |
| a s k |
| m a s k |

the first letter
rhymes with **has**
to question
a cover for the face

The Latest Style Write sentences that tell what the people in the picture are saying. Use the words **fabric, cape, gown,** and **vest.**
Answers will vary.

_____
_____
_____

7

Skill: Children will practice spelling words with the /ā/ sound and words related to the theme of costumes.

Home Use: Help your child practice the spelling words by having him or her complete the activities on this page. Check the completed page, and have your child practice saying and spelling any misspelled words.

Practice Master and Test Answers

197

PRACTICE B
Spelling the Short e Sound

Basic Words
1. pet
2. leg
3. ten
4. yes
5. bed
6. help
7. set
8. went
9. pen
10. wet
Elephant Words
any
said

Hink Pink Write the Basic Word that answers the question and rhymes with the word in dark print.

1. What is a doctor for animals? a **vet** _____ pet
2. What is a blushing cot? a **red** _____ bed
3. What does a chicken write with? a **hen** _____ pen
4. What is a damp plane? a **jet** _____ wet
5. What do you need to lift a hippo? _____ **men** ten
6. What is a ready fish trap? a **net** _____ set

1. pet
2. bed
3. pen
4. wet
5. ten
6. set

Proofreading 7–12. Find and cross out six Basic or Elephant Words that are spelled wrong in this story. Write each word correctly.

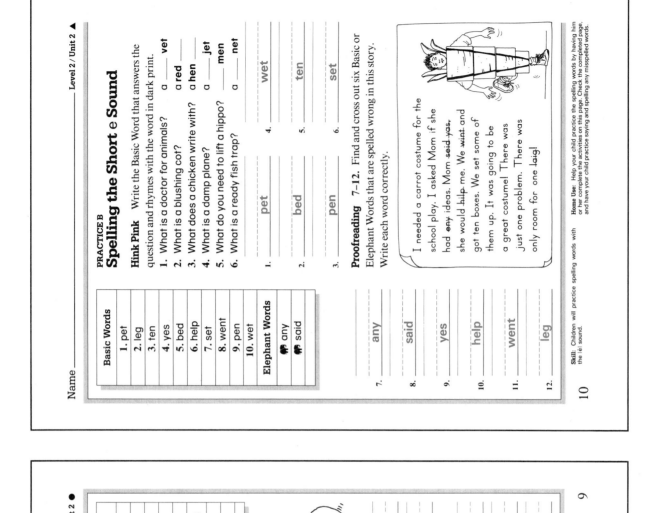

I needed a carrot costume for the school play. I asked Mom if she had eny ideas. Mom sed yes, she would hilp me. We wint and got ten boxes. We set some of them up. It was going to be a great costume! There was just one problem. There was only room for one laig!

7. any
8. said
9. yes
10. help
11. went
12. leg

10

Skill: Children will practice spelling words with the /e/ sound.

Home Use: Help your child practice the spelling words by having him or her complete the activities on this page. Check the completed page, and have your child practice saying and spelling any misspelled words.

PRACTICE A
Spelling the Short e Sound

Basic Words
1. pet
2. leg
3. ten
4. yes
5. bed
Elephant Words
any
said

Summing Up

The vowel sound in **pet** and **leg** is called the short **e** sound. The short **e** sound may be spelled **e**.

Busy Bee Write the letter or letters that spell the short **e** sound to finish each Basic or Elephant Word. Color the two words in which the short **e** sound is not spelled **e**.

p e t   t e n   y e s   a n y   s a i d

Now write the words in ABC order.

1. any
2. bed
3. pet
4. said

b e d   t e n   y e s

5. ten
6. yes
7. bed
8. leg
9. ten

Three of a Kind Write the Basic Word that finishes each group.

7. table, _____, chair
8. arm, _____, foot
9. five, _____, twenty

9

Skill: Children will practice spelling words with the /e/ sound.

Home Use: Help your child practice the spelling words by having him or her complete the activities on this page. Check the completed page, and have your child practice saying and spelling any misspelled words.

Unit 2 Test: Spelling the Short e Sound

Read each sentence. Is the underlined word spelled right or wrong? Mark your answer.

	Right	Wrong
Sample: Do you want the red <u>bike</u>?	●	○

Items 1–7 test Basic Words 1–5 and the Elephant Words.
Items 8–12 test Basic Words 6–10.

	Right	Wrong
1. Are there <u>eny</u> peanuts left?	○	●
2. Can you hop on one <u>leg</u>?	●	○
3. My birthday is in <u>ten</u> days.	●	○
4. Did Mrs. Grey say <u>yas</u>?	○	●
5. I have a worm for a <u>pet</u>.	●	○
6. It is time to go to <u>bedd</u>.	○	●
7. Did you hear what she <u>said</u>?	●	○
8. Frank has a new green <u>penn</u>.	○	●
9. Carlos will <u>set</u> the table.	●	○
10. We <u>wint</u> to feed the ducks today.	○	●
11. Adam was happy to <u>halp</u> Sara.	○	●
12. My shoes got <u>wet</u> in the puddle.	●	○

12

PRACTICE C
Spelling the Short e Sound

Welcome to the Zoo Pretend you are a guide at a zoo. Draw the path you would take to visit the animals in ABC order. **Sample answer:**

Challenge Words
1. penguin
2. elk
Theme Vocabulary
3. snail
4. parrot
5. hamster
6. lizard

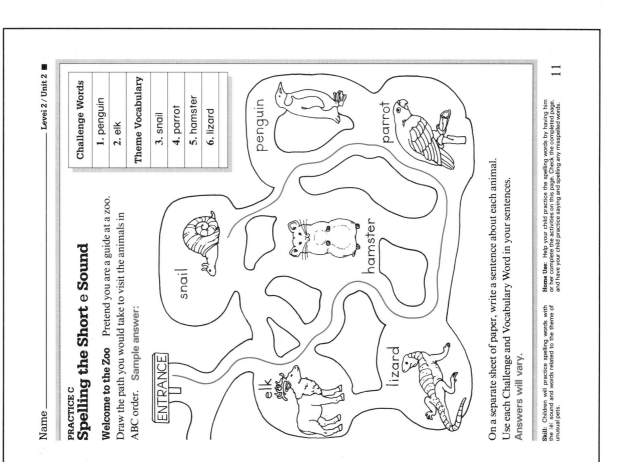

On a separate sheet of paper, write a sentence about each animal. Use each Challenge and Vocabulary Word in your sentences. **Answers will vary.**

Skill: Children will practice spelling words with the /ĕ/ sound and words related to the theme of unusual pets.

Home Use: Help your child practice the spelling words by having him or her complete the activities on this page. Check the completed page, and have your child practice saying and spelling any misspelled words.

11

Practice Master and Test Answers

PRACTICE B
Spelling the Short i Sound

Basic Words
1. pig
2. win
3. is
4. six
5. his
6. if
7. hit
8. fix
9. pin
10. dig

Elephant Words
been
I

Fill-In Fun Write the missing Basic or Elephant Word.

1. needle and _____   4. Mike and _____
2. _____ or lose   5. _____ or miss
3. _____ and seven   6. _____ and hers

1. pin
2. win
3. six
4. I
5. hit
6. his

Tick-Tack-Code Use the code below to write Basic or Elephant Words. Look at the letters and the shape of the lines around each letter.

b	d	g
f	i / e	n
p	s	x

Example: p i n = pin

7. fix
8. is
9. dig
10. been
11. pig
12. if

Skill: Children will practice spelling words with the |i| sound.

Home Use: Help your child practice the spelling words by having him or her complete the activities on this page. Check the completed page, and have your child practice saying and spelling any misspelled words.

PRACTICE A
Spelling the Short i Sound

Basic Words
1. pig
2. win
3. is
4. six
5. his

Elephant Words
been
I

Summing Up

The vowel sound in **pig** and **is** is called the short **i** sound. The short **i** sound may be spelled **i**.

Shady Words Color each box that has a word in which the short **i** sound is spelled **i**. Color green the box that has the word in which the short **i** sound is not spelled **i**. Write the words.

six	his	win
cat	set	win
fun	been	hop
win	pig	is

Order of answers may vary.

1. six   3. win
2. his   4. been

Look at the shape of the boxes you colored. Write the Elephant Word you see. _____ I

Silly Rhymes Finish these silly sentences. Write a Basic Word to rhyme with the word in dark print.

8. My pet _____ ate a **fig**.
9. Can you **mix** _____ eggs with water?
10. How did you _____ a safety **pin**?

5. win
6. pig
7. is
8. pig
9. six
10. win

Skill: Children will practice spelling words with the |i| sound.

Home Use: Help your child practice the spelling words by having him or her complete the activities on this page. Check the completed page, and have your child practice saying and spelling any misspelled words.

Unit 3 Test: Spelling the Short i Sound

Read each sentence. Is the underlined word spelled right or wrong? Mark your answer.

Sample:

Sasha <u>did</u> her work.

        Right **Wrong**

         ●   ○

Items 1–7 test Basic Words 1–5 and the Elephant Words.
Items 8–12 test Basic Words 6–10.

        Right **Wrong**

1. Who will win the new book?   ● ○
2. Jory has <u>benn</u> very busy.   ○ ●
3. Tony gave the book to <u>hiz</u> sister.   ○ ●
4. Aunt Brenda just fed the <u>pig</u>.   ● ○
5. This <u>iss</u> my teacher Mr. Taylor.   ○ ●
6. Lou asked if <u>I</u> would go to the game.   ● ○
7. There are <u>sics</u> boys on my team.   ○ ●
8. Will you <u>fix</u> my radio?   ● ○
9. I will be happy <u>iv</u> you visit.   ○ ●
10. Andy can <u>deg</u> a hole in the sand.   ○ ●
11. That <u>pin</u> is sharp.   ● ○
12. Chen was able to hit the ball.   ● ○

16

PRACTICE C
Spelling the Short i Sound

Who's Who   Rona is at a fair. She needs to find four people she has never met. Write the missing Challenge or Vocabulary Word for each clue.

Challenge Words
1. quilt
2. picnic
Theme Vocabulary
3. ribbon
4. booth
5. ring
6. judge

1. Meg and Eve are standing on either side of the ticket _____.
2. Meg has a _____ in her hair.
3. Eve is carrying a _____ basket.
4. Ike and Meg are standing on a large _____ that they made.
5–6. Dave is holding a round _____ that a _____ gave him for winning a race.

1. ___booth___
2. ___ribbon___
3. ___picnic___
4. ___quilt___
5. ___ring___
6. ___judge___

Then use the clues to write the name of each person.

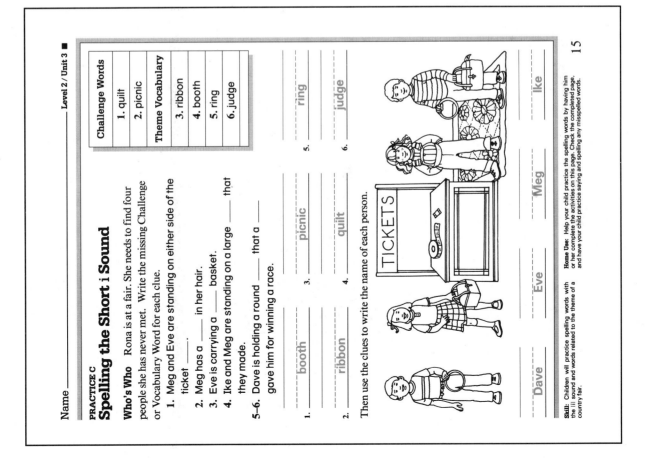

___Dave___   ___Eve___   ___Meg___   ___Ike___

Skill: Children will practice spelling words with the [i] sound and words related to the theme of a country fair.

Home Use: Help your child practice the spelling words by having him or her complete the activities on this page. Check the completed page, and have your child practice saying and spelling any misspelled words.

15

202

PRACTICE B
Spelling the Short o Sound

Basic Words
1. job
2. pot
3. nod
4. top
5. not
6. dot
7. fox
8. mop
9. spot
10. hop
Elephant Word
🐘 of

Buckle Up! All of the seat belts need to be closed. Draw lines to match the parts of the seat belts to spell Basic or Elephant Words. Write the words.

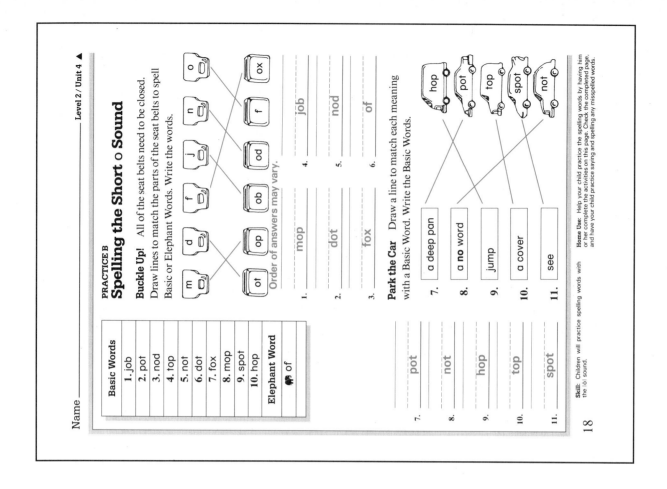

Order of answers may vary.

1. _____ mop

2. _____ dot

3. _____ fox

4. _____ job

5. _____ nod

6. _____ of

Park the Car Draw a line to match each meaning with a Basic Word. Write the Basic Words.

7. | a deep pan | _____ pot

8. | a **no** word | _____ not

9. | jump | _____ hop

10. | a cover | _____ top

11. | see | _____ spot

18

Skill: Children will practice spelling words with the /o/ sound.

Home Use: Help your child practice the spelling words by having him or her complete the activities on this page. Check the completed page, and have your child practice saying and spelling any misspelled words.

PRACTICE A
Spelling the Short o Sound

Summing Up

The vowel sound in **job** and **pot** is called the short **o** sound. The short **o** sound may be spelled **o**.

Basic Words
1. job
2. pot
3. nod
4. top
5. not
Elephant Word
🐘 of

Short o Nest Use the consonant letters on the eggs and the letter **o** to write four Basic Words. Draw a line under the letter that spells the short **o** sound in each word. Order of answers may vary.

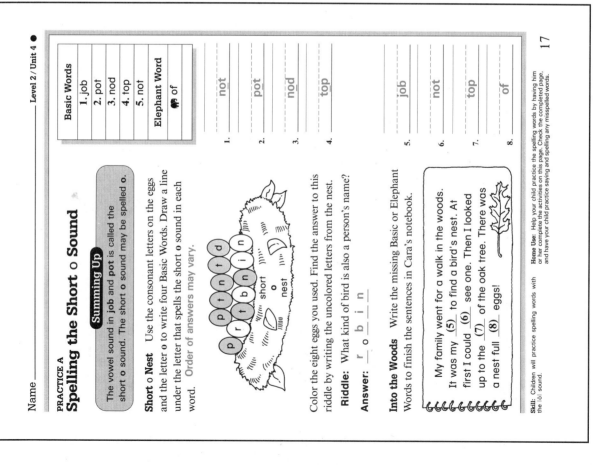

1. _____ n o t

2. _____ p o t

3. _____ n o d

4. _____ t o p

Color the eight eggs you used. Find the answer to this riddle by writing the uncolored letters from the nest.

Riddle: What kind of bird is also a person's name?

Answer: r o b i n

Into the Woods Write the missing Basic or Elephant Words to finish the sentences in Cara's notebook.

My family went for a walk in the woods. It was my **(5)** to find a bird's nest. At first I could **(6)** see one. Then I looked up to the **(7)** of the oak tree. There was a nest full **(8)** eggs!

5. _____ job

6. _____ not

7. _____ top

8. _____ of

17

Skill: Children will practice spelling words with the /o/ sound.

Home Use: Help your child practice the spelling words by having him or her complete the activities on this page. Check the completed page, and have your child practice saying and spelling any misspelled words.

PRACTICE C
Spelling the Short o Sound

Word Pairs Write the words that complete each pair of sentences. Use a Challenge or Vocabulary Word in each pair.

Challenge Words
1. block
2. hospital

Theme Vocabulary
3. careful
4. injure
5. exit
6. alarm

1–2. A teacher works in a _____.
A doctor works in a _____.

1. _____ school
2. _____ hospital

3–4. You smell thick, black _____.
You hear the fire _____.

3. _____ smoke
4. _____ alarm

5–6. You can walk out an _____.
You can walk in an _____.

5. _____ exit
6. _____ entrance

Best Sellers Write the missing Challenge or Vocabulary Word for each book title. Use capital letters correctly.

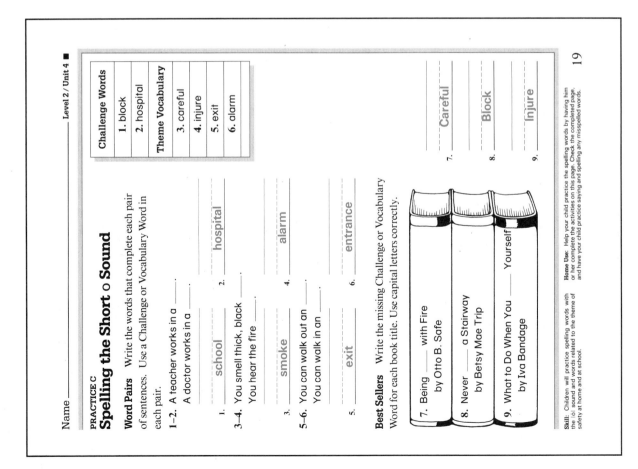

7. _____ **Careful** with Fire
by Otto B. Safe

8. Never _____ **Block** a Stairway
by Betsy Mae Trip

9. What to Do When You _____ **Injure** Yourself
by Iva Bandage

Skill: Children will practice spelling words with the /o/ sound and words related to the theme of safety at home and at school.

Home Use: Help your child practice the spelling words by having him or her complete the activities on this page. Check the completed page, and have your child practice saying and spelling any misspelled words.

19

Unit **4** Test: Spelling the Short o Sound

Each item below gives three spellings of a word. Choose the correct spelling. Mark the letter for that word.

Sample:
a. boks   **b.** bux   **c.** box

ANSWERS
ⓐ ⓑ ●

Items 1–6 test Basic Words 1–5 and the Elephant Word.
Items 7–11 test Basic Words 6–10.

1. **a.** not   **b.** nott   **c.** nat   ● ⓑ ⓒ
2. **a.** top   **b.** topp   **c.** toop   ● ⓑ ⓒ
3. **a.** ov   **b.** of   **c.** uf   ⓐ ● ⓒ
4. **a.** pott   **b.** patt   **c.** pot   ⓐ ⓑ ●
5. **a.** job   **b.** jub   **c.** jobb   ● ⓑ ⓒ
6. **a.** nod   **b.** nodd   **c.** nud   ● ⓑ ⓒ
7. **a.** hopp   **b.** hop   **c.** hup   ⓐ ● ⓒ
8. **a.** dott   **b.** dat   **c.** dot   ⓐ ⓑ ●
9. **a.** sput   **b.** spot   **c.** spott   ⓐ ● ⓒ
10. **a.** mup   **b.** mopp   **c.** mop   ⓐ ⓑ ●
11. **a.** foks   **b.** fex   **c.** fox   ⓐ ⓑ ●

20

Practice Master and Test Answers

PRACTICE A
Spelling the Short u Sound

Basic Words
1. sun
2. mud
3. bug
4. fun
5. but
Elephant Words
🐘 some
🐘 from

Summing Up

The vowel sound in **sun** and **mud** is called the short **u** sound. The short **u** sound may be spelled **u**.

Picture This Write the letter that begins each picture name. Make Basic Words.

1. 🐘 + ☂ + = _____ bug
2. 🧦 + ☂ + = _____ sun
3. 🦋 + ☂ + = _____ but
4. 🦔 + ☂ + = _____ mud

Riddles Write a Basic or Elephant Word to finish each riddle. Then see if you can think of the answer to each riddle.

5. What fruit cannot lie in the hot _____ ?   _____ sun
6. When do _____ cars get angry?   _____ some
7. What kind of music do dads have _____ singing?   _____ fun
8. How can you keep a skunk _____ smelling?   _____ from

Riddle Answers: 5. a banana because it peels 6. when they come to a crossroad 7. pop music 8. hold its nose

Skill: Children will practice spelling words with the /ŭ/ sound.

Home Use: Help your child practice the spelling words by having him or her complete the activities on this page. Check the completed page, and have your child practice saying and spelling any misspelled words.

21

PRACTICE B
Spelling the Short u Sound

Basic Words
1. sun
2. mud
3. bug
4. fun
5. but
6. hug
7. bun
8. nut
9. bus
10. rug
Elephant Words
🐘 some
🐘 from

Word Search Write a word for each clue. Then circle each word in the puzzle. Look across and down.

1. a machine to drive
2. a good time
3. wet dirt
4. a kind of seed
5. a floor covering
6. an insect
7. a few
8. a bright star

1. _____ bus
2. _____ fun
3. _____ mud
4. _____ nut

5. _____ rug
6. _____ bug
7. _____ some
8. _____ sun

x	a	s	o	m	e	r	b	u	s
p	n	u	t	u	p	i	r	u	g
f	u	n	v	d	w	o	g	g	l
							o	u	b

Proofreading 9–12. Find and cross out four Basic or Elephant Words that are spelled wrong in Shirley's list. Write each word correctly.

- Eat a bunn for breakfast.
- Get some money frome Dad.
- Have fun at the park, bot do not stay late.
- Walk in the mud. Do not walk on the rug.
- Give Mom a heg.

9. _____ bun
10. _____ from
11. _____ but
12. _____ hug

22

Skill: Children will practice spelling words with the short /ŭ/ sound.

Home Use: Help your child practice the spelling words by having him or her complete the activities on this page. Check the completed page, and have your child practice saying and spelling any misspelled words.

Name _____

Unit 5 Test: Spelling the Short u Sound

Each item below gives three spellings of a word. Choose the correct spelling. Mark the letter for that word.

ANSWERS
(a) (b) ●

Sample:
a. upp   b. up   c. op

Items 1–7 test Basic Words 1–5 and the Elephant Words.
Items 8–12 test Basic Words 6–10.

#	a.	b.	c.
1.	but	bott	buut
2.	mudd	med	mud
3.	frum	from	fromm
4.	buug	bug	bugg
5.	fun	fen	fonn
6.	som	sume	some
7.	sun	sonn	sunn
8.	bon	bun	bund
9.	heg	hugg	hug
10.	nut	nutt	nott
11.	rog	ruug	rug
12.	bas	bus	bos

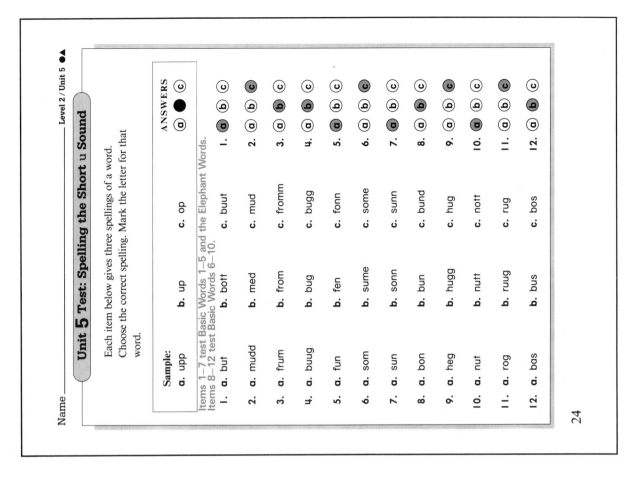

24

Name _____

PRACTICE C
Spelling the Short u Sound

What Class   Think how the words in each group are alike. Write the missing Challenge or Vocabulary Words. In the box below each group, write a Vocabulary Word that tells about all the things in the group.
Order of answers for 1–2 may vary.

spring	lightning
fall	rain
1. summer	wind
2. winter	4. thunder

3. season → 5. weather

Challenge Words
1. thunder
2. puddle

Theme Vocabulary
3. summer
4. winter
5. season
6. weather

Double Trouble   Write a word pair for each clue. Use one Challenge or Vocabulary Word in each word pair.

a small pool of water and dirt
6. m u d   p u d d l e

a place to learn in July
7. s u m m e r   s c h o o l

skiing, sledding, and ice hockey
8. w i n t e r   s p o r t s

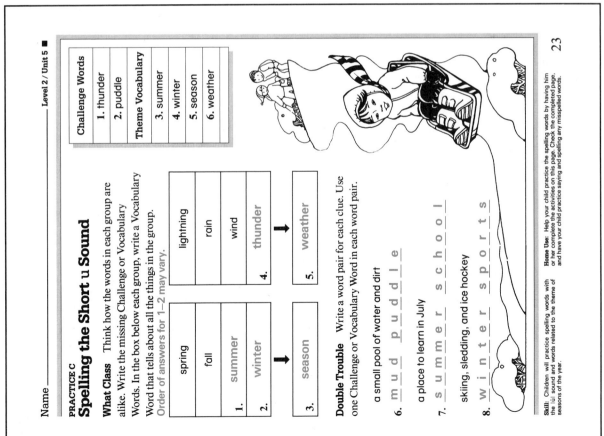

Skill: Children will practice spelling words with the /u/ sound and words related to the theme of seasons of the year.

Home Use: Help your child practice the spelling words by having him or her complete the activities on this page. Check the completed page, and have your child practice saying and spelling any misspelled words.

23

Practice Master and Test Answers

Unit 6 Review: Test A

Read each sentence. One of the underlined words in each sentence is spelled wrong. Mark the letter for that word.

Sample:

My purple boot has mod on it.
   a   b

ANSWERS
(a) ●

This test reviews Basic Words 1–5 and Elephant Words from Units 1–5.

1. Does Simon have a fon job?
      a   b   1. (a) (b)
2. Della has a pig for a pett.
      a   b   2. (a) (b)
3. If I nod, my het will fall off.
      a   b   3. (a) (b)
4. Kay put som plums in the bag.
      a   b   4. (a) (b)
5. The leg of the table es broken.
      a   b   5. (a) (b)
6. I have bein playing in the sun.
      a   b   6. (a) (b)
7. That bugg has six legs.
      a   b   7. (a) (b)
8. Is there any soup in the pott?
      a   b   8. (a) (b)
9. I sat up in bed az the alarm rang.
      a   b   9. (a) (b)
10. I em not riding my bike today.
       a   b   10. (a) (b)
11. Reba ran but she did not wen.
       a   b   11. (a) (b)
12. Paul's bus woz ten minutes late.
       a   b   12. (a) (b)

Unit 6 Review: Test B

Read each sentence. One of the underlined words in each sentence is spelled wrong. Mark the letter for that word.

Sample:

Fran will halp me to pin the flower.
   a   b

ANSWERS
● (b)

This test reviews Basic Words 6–10 and Elephant Words from Units 1–5.

1. Lin was saad when we went home.
      a   b   1. (a) (b)
2. Ella ran to give Grandma a hugg.
      a   b   2. (a) (b)
3. Jon will hop ef you ask him.
      a   b   3. (a) (b)
4. Erin het the ball with the bat.
      a   b   4. (a) (b)
5. Tim sat in wat paint.
      a   b   5. (a) (b)
6. Did you sett my pen on the desk?
      a   b   6. (a) (b)
7. Can she fix the sput?
      a   b   7. (a) (b)
8. What bus does Kerry wunt to take?
      a   b   8. (a) (b)
9. Move the rog from Ivan's room.
      a   b   9. (a) (b)
10. May I use any mmop or broom?
       a   b   10. (a) (b)
11. Vito saed he saw a fox.
       a   b   11. (a) (b)
12. Watch the animal deg for the nut.
       a   b   12. (a) (b)

PRACTICE A
Vowel-Consonant-e Spellings

Basic Words
1. five
2. late
3. nine
4. made
5. side
Elephant Words
🐘 give
🐘 have

Summing Up

The vowel sounds in **late** and **five** are called the long **a** and the long **i** sounds. These long vowel sounds may be spelled by the vowel-consonant-**e** pattern.

A Fine Bunch Help Mickie. Write the words from his bananas under the correct sounds. Order of answers may vary.

bananas: side have made give late nine

long i

1. ___side___

2. ___nine___

long a

3. ___made___

4. ___late___

short a or short i

5. ___have___

6. ___give___

Monkey Rhymes Write the Basic Word for each set of clues.

7. If is a monkey that is not on time.
   If rhymes with **date**.   7. ___late___

8. If is one more than four monkeys.
   If rhymes with **dive**.   8. ___five___

9. If is not a monkey's front or back.
   If rhymes with **wide**.   9. ___side___

Skill: Children will practice spelling words with the /ā/ and the /ī/ sounds.

Home Use: Help your child practice the spelling words by having him or her complete the activities on this page. Check the completed page, and have your child practice saying and spelling any misspelled words.

PRACTICE B
Vowel-Consonant-e Spellings

Basic Words
1. five
2. late
3. nine
4. made
5. side
6. ate
7. fine
8. same
9. hide
10. line
Elephant Words
🐘 give
🐘 have

Crossword Clues Write a Basic or Elephant Word for each clue.

(crossword grid with answers: made, it, nine, five, side, have, ...)

Across

2. built
5. almost ten
6. not the top or bottom
7. to own

Down

1. a long, thin mark
3. rhymes with **late**
4. less than six

In the Family Write the Basic or Elephant Word that is the opposite of the word in dark print.

8. Mr. Opposite is always **early**.
   Mrs. Opposite is always ___late___.   8. ___late___

9. Mr. Opposite wears a **different** hat every day.
   Mrs. Opposite always wears the ___same___ one.   9. ___same___

10. Mr. Opposite wants to **get** some new books.
    Mrs. Opposite wants to ___give___ away her old ones. 10. ___give___

11. Mr. Opposite likes to **show** his paintings.
    Mrs. Opposite likes to ___hide___ hers.   11. ___hide___

12. Mr. Opposite thinks the weather is **awful**.
    Mrs. Opposite thinks it is just ___fine___.   12. ___fine___

Skill: Children will practice spelling words with the /ā/ and the /ī/ sounds.

Home Use: Help your child practice the spelling words by having him or her complete the activities on this page. Check the completed page, and have your child practice saying and spelling any misspelled words.

Practice Master and Test Answers

207

Level 2 / Unit 7 ●▲

Unit 7 Test: Vowel-Consonant-e Spellings

Read each sentence. Is the underlined word spelled right or wrong? Mark your answer.

	Right	Wrong
Sample:		
Freda <u>gave</u> me a funny hat.	●	○

Items 1–7 test Basic Words 1–5 and the Elephant Words.
Items 8–12 test Basic Words 6–10.

		Right	Wrong
1.	Wave from the <u>sied</u> of the road.	○	●
2.	The library has nine <u>new</u> books.	●	○
3.	Bruno is never <u>late</u> for school.	●	○
4.	Edith <u>moad</u> a big mistake.	○	●
5.	I will have another <u>muffin</u>.	●	○
6.	They will <u>leave</u> in five minutes.	●	○
7.	Will Gabe <u>gife</u> you his skates?	○	●
8.	Draw a red line across the <u>paper</u>.	●	○
9.	Who will <u>hied</u> the gift?	○	●
10.	Nelson <u>ate</u> all of his dinner.	●	○
11.	Stan and Nina have the <u>saem</u> shoes.	○	●
12.	You did a <u>finn</u> job on the report.	○	●

36

Level 2 / Unit 7 ■

PRACTICE C
Vowel-Consonant-e Spellings

Challenge Words
1. mistake
2. write
Theme Vocabulary
3. pupil
4. absent
5. locker
6. gym

School Books Write the missing Challenge or Vocabulary Word for each book title. Use capital letters.

1. How to Be a Smart _____ by Iva Brain
2. Games to Play in the _____ by P. E. Time
3. How to Correct a _____ by E. Raser

1. ____Pupil____ 3. ____Mistake____

2. ____Gym____

Addagrams Write a word for each clue. Then write the correct letters in the numbered boxes. The letters will spell a Challenge or Vocabulary Word.

4. a rubber wheel = $\frac{t}{4}\frac{i}{3}\frac{r}{2}\frac{e}{5}$

   a thin piece of metal = $\frac{w}{1}\frac{i}{3}\frac{r}{2}\frac{e}{5}$

1	2	3	4	5
w	r	i	t	e

5. something a key fits = $\frac{l}{1}\frac{o}{2}\frac{c}{3}\frac{k}{4}$

   the middle of an apple = $\frac{c}{3}\frac{o}{2}\frac{r}{6}\frac{e}{5}$

1	2	3	4	5	6
l	o	c	k	e	r

6. an animal that flies = $\frac{b}{2}\frac{a}{1}\frac{t}{6}$

   mailed = $\frac{s}{3}\frac{e}{4}\frac{n}{5}\frac{t}{6}$

1	2	3	4	5	6
a	b	s	e	n	t

Skill: Children will practice spelling words with the vowel-consonant-e pattern and words related to the theme of schools.

Home Use: Help your child practice the spelling words by having him or her complete the activities on this page. Check the completed page, and have your child practice saying and spelling any misspelled words.

35

PRACTICE A
More Vowel-Consonant-e Spellings

Basic Words
1. bone
2. nose
3. use
4. these
5. rope
Elephant Words
🐘 one
🐘 goes

Summing Up

The vowel sounds in **bone**, **use**, and **these** are called the long **o**, the long **u**, and the long **e** vowel sounds. These long vowel sounds may be spelled by the vowel-consonant-**e** pattern.

Puzzle Play Write the missing Basic or Elephant Words. Use the letters in the boxes to spell the name of a kind of bird.

1. My dog g̲ o̲ e̲ s̲ into the yard every day.

2. Fang digs o̲ n̲ e̲ hole in the dirt.

3. He puts his tasty b̲ o̲ n̲ e̲ inside.

4. He sniffs it with his n̲ o̲ s̲ e̲ .

5. Fang never fills in t̲ h̲ e̲ s̲ e̲ holes.

Secret Word: g̲ o̲ o̲ s̲ e̲

Bingo! Color each box that has a word with the long **o**, the long **u**, or the long **e** vowel sound. Write the words that make a row. Order of answers may vary.

fox	pot	bus	these	hug
these	rope	bone	goes	use
nose	some	sun	rope	from
fun	bone	hop	mud	these

6. _____these_____

7. _____rope_____

8. _____bone_____

9. ____(goes)____

10. _____use_____

Now circle the word you wrote that does not have the vowel-consonant-e pattern.

Skill: Children will practice spelling words with the /ō/, the /ū/, and the /ē/ sounds.

Home Use: Help your child practice the spelling words by having him or her complete the activities on this page. Check the completed page, and have your child practice saying and spelling any misspelled words.

PRACTICE B
More Vowel-Consonant-e Spellings

Basic Words
1. bone
2. nose
3. use
4. these
5. rope
6. home
7. cute
8. close
9. hope
10. those
Elephant Words
🐘 one
🐘 goes

Letter Math Add and take away letters to make Basic Words. Write the words.

1. the − e + ose = ? _____those_____

2. cap − ap + ute = ? _____cute_____

3. clay − ay + ose = ? _____close_____

4. hip − ip + ome = ? _____home_____

5. hat − at + ope = ? _____hope_____

6. big − ig + one = ? _____bone_____

Proofreading 7–12. Find and cross out six Basic or Elephant Words that are spelled wrong in these airplane messages. Write each word correctly.

Do not let your ~~noz~~ burn.
Please ~~yuos~~ Ray's sun cream.

We hope you will visit Dave's Store.
We sell ladders, paint, and ~~rop~~!

Take home Mia's handmade hats for two dollars! You can't beat ~~theez~~ prices.

Everyone ~~gose~~ to Patty's Pizza!
Buy two for the price of ~~wun~~!

7. _____nose_____

8. _____use_____

9. _____rope_____

10. _____these_____

11. _____goes_____

12. _____one_____

Skill: Children will practice spelling words with the /ō/, the /ū/, and the /ē/ sounds.

Home Use: Help your child practice the spelling words by having him or her complete the activities on this page. Check the completed page, and have your child practice saying and spelling any misspelled words.

Unit 8 Test: More Vowel-Consonant-e Spellings

Each item below gives three spellings of a word. Choose the correct spelling. Mark the letter for that word.

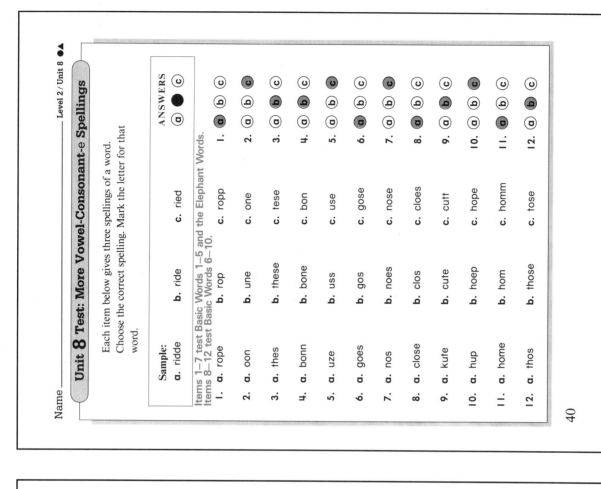

Sample:

a. ridde   b. ride   c. ried

ANSWERS
a ● c

Items 1–7 test Basic Words 1–5 and the Elephant Words.
Items 8–12 test Basic Words 6–10.

#	a	b	c	Answer
1.	a. rope	b. rop	c. ropp	a b c
2.	a. oon	b. une	c. one	a b c
3.	a. thes	b. these	c. tese	a b c
4.	a. bonn	b. bone	c. bon	a b c
5.	a. uze	b. uss	c. use	a b c
6.	a. goes	b. gos	c. gose	a b c
7.	a. nos	b. noes	c. nose	a b c
8.	a. close	b. clos	c. cloes	a b c
9.	a. kute	b. cute	c. cutt	a b c
10.	a. hup	b. hoep	c. hope	a b c
11.	a. home	b. hom	c. homm	a b c
12.	a. thos	b. those	c. tose	a b c

PRACTICE C
More Vowel-Consonant-e Spellings

Say It with Pictures   You can draw letters to show the meanings of the words they spell. Look at the example. Make a drawing for each Challenge and Vocabulary Word. Then write the word.
Drawings and order of answers may vary.

Example:

ate

Challenge Words
1. globe
2. mule
Theme Vocabulary
3. huge
4. sharp
5. reptile
6. fossil

1. globe

2. mule

3. huge

4. sharp

5. reptile

6. fossil

Skill: Children will practice spelling words with the vowel-consonant-e pattern and words related to the theme of dinosaurs.

Home Use: Help your child practice the spelling words by having him or her complete the activities on this page. Check the completed page, and have your child practice saying and spelling any misspelled words.

PRACTICE B
Words with Consonant Clusters

Basic Words
1. trip
2. swim
3. step
4. nest
5. club
6. stone
7. next
8. brave
9. glad
10. lost

Puzzle Play Write a Basic Word for each clue. Use the letters in the boxes to spell two words that tell what the bee in the cartoon is.

1. a heavy stick of wood   c l u **b**
2. where birds live   n **e** s t
3. to float or move in water   **s** w i m
4. coming right after   n e x **t**
5. put a foot forward   **s** t e p
6. not afraid   b **r** a v e
7. happy   g l **a** d
8. the opposite of **found**   l **l** o s t
9. a piece of rock   s t **o** n e
10. vacation   t **r** i p

Secret Words:
the **b e s t   s p e l l e r**

EXTRA! Draw your own cartoon. Write a word pair to tell about it. Use at least one Basic Word.

42

Skill: Children will practice spelling words with consonant clusters.

Home Use: Help your child practice the spelling words by having him or her complete the activities on this page. Check the completed page, and have your child practice saying and spelling any misspelled words.

PRACTICE A
Words with Consonant Clusters

Basic Words
1. trip
2. swim
3. step
4. nest
5. club

Summing Up

A **consonant cluster** is two consonant letters whose sounds are blended together. Some consonant clusters are **tr**, **sw**, **st**, **cl**, **xt**, **br**, and **gl**.

Juggling Act Color the balls with consonant clusters. Draw a line from each cluster to an ending to make a Basic Word. Then write the word. Order of answers may vary.

1. swim
2. step
3. trip
4. club

Word Search Write a Basic Word for each clue. Then circle each word. Look across and down.

5. a bird's home
6. a way of walking
7. to move through water
8. a journey

5. nest
6. step
7. swim
8. trip

41

Skill: Children will practice spelling words with consonant clusters.

Home Use: Help your child practice the spelling words by having him or her complete the activities on this page. Check the completed page, and have your child practice saying and spelling any misspelled words.

Practice Master and Test Answers

Unit 9 Test: Words with Consonant Clusters

Read each sentence. Find the correctly spelled word to complete each sentence. Mark the letter next to that word.

Sample:

Jack did not ____ on the ice.

● slip   (b) slep   (c) slup

ANSWERS

Items 1–5 test Basic Words 1–5. Items 6–10 test Basic Words 6–10.

1. Al took one bag on his ____.   (a) trep   (b) tripp   (c) trip

2. Our ____ went to the park.   (a) club   (b) culb   (c) clubb

3. Do not ____ on a wet floor.   (a) stap   (b) step   (c) stip

4. Eva came to ____ in the pool.   (a) swem   (b) swom   (c) swim

5. I saw a robin's ____.   (a) nest   (b) nist   (c) nesst

6. Kyle threw the flat ____.   (a) ston   (b) stone   (c) stune

7. Lee ____ her new book.   (a) loct   (b) lostt   (c) lost

8. The ____ bus will come soon.   (a) next   (b) nixt   (c) naxt

9. I am ____ everyone had fun.   (a) gald   (b) glad   (c) gladd

10. The ____ girl saved Susan.   (a) brev   (b) brave   (c) berav

44

PRACTICE C
Words with Consonant Clusters

Who Did It? Read the story and the clues. Write the missing Challenge and Vocabulary Words for the clues.

Challenge Words
1. branches
2. storm
Theme Vocabulary
3. gear
4. cabin
5. clearing
6. camper

Four hikers stayed in a small hut in the woods. The last hiker to leave the next morning forgot to close the door. A raccoon got in and ate all the food. Who forgot to close the door?

Clues

1. Jane put her camping ____ in her pack.

2. She went out the ____ door at seven o'clock.

3. Cleo, the oldest ____, left ten minutes after Jane did.

4. She crossed a ____ that had no trees.

5. Twenty minutes after Cleo left, Sue went off to gather twigs and ____.

6. Ten minutes before Sue left, Tina left to give everyone raincoats in case of a ____.

1. _____ gear _____

2. _____ cabin _____

3. _____ camper _____

4. _____ clearing _____

5. _____ branches _____

6. _____ storm _____

Now write the time each hiker left the hut.

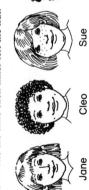

Jane	Cleo	Sue	Tina
7:00	7:10	7:30	7:20

Who forgot to close the door? _____ Sue _____

Skill: Children will practice spelling words with consonant clusters and words related to the theme of camping and hiking.

Home Use: Help your child practice the spelling words by having him or her complete the activities on this page. Check the completed page, and have your child practice saying and spelling any misspelled words.

43

Name _____

PRACTICE A
Words Spelled with k or ck

Summing Up

The words **lake** and **rock** end with the same consonant sound. This consonant sound may be spelled **k** or **ck**.

Basic Words
1. lake
2. rock
3. ask
4. pick
5. truck

Letter Load Look at the spelling clue at the front of each truck. Then write the Basic Word for each picture.

k
1. ask   2. lake

ck
3. pick   4. truck   5. rock

Letter Drop Write the Basic Word that rhymes with the word in dark print to finish each poem.

6. To hide my face, I wear a **mask**. If you want to see me, you must _____ ask
7. Snow is falling. I saw a **flake**. Is snow falling on the _____? lake
8. Thunder boomed and lightning **struck**. The rain splashed all around the _____. truck

Skill: Children will practice spelling words that end with **k** or **ck**.

Home Use: Help your child practice the spelling words by having him or her complete the activities on this page. Check the completed page, and have your child practice saying and spelling any misspelled words.

Name _____

PRACTICE B
Words Spelled with k or ck

Basic Words
1. lake
2. rock
3. ask
4. pick
5. truck
6. black
7. back
8. bake
9. clock
10. kick

Riddles Write a Basic Word to finish each riddle. Then see if you can think of the answer to each riddle.

1. What kind of trees grow near an ocean or a _____? lake
2. What did the big hand on the _____ say to the little hand? clock
3. What question did the little hand _____ the big hand? ask
4. Why are cooks mean when they _____ a cake? bake
5. What happens when you _____ a blue rock into the Red Sea? kick

Proofreading 6–10. Find and cross out five Basic Words that are spelled wrong on these signs. Write each word correctly. Begin each word with a capital letter.

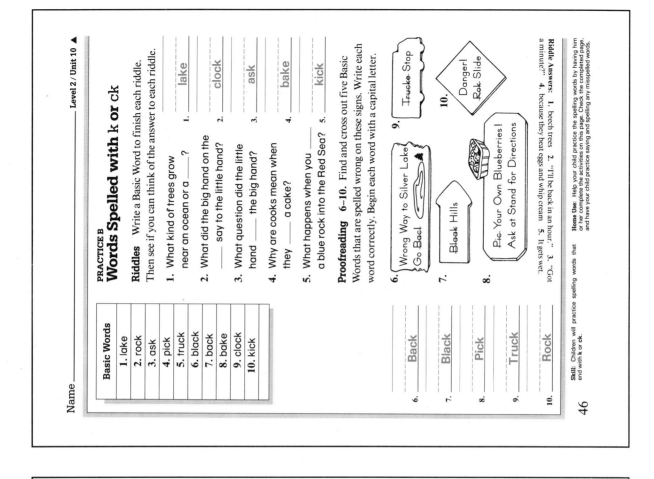

6. Wrong Way to Silver Lake Go Bacl — Back
7. Blaak Hills — Black
8. Pic Your Own Blueberries! Ask at Stand for Directions — Pick
9. Trucke Stop — Truck
10. Danger! Rok Slide — Rock

Riddle Answers: 1. beech trees 2. "I'll be back in an hour." 3. "Got a minute?" 4. because they beat eggs and whip cream 5. It gets wet.

Skill: Children will practice spelling words that end with **k** or **ck**.

Home Use: Help your child practice the spelling words by having him or her complete the activities on this page. Check the completed page, and have your child practice saying and spelling any misspelled words.

Practice Master and Test Answers

Unit 10 Test: Words Spelled with k or ck

Read each sentence. Is the underlined word spelled right or wrong? Mark your answer.

Sample:
Peter flew his new kite.

	Right	Wrong
	●	○

Items 1–5 test Basic Words 1–5. Items 6–10 test Basic Words 6–10.

	Right	Wrong
1. Hans fed the ducks at the lake.	●	○
2. Which box would you pik?	○	●
3. Val has to asck her mother.	○	●
4. My brother drives a truck.	●	○
5. Troy found an interesting rok.	○	●
6. I often use my black pen.	●	○
7. Norma can kik the ball very far.	○	●
8. Read the clock on the wall.	●	○
9. What will you bake for the party?	●	○
10. Damon will be bak after lunch.	○	●

48

PRACTICE C
Words Spelled with k or ck

Crossword Clues Write the Challenge and Vocabulary Words in the puzzle. Then write a clue for each Across word and each Down word.

Challenge Words
1. dock
2. snake

Theme Vocabulary
3. wade
4. shore
5. brook
6. flow

(crossword puzzle grid with answers: b r o o k / f l o w / s n a k e / h / d o c k / r / w a d e)

Across

Answers will vary.

1. _____
2. _____
3. _____
4. _____

Down

3. _____
5. _____

Skill: Children will practice spelling words that end with k or ck and words related to the theme of rivers and lakes.

Home Use: Help your child practice the spelling words by having him or her complete the activities on this page. Check the completed page, and have your child practice saying and spelling any misspelled words.

47

214

Name _____

PRACTICE B
Words with Double Consonants

Basic Words
1. bell
2. off
3. dress
4. add
5. hill
6. well
7. egg
8. will
9. grass
10. tell

Tick-Tack-Code Use the code below to write Basic Words. Look at the letters and the shape of the lines around each letter.

	b	d	e
w			l
t	r		s

1. well
2. tell
3. dress
4. bell

Mother Goose Times Write the missing Basic Words in these headlines. Begin each word with a capital letter.

Humpty Dumpty Falls (5) Wall

Goose Lays Gold (6) in Green (7)

Jack and Jill Climb (8) ! Jack Hurt in Fall!

Tommy Tucker (9) Sing for His Supper

Snow White Can't Count! Dwarfs Don't (10) up to Seven

5. Off
6. Egg
7. Grass
8. Hill
9. Will
10. Add

50

Skill: Children will practice words that end with double consonants.

Home Use: Help your child practice the spelling words by having him or her complete the activities on this page. Check the completed page. and have your child practice saying and spelling any misspelled words.

Name _____

PRACTICE A
Words with Double Consonants

Summing Up

In words like **bell**, **off**, and **dress**, the final consonant sound is spelled with two letters that are the same.

Basic Words
1. bell
2. off
3. dress
4. add
5. hill

How Charming! Write the missing final consonants. Then write the words in ABC order.

be l l   hi l l   a d d   dre s s

1. add
2. bell
3. dress
4. hill

Silly Songs Write a Basic Word to complete each song title. Begin each word with a capital letter.

5. I Would Climb Any ___ Hill ___ for Your Smile

6. Just Dance Until the Music Is Turned ___ Off ___

7. I Hear a ___ Bell ___ Ringing in My Heart

8. Let's ___ Dress ___ Up for the Party

49

Skill: Children will practice spelling words that end with double consonants.

Home Use: Help your child practice the spelling words by having him or her complete the activities on this page. Check the completed page. and have your child practice saying and spelling any misspelled words.

Practice Master and Test Answers

Unit 11 Test: Words with Double Consonants

Each item below gives three spellings of a word.
Choose the correct spelling. Mark the letter for that word.

			ANSWERS
Sample:			
a. fil	b. fill	c. fiil	ⓐ ● ⓒ

Items 1–5 test Basic Words 1–5. Items 6–10 test Basic Words 6–10.

	a.	b.	c.	ANSWERS
1.	a. off	b. ofv	c. ovf	ⓐ ⓑ ⓒ
2.	a. hil	b. holl	c. hill	ⓐ ⓑ ⓒ
3.	a. ders	b. dress	c. dres	ⓐ ⓑ ⓒ
4.	a. bel	b. behl	c. bell	ⓐ ⓑ ⓒ
5.	a. add	b. adb	c. aad	ⓐ ⓑ ⓒ
6.	a. wel	b. well	c. wehl	ⓐ ⓑ ⓒ
7.	a. gras	b. gress	c. grass	ⓐ ⓑ ⓒ
8.	a. egg	b. eg	c. igg	ⓐ ⓑ ⓒ
9.	a. tel	b. tell	c. ttel	ⓐ ⓑ ⓒ
10.	a. will	b. wwil	c. wil	ⓐ ⓑ ⓒ

52

PRACTICE C

Words with Double Consonants

Mystery Music Find out what instrument each boy plays. Use the clues and the chart. Mark an **X** in the boxes under the instruments each boy does not play. Draw a star in the box that shows the instrument each boy does play.

Challenge Words
1. brass
2. skill
Theme Vocabulary
3. tune
4. harp
5. tuba
6. pit

Clues

- Each boy plays a different instrument.
- No boy's name begins with the same letter as the instrument he plays.
- Ted does not play the violin.

	harp	tuba	violin
Hal	X	X	☆
Ted	☆	X	X
Vic	X	☆	X

Write each missing Challenge Word, Vocabulary Word, or boy's name to finish the story. Use the chart to help you.

At two o'clock, the boys took their seats in the orchestra __(1)__. Soon, __(2)__ began to __(3)__ his violin. Then Ted plucked at the strings of his __(4)__. Finally, __(5)__ put the __(6)__ to his mouth and blew a few notes. He was proud of his shiny __(7)__ instrument. He hoped he had the __(8)__ to play it well.

1. _pit_

2. _Hal_

3. _tune_

4. _harp_

5. _Vic_

6. _tuba_

7. _brass_

8. _skill_

Skill: Children will practice spelling words that end with double consonants and words related to the theme of songs and instruments.

Home Use: Help your child practice the spelling words by having him or her complete the activities on this page. Check the completed page, and have your child practice saying and spelling any misspelled words.

51

216

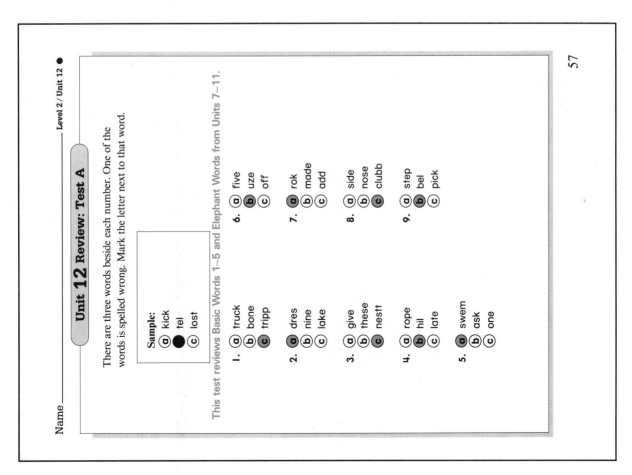

Name _____

Unit 12 Review: Test A

There are three words beside each number. One of the words is spelled wrong. Mark the letter next to that word.

Sample:
- (a) kick
- (b) tel ●
- (c) lost

This test reviews Basic Words 1–5 and Elephant Words from Units 7–11.

1. (a) truck (b) bone (c) tripp ●
2. (a) dres ● (b) nine (c) lake
3. (a) give (b) these (c) nestt ●
4. (a) rope (b) hil ● (c) late
5. (a) swem ● (b) ask (c) one
6. (a) five (b) uze ● (c) off
7. (a) rok ● (b) made (c) add
8. (a) side (b) nose (c) clubb ●
9. (a) step (b) bel ● (c) pick

57

Name _____

Unit 12 Review: Test B

There are three words beside each number. One of the words is spelled wrong. Mark the letter next to that word.

Sample:
- (a) dress
- (b) swim
- (c) truc ●

This test reviews Basic Words 6–10 and Elephant Words from Units 7–11.

1. (a) brave (b) gras ● (c) cute
2. (a) bak ● (b) ate (c) kick
3. (a) hide (b) close (c) eg ●
4. (a) lost (b) wel ● (c) those
5. (a) black (b) tell (c) ston ●
6. (a) homm ● (b) glad (c) same
7. (a) bake (b) nixt ● (c) clock
8. (a) fien ● (b) have (c) hope
9. (a) line (b) goes (c) wil ●

58

Practice Master and Test Answers

217

PRACTICE A
More Long a Spellings

Summing Up

The vowel sound in **way** and **train** is the long **a** sound. The long **a** sound may be spelled **ay** or **ai**.

Basic Words
1. train
2. way
3. mail
4. play
5. trail
Elephant Words
🐘 they
🐘 great

What a Place! Write the letters that spell the long **a** sound to finish each word. Color the two signs in which the long **a** sound is not spelled **ay** or **ai**.

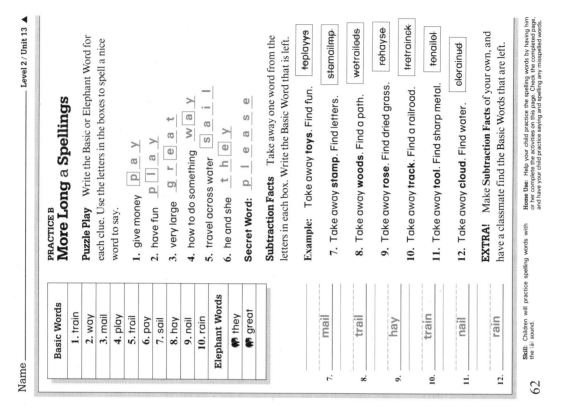

Tr a i n Station — M a i l Box — Gr e a t Road — One W a y — Pl a y Time — Children are welcome if th e y are with a grown-up.

Now write the words you made.   Order of answers may vary.

1. Way
2. Mail
3. Train
4. Great
5. Play
6. they

Fine Rhymes Finish these sentences. Write a Basic Word to rhyme with the word in dark print.

7. If it starts to **rain** will you ride the _____?
8. It is fun to **sail** and to walk on the _____.
9. We **may** go this _____.

7. train
8. trail
9. way

Skill: Children will practice spelling words with the /ā/ sound.

Home Use: Help your child practice the spelling words by having him or her complete the activities on this page. Check the completed page, and have your child practice saying and spelling any misspelled words.

61

PRACTICE B
More Long a Spellings

Basic Words
1. train
2. way
3. mail
4. play
5. trail
6. pay
7. sail
8. hay
9. nail
10. rain
Elephant Words
🐘 they
🐘 great

Puzzle Play Write the Basic or Elephant Word for each clue. Use the letters in the boxes to spell a nice word to say.

1. give money p a y
2. have fun p l a y
3. very large g r e a t
4. how to do something w a y
5. travel across water s a i l
6. he and she t h e y

Secret Word: p l e a s e

Subtraction Facts Take away one word from the letters in each box. Write the Basic Word that is left.

Example: Take away **toys**. Find fun. toplayys

7. Take away **stamp**. Find letters. stemailp
8. Take away **woods**. Find a path. wotrailods
9. Take away **rose**. Find dried grass. rohayse
10. Take away **track**. Find a railroad. tratrainck
11. Take away **tool**. Find sharp metal. tonailol
12. Take away **cloud**. Find water. clorainud

EXTRA! Make **Subtraction Facts** of your own, and have a classmate find the Basic Words that are left.

7. mail
8. trail
9. hay
10. train
11. nail
12. rain

Skill: Children will practice spelling words with the /ā/ sound.

Home Use: Help your child practice the spelling words by having him or her complete the activities on this page. Check the completed page, and have your child practice saying and spelling any misspelled words.

62

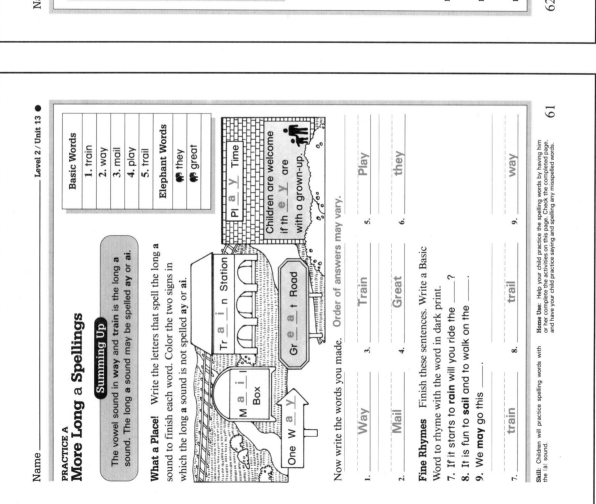

Name _____

Unit 13 Test: More Long a Spellings

Read each sentence. Find the correctly spelled word to complete each sentence. Mark the letter next to that word.

Sample:

We spent the ____ at home.

ANSWERS

ⓐ dai　ⓑ dae　● day

Items 1–7 test Basic Words 1–5 and the Elephant Words.
Items 8–12 test Basic Words 6–10.

1. We ____ on the swings.　ⓐ plae　● play　ⓒ plai

2. Henry sang on his ____ home.　● way　ⓑ wai　ⓒ wey

3. My aunts said ____ like her.　ⓐ thay　ⓑ thaye　● they

4. Jon will follow the ____ .　ⓐ tral　● trail　ⓒ trayl

5. Do you ride on the ____ ?　ⓐ tran　ⓑ trayn　● train

6. Mr. Davis is a ____ teacher.　ⓐ gret　● great　ⓒ grayt

7. I got a card in the ____ .　● mail　ⓑ mal　ⓒ mael

8. He ran quickly in the ____ .　ⓐ raen　● rane　ⓒ rain

9. Leon will ____ on the lake.　ⓐ sail　ⓑ sayl　ⓒ sael

10. Do horses eat ____ ?　ⓐ hae　● hay　ⓒ hai

11. I will ____ for your ticket.　ⓐ pai　ⓑ paiy　● pay

12. Don't step on that ____ !　● nail　ⓑ nayl　ⓒ nale

64

Name _____

PRACTICE C
More Long a Spellings

Word Sets　Write the missing words to complete each sentence. Use two Challenge Words in the first set and two Vocabulary Words in the second set.

Challenge Words
1. railroad
2. subway

Theme Vocabulary
3. caboose
4. engine
5. crossing
6. coach

1–2. Most ____ tracks run on top of the ground.
Most ____ tracks run under the ground.

1. _____railroad_____　2. ____subway____

3–4. The passengers in the ____ sit and read.
The crew in the ____ cook and sleep.

3. _____coach_____　4. ____caboose____

Words in Common　Write a word pair for each clue. Use a Challenge or Vocabulary Word in each pair. Write each word beside the correct number. The words in dark print will help you.

Example: mail that travels by **air**
a **carrier** who delivers **mail**

air	mail	carrier

5–6. the place where **deer cross** a street

6–7. a **guard** who helps children **cross** a street

8–9. a **train** that runs along **railroad** tracks

9–10. an **engine** that pulls a **train**

5.	deer	6.	crossing	7.	guard
8.	railroad	9.	train	10.	engine

Skill: Children will practice spelling words with the /ā/ sound and words related to the theme of trains.

Home Use: Help your child practice the spelling words by having him or her complete the activities on this page. Check the completed page, and have your child practice saying and spelling any misspelled words.

63

PRACTICE B
More Long e Spellings

Basic Words
1. clean
2. keep
3. please
4. green
5. we
6. be
7. eat
8. tree
9. mean
10. read
Elephant Words
👥 the
👥 people

Crossword Clues Write a Basic or Elephant Word for each clue.

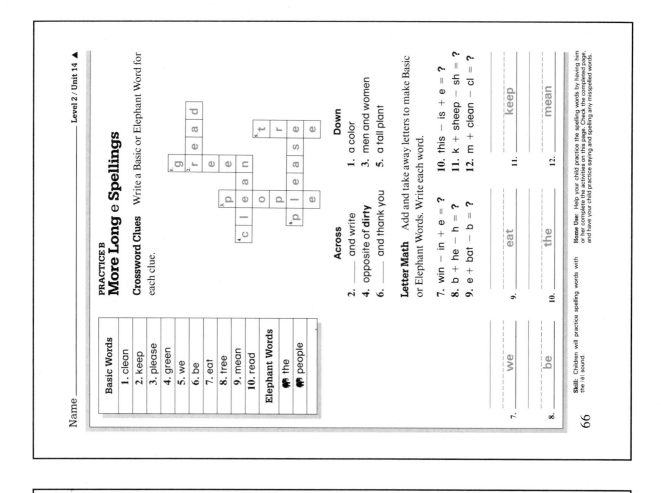

Across

2. ___ and write
4. opposite of **dirty**
6. ___ and thank you

Down

1. a color
3. men and women
5. a tall plant

Letter Math Add and take away letters to make Basic or Elephant Words. Write each word.

7. win – in + e = ?
8. b + he – h = ?
9. e + bat – b = ?
10. this – is + e = ?
11. k + sheep – sh = ?
12. m + clean – cl = ?

7. __we__
8. __be__
9. __eat__
10. __the__
11. __keep__
12. __mean__

Skill: Children will practice spelling words with the |ē| sound.

Home Use: Help your child practice the spelling words by having him or her complete the activities on this page. Check the completed page, and have your child practice saying and spelling any misspelled words.

PRACTICE A
More Long e Spellings

Summing Up

The vowel sound in **we**, **keep**, and **clean** is the long **e** sound. The long **e** sound may be spelled **e**, **ee**, or **ea**.

Catch a Shooting Star Write each Basic Word under the star with the matching spelling for the long **e** sound.
Order of answers may vary.

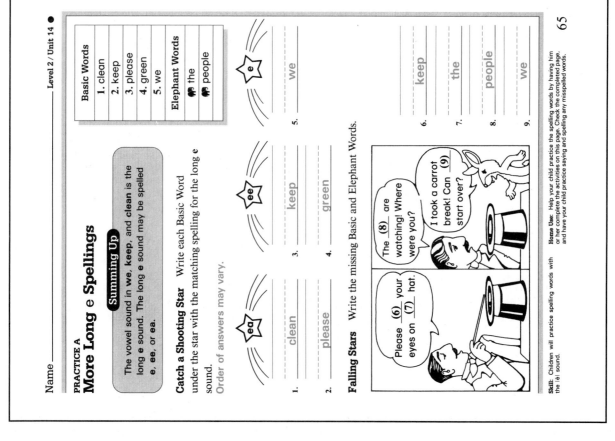

ea
1. __clean__
2. __please__

ee
3. __keep__
4. __green__

e
5. __we__

Falling Stars Write the missing Basic and Elephant Words.

Please __(6)__ your eyes on __(7)__ hat.

The __(8)__ are watching! Where were you?

I took a carrot break! Can __(9)__ start over?

6. __keep__
7. __the__
8. __people__
9. __we__

Skill: Children will practice spelling words with the |ē| sound.

Home Use: Help your child practice the spelling words by having him or her complete the activities on this page. Check the completed page, and have your child practice saying and spelling any misspelled words.

220

Unit 14 Test: More Long e Spellings

Read each sentence. Is the underlined word spelled right or wrong? Mark your answer.

	Right	Wrong
Sample: We put our feet in the water.	●	○

Items 1–7 test Basic Words 1–5 and the Elephant Words.
Items 8–12 test Basic Words 6–10.

		Right	Wrong
1.	Tyler will try to keap quiet.	○	●
2.	Is your house white or grene?	○	●
3.	Rex asked for the answer.	●	○
4.	Will you please do this?	●	○
5.	Chris has to cleen his room.	○	●
6.	Can we join you on the trip?	●	○
7.	Some peeple work in the city.	○	●
8.	Lou has a fruit trea in his yard.	○	●
9.	What book did you read this week?	●	○
10.	Kara will be home soon.	●	○
11.	Ethan loves to eet corn.	○	●
12.	That was a mean thing to do.	●	○

68

PRACTICE C
More Long e Spellings

Signs of the Times Write what you think it says on each sign. Use a Challenge or Vocabulary Word for each sign. Use capital letters correctly.

Challenge Words
1. stream
2. street
Theme Vocabulary
3. trash
4. dump
5. collect
6. sewer

Example:

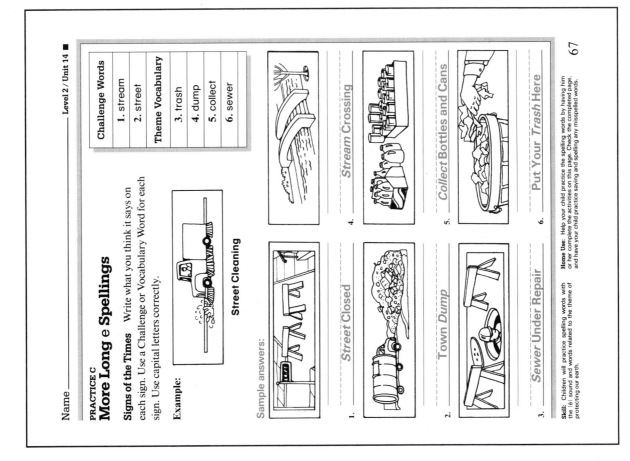

Street Cleaning

Sample answers:

1. **Street** Closed

2. **Town** *Dump*

3. *Sewer* Under Repair

4. *Stream* Crossing

5. *Collect* Bottles and Cans

6. Put Your *Trash* Here

67

Skill: Children will practice spelling words with the /ē/ sound and words related to the theme of protecting our earth.

Home Use: Help your child practice the spelling words by having him or her complete the activities on this page. Check the completed page, and have your child practice saying and spelling any misspelled words.

Practice Master and Test Answers

221

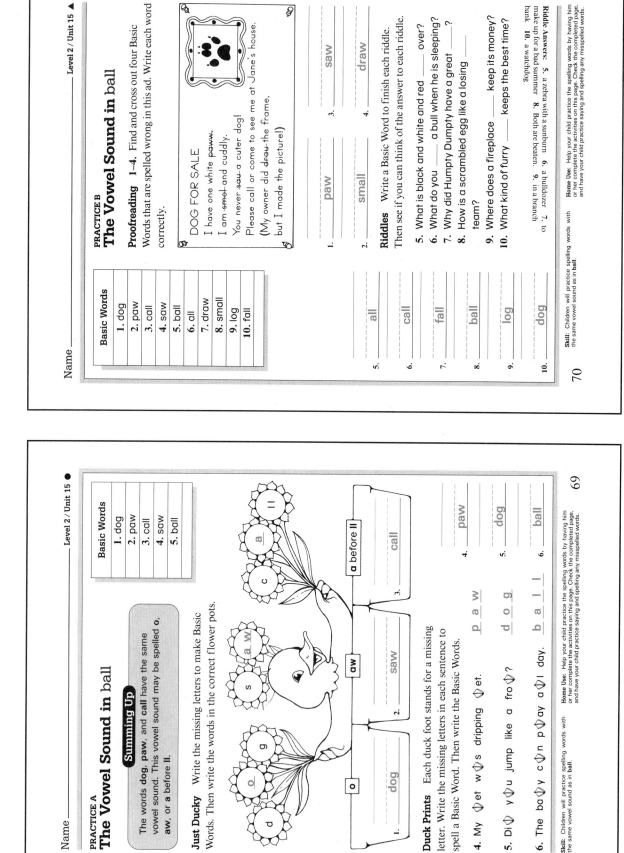

Name _____

Level 2 / Unit 15 ▲

PRACTICE B
The Vowel Sound in ball

Basic Words
1. dog
2. paw
3. call
4. saw
5. ball
6. all
7. draw
8. small
9. log
10. fall

Proofreading 1–4. Find and cross out four Basic Words that are spelled wrong in this ad. Write each word correctly.

DOG FOR SALE
I have one white ~~paw~~.
I am ~~smel~~ and cuddly.
You never ~~sau~~ a cuter dog!
Please call or come to see me at Jane's house.
(My owner did ~~drau~~ the frame, but I made the picture!)

1. _____ paw   3. _____ saw
2. _____ small   4. _____ draw

5. _____ all
6. _____ call
7. _____ fall
8. _____ ball
9. _____ log
10. _____ dog

Riddles Write a Basic Word to finish each riddle. Then see if you can think of the answer to each riddle.

5. What is black and white and red _____ over?
6. What do you _____ a bull when he is sleeping?
7. Why did Humpty Dumpty have a great _____?
8. How is a scrambled egg like a losing team?
9. Where does a fireplace _____ keeps its money?
10. What kind of furry _____ keeps the best time?

Riddle Answers: 5. a zebra with a sunburn 6. a bulldozer 7. to make up for a bad summer 8. Both are beaten. 9. in a branch bank 10. a watchdog

70

Skill: Children will practice spelling words with the same vowel sound as in **ball**.

Home Use: Help your child practice the spelling words by having him or her complete the activities on this page. Check the completed page, and have your child practice saying and spelling any misspelled words.

Name _____

Level 2 / Unit 15 ●

PRACTICE A
The Vowel Sound in ball

Summing Up

The words **dog**, **paw**, and **call** have the same vowel sound. This vowel sound may be spelled **o**, **aw**, or **a before ll**.

Basic Words
1. dog
2. paw
3. call
4. saw
5. ball

Just Ducky Write the missing letters to make Basic Words. Then write the words in the correct flower pots.

c a ll

s aw

o g d

o
1. _____ dog

aw
2. _____ saw
3. _____ call

a before ll

Duck Prints Each duck foot stands for a missing letter. Write the missing letters in each sentence to spell a Basic Word. Then write the Basic Words.

4. My ◇et w◇s dripping ◇et.   4. _____ paw

5. Di◇ y◇u jump like a fro◇?   5. _____ dog

6. The ba◇y c◇n p◇ay ◇◇ day.   6. _____ ball

p a w
d o g
b a l l

69

Skill: Children will practice spelling words with the same vowel sound as in **ball**.

Home Use: Help your child practice the spelling words by having him or her complete the activities on this page. Check the completed page, and have your child practice saying and spelling any misspelled words.

PRACTICE C
The Vowel Sound in ball

Word Towers Start at the top of each tower. Add one letter to write the next word. Put the letters in the order that spells the word for each clue. The last word in each tower is a Challenge Word.

Challenge Words
1. stall
2. claw
Theme Vocabulary
3. clip
4. healthy
5. ill
6. cure

Clues

1.

| a |
l	a
a	l	l
t	a	l	l
s	t	a	l	l

the first letter of the alphabet

a musical note

everything

opposite of **short**

a place in a barn

2.

| a |
l	a
l	a	w
c	l	a	w

the first letter of the alphabet

a musical note

a rule

a nail of an animal's foot

Animal Helpers Read each sign. Write a sentence telling what each person can do to help your pet. Use all of the Vocabulary Words in your sentences. Write your answers on a separate sheet of paper. Answers will vary.

3. Haircuts for Dogs!
Ms. Chan

4. Help Your Pet
Stay Well!
Dr. Veto

5. Animal Exercise
Gym!
Mr. Mann

Skill: Children will practice spelling words with the vowel sound in **ball** and words related to the theme of animal doctor.

Home Use: Help your child practice the spelling words by having him or her complete the activities on this page. Check the completed page, and have your child practice saying and spelling any misspelled words.

71

Unit 15 Test: The Vowel Sound in ball

Each item below gives three spellings of a word. Choose the correct spelling. Mark the letter for that word.

Sample:
a. wal   b. wawl   c. wall

ANSWERS
ⓐ ⓑ ●

Items 1–6 test Basic Words 1–5. Items 6–10 test Basic Words 6–10.

1. a. paw	b. po	c. pawe	1. ● ⓑ ⓒ
2. a. cawl	b. cal	c. call	2. ⓐ ⓑ ●
3. a. sawe	b. saw	c. sa	3. ⓐ ● ⓒ
4. a. dolg	b. dawg	c. dog	4. ⓐ ⓑ ●
5. a. ball	b. bal	c. bol	5. ● ⓑ ⓒ
6. a. logg	b. log	c. lawg	6. ⓐ ● ⓒ
7. a. droh	b. dro	c. draw	7. ⓐ ⓑ ●
8. a. fawl	b. fall	c. fal	8. ⓐ ● ⓒ
9. a. small	b. smal	c. smawl	9. ● ⓑ ⓒ
10. a. oll	b. al	c. all	10. ⓐ ⓑ ●

72

Practice Master and Test Answers

223

PRACTICE B
Words Spelled with sh or ch

Basic Words
1. sheep
2. chase
3. wish
4. much
5. chop
6. each
7. dish
8. such
9. wash
10. ship
Elephant Words
🐘 catch
🐘 sure

Dot-to-Dot 1–4. Find what race cars do. Connect the dots to spell Basic Words. Then write the words.

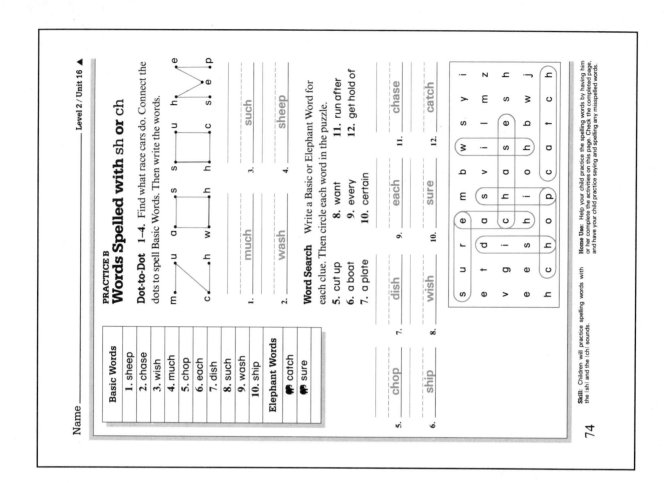

1. _____ much
2. _____ wash
3. _____ such
4. _____ sheep

Word Search Write a Basic or Elephant Word for each clue. Then circle each word in the puzzle.

5. cut up _____ chop
6. a boat _____ ship
7. a plate _____ dish
8. want _____ wish
9. every _____ each
10. certain _____ sure
11. run after _____ chase
12. get hold of _____ catch

s	u	r	e	m	b	w	s	y	i
e	t	d	a	s	v	i	l	m	z
v	g	i	c	h	a	s	e	s	h
e	e	s	h	i	o	h	b	w	j
h	c	h	o	p	c	a	t	c	h

74

Skill: Children will practice spelling words with the |sh| and the |ch| sounds.

Home Use: Help your child practice the spelling words by having him or her complete the activities on this page. Check the completed page, and have your child practice saying and spelling any misspelled words.

PRACTICE A
Words Spelled with sh or ch

Basic Words
1. sheep
2. chase
3. wish
4. much
5. chop
Elephant Words
🐘 catch
🐘 sure

Summing Up

The sound that begins **sheep** and ends **wish** may be spelled **sh**. The sound that begins **chase** and ends **much** may be spelled **ch**.

A Penny Saved 1–6. Write the letter or letters that spell the **sh** or the **ch** sound to finish each word. Draw a line from each coin to the correct bank. Color the two words in which the **sh** and **ch** sounds are not spelled **sh** or **ch**.

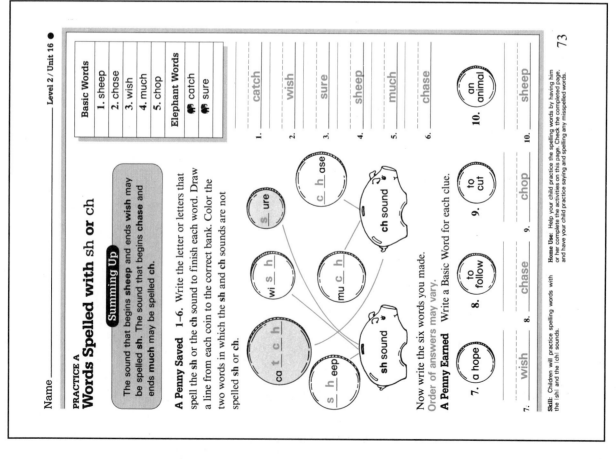

1. _____ catch
2. _____ wish
3. _____ sure
4. _____ sheep
5. _____ much
6. _____ chase

Now write the six words you made.
Order of answers may vary.

A Penny Earned Write a Basic Word for each clue.

7. a hope _____
8. to follow _____
9. to cut _____
10. an animal _____

7. _____ wish
8. _____ chase
9. _____ chop
10. _____ sheep

73

Skill: Children will practice spelling words with the |sh| and the |ch| sounds.

Home Use: Help your child practice the spelling words by having him or her complete the activities on this page. Check the completed page, and have your child practice saying and spelling any misspelled words.

Unit 16 Test: Words Spelled with sh or ch

Read each sentence. Find the correctly spelled word to complete each sentence. Mark the letter next to that word.

Sample:

Patti said ____ would be here.

ⓐ shee   ⓑ che   ● she

ANSWERS

Items 1–7 test Basic Words 1–5 and the Elephant Words.
Items 8–12 test Basic Words 6–10.

1. I will count the ____.   ⓐ chepe   **ⓑ** sheep   ⓒ shep

2. Dina will ____ the wood.   **ⓐ** chop   ⓑ chope   ⓒ chob

3. How ____ did it cost?   ⓐ mushe   ⓑ moch   **ⓒ** much

4. Scruffy likes to ____ cars.   **ⓐ** chas   ⓑ chaze   ⓒ chase

5. Are you ____ of that?   ⓐ sure   ⓑ shor   ⓒ chure

6. Joy made a ____.   ⓐ wich   **ⓑ** wish   ⓒ wesh

7. Doug tried to ____ the ball.   ⓐ cech   ⓑ catsh   **ⓒ** catch

8. That is ____ a great book!   **ⓐ** such   ⓑ sush   ⓒ soch

9. Give a horn to ____ child.   ⓐ ech   **ⓑ** each   ⓒ eech

10. Terry gave me a pretty ____.   **ⓐ** dish   ⓑ dich   ⓒ desh

11. A ____ took them home again.   ⓐ shup   **ⓑ** ship   ⓒ shipp

12. Carl had to ____ his hands.   ⓐ wach   ⓑ wosh   **ⓒ** wash

---

PRACTICE C
Words Spelled with sh or ch

Cattle Drive Write the name of each numbered cow. Use the clues in the story to help you.

At ten o'clock in the morning, Farmer Dell took his cows to the field. The cows walked in a single line. Lucky was ahead of Queen. Star was first in line. Lucky was behind Basil, and Basil was behind Star. The last cow kept stopping to nibble grass along the way. Finally, the farmer yelled at her to join the other cows.

Challenge Words
1. shout
2. lunch

Theme Vocabulary
3. graze
4. cattle
5. herd
6. stray

1. ____Star____

2. ____Basil____

3. ____Lucky____

4. ____Queen____

Roundup Write the missing Challenge and Vocabulary Words. Use the information from the story above and your answers to numbers 1–4.

5. Lucky, Queen, Star, and Basil are ____.

6. A group of cows is called a ____.

7. Farmer Dell took the cows out before ____.

8. He took the cows to ____ on some grass.

9. Queen was a ____ cow.

10. Farmer Dell had to ____ at the last cow in line.

5. ____cattle____   7. ____lunch____   9. ____stray____

6. ____herd____   8. ____graze____   10. ____shout____

Skill: Children will practice spelling words with the /sh/ and the /ch/ sounds and words related to the theme of ranching.

Home Use: Help your child practice the spelling words by having him or her complete the activities on this page. Check the completed page, and have your child practice saying and spelling any misspelled words.

Practice Master and Test Answers

PRACTICE B
Words Spelled with th or wh

Basic Words
1. teeth
2. when
3. then
4. wheel
5. with
6. what
7. than
8. while
9. them
10. which

Dots and Dashes Use the Morse Code below to write Basic Words.

∎∙ = a	∙∙∙∙ = h	∎ = t
∙ = e	∎∙ = n	∙∎∎ = w

Example: ∎ ∙∙∙∙ ∙ **the**

1. ∎ ∙∙∙∙ ∙ ∎ _____ then
2. ∙∎∎ ∙∙∙∙ ∎∙ ∎ _____ what
3. ∎ ∙∙∙∙ ∎∙ _____ than
4. ∎ ∙ ∙ ∎ ∙∙∙∙ _____ teeth

Proofreading 5–10. Find and cross out six Basic Words that are spelled wrong in this note. Write each word correctly.

To: Billy   From: Mom

It's time to clean your room! It may take you less than an hour. Here is what I want you to do.
1. Please pick up your toys.
   Do not put them in the bathtub!
2. Let me know which toys need to be fixed.
3. Dust with a clean rag!
4. Tell me when you finish. I will check your room wile you play.

P.S. The weel to your truck is in the sink.

5. _____ them
6. _____ which
7. _____ with
8. _____ when
9. _____ while
10. _____ wheel

78

Skill: Children will practice spelling words with the /hw/, the /th/, and the /th/ sounds.

Home Use: Help your child practice the spelling words by having him or her complete the activities on this page. Check the completed page, and have your child practice saying and spelling any misspelled words.

PRACTICE A
Words Spelled with th or wh

Basic Words
1. teeth
2. when
3. then
4. wheel
5. with

Summing Up

The sounds that begin **then** and end **teeth** may be spelled **th**. The sound that begins **when** may be spelled **wh**.

No Clues Puzzle Complete each puzzle. Write the Basic Words that have the spelling shown in each bulb. Color the squares that have the letters **wh** or **th**.

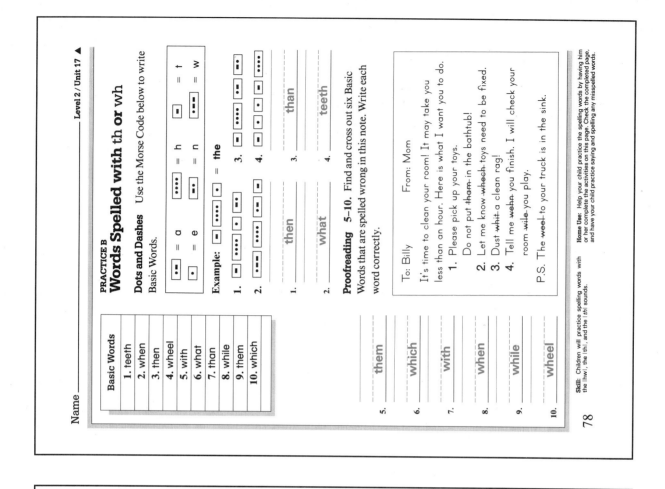

Bright Ideas Think how the words in each group are alike. Write the missing Basic Words.

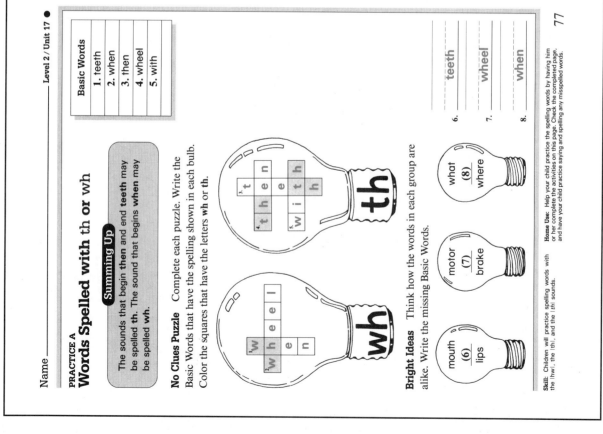

mouth
(6) _____ teeth
lips

motor
(7) _____ wheel
brake

what
(8) _____ when
where

6. _____ teeth
7. _____ wheel
8. _____ when

77

Skill: Children will practice spelling words with the /hw/, the /th/, and the /th/ sounds.

Home Use: Help your child practice the spelling words by having him or her complete the activities on this page. Check the completed page, and have your child practice saying and spelling any misspelled words.

Name _____

PRACTICE C
Words Spelled with th or wh

Say It with Pictures You can draw letters to show the meanings of the words they spell. Look at the example. Make a drawing for each Challenge and Vocabulary Word. Then write the words.
Drawings and order of answers may vary.

Challenge Words
1. mouth
2. whistle
Theme Vocabulary
3. toothbrush
4. rinse
5. roots
6. braces

Example:

wheel

1. _____ mouth

2. _____ whistle

3. _____ toothbrush

4. _____ rinse

5. _____ roots

6. _____ braces

Skill: Children will practice spelling words with the |hw|, the |th|, and the |th| sounds and words related to the theme of dentist.

Home Use: Help your child practice the spelling words by having him or her complete the activities on this page. Check the completed page, and have your child practice saying and spelling any misspelled words.

79

Name _____

Unit 17 Test: Words Spelled with th or wh

Read each sentence. Is the underlined word spelled right or wrong? Mark your answer.

Sample:
She used a can of white paint.

	Right	Wrong
	●	○

Items 1–5 test Basic Words 1–5. Items 6–10 test Basic Words 6–10.

		Right	Wrong
1.	Kendi put a new weel on my bike.	○	●
2.	What did he say then?	●	○
3.	Mona went there whith us.	○	●
4.	The baby has two teeth.	●	○
5.	Dave left wen the movie ended.	○	●
6.	They waited whil I ran.	○	●
7.	I am taller than you are.	●	○
8.	Do you know wich is yours?	○	●
9.	Call them on the phone.	●	○
10.	Joshua knows what to buy.	●	○

80

Practice Master and Test Answers

227

Unit 18 Review: Test A

Read the three word groups. Find the underlined word that is spelled wrong. Mark the letter for that word.

Sample:
- (a) ● will <u>stae</u> away
- (b) a new day
- (c) black and white

This test reviews Basic Words 1–5 and Elephant Words from Units 13–17.

1. (a) wood to chop
   (b) ● a cat's <u>pau</u> print
   (c) to keep quiet

2. (a) ● a <u>traen</u> ticket
   (b) now and then
   (c) green grass

3. (a) to run and play
   (b) the big dog
   (c) ● too <u>mach</u>

4. (a) ● to throw or <u>cach</u>
   (b) two new teeth
   (c) a nature trail

5. (a) to be sure
   (b) saw the book
   (c) ● a car's <u>weel</u>

6. (a) the wrong way
   (b) ● a loud <u>caul</u>
   (c) with my friends

7. (a) ● to make a <u>wich</u>
   (b) where and when
   (c) in the mail

8. (a) the answer
   (b) ● a <u>greit</u> job
   (c) two sheep

9. (a) Sam and they
   (b) please and thank you
   (c) ● <u>cleen</u> dishes

10. (a) ● to <u>shase</u> away
    (b) a bat and a ball
    (c) you and we

Unit 18 Review: Test B

Read the three word groups. Find the underlined word that is spelled wrong. Mark the letter for that word.

Sample:
- (a) she and he
- (b) ● with both <u>feit</u>
- (c) a warm <u>bath</u>

This test reviews Basic Words 6–10 and Elephant Words from Units 13–17.

1. (a) to fall off
   (b) food to eat
   (c) ● a <u>lawg</u> cabin

2. (a) for a while
   (b) to wash and dry
   (c) ● <u>al</u> in a row

3. (a) ● <u>rayn</u> and snow
   (b) more than that
   (c) sure enough

4. (a) a sail on a boat
   (b) ● <u>eash</u> and every
   (c) on a ship

5. (a) ● <u>tha</u> good news
   (b) a ball to catch
   (c) no such thing

6. (a) a bill to pay
   (b) ● <u>meen</u> and nasty
   (c) the tall tree

7. (a) a nail in the wall
   (b) to be happy
   (c) ● <u>smoll</u> wonder

8. (a) different people
   (b) ● <u>wat</u> to say
   (c) from them

9. (a) ● <u>hai</u> for horses
   (b) books to read
   (c) paper to draw on

10. (a) a great job
    (b) which way
    (c) ● a cup and a <u>dich</u>

Practice Master and Test Answers

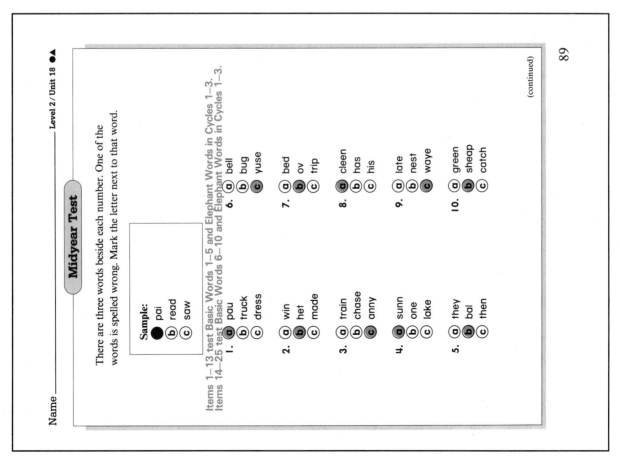

Midyear Test

There are three words beside each number. One of the words is spelled wrong. Mark the letter next to that word.

Sample:
● pai
b read
c saw

Items 1–13 test Basic Words 1–5 and Elephant Words in Cycles 1–3.
Items 14–25 test Basic Words 6–10 and Elephant Words in Cycles 1–3.

1. a pau   b truck   c dress
2. a win   **b het**   c made
3. a train   b chase   **c anny**
4. **a sunn**   b one   c lake
5. a they   **b bal**   c then

6. a bell   b bug   **c yuse**
7. a bed   **b ov**   c trip
8. **a cleen**   b has   c his
9. a late   b nest   **c waye**
10. a green   **b sheep**   c catch

(continued)

89

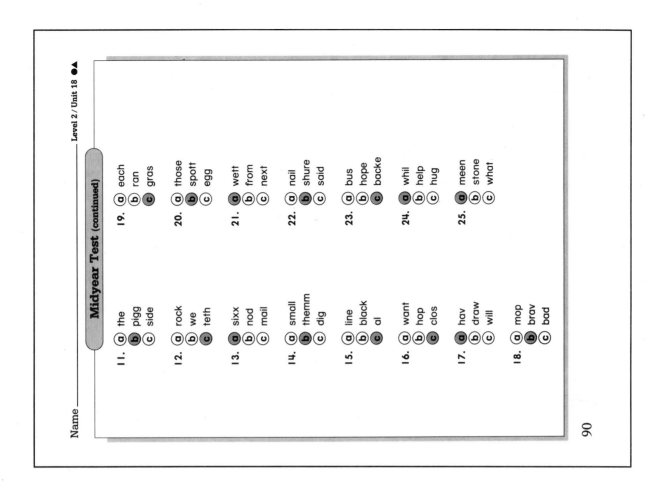

Midyear Test (continued)

11. a the   **b pigg**   c side
12. a rock   b we   **c teth**
13. **a sixx**   b nod   c mail
14. a small   **b themm**   c dig
15. a line   b black   **c al**
16. a want   b hop   **c clos**
17. **a hav**   b draw   c will
18. a mop   **b brav**   c bad

19. a each   b ran   **c gras**
20. a those   **b spott**   c egg
21. **a wett**   b from   c next
22. a nail   **b shure**   c said
23. a bus   b hope   **c backe**
24. **a whil**   b help   c hug
25. **a meen**   b stone   c what

90

229

PRACTICE B
Words That End with nd, ng, or nk

Basic Words
1. king
2. thank
3. hand
4. sing
5. and
6. think
7. bring
8. long
9. end
10. thing

Silly Rhymes Finish these silly sentences. Write a Basic Word to rhyme with the word in dark print.

1. The royal _____ ate a chicken **wing**.
2. Can you _____ your piggy **bank**?
3. I sang a **song** that was too _____!
4. I built a house of **sand** with one _____.
5. Why did you _____ your new gold **ring**?
6. Do you _____ this rock will **sink**?

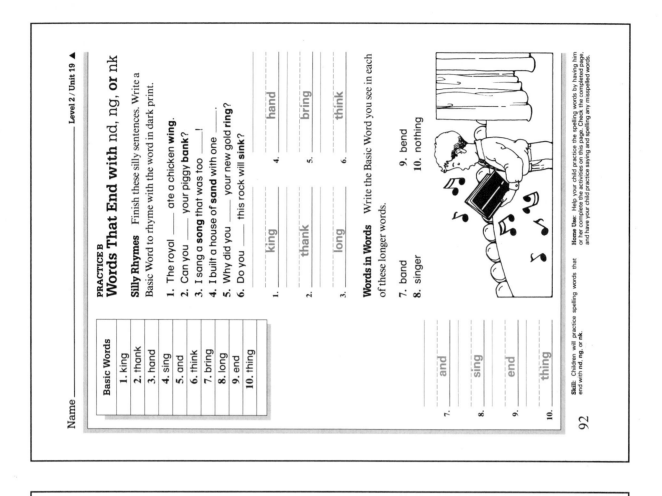

Words in Words Write the Basic Word you see in each of these longer words.

7. band
8. singer
9. bend
10. nothing

1. king   4. _____ hand
2. thank   5. _____ bring
3. long   6. _____ think

7. _____ and
8. _____ sing
9. _____ end
10. _____ thing

Skill: Children will practice spelling words that end with **nd**, **ng**, or **nk**.

Home Use: Help your child practice the spelling words by having him or her complete the activities on this page. Check the completed page, and have your child practice saying and spelling any misspelled words.

PRACTICE A
Words That End with nd, ng, or nk

Summing Up

You hear the sounds of **n** and **d** in words that end with the consonant cluster **nd**.
You may not hear the sound of **n** in words that end with the consonants **ng** or **nk**.

Basic Words
1. king
2. thank
3. hand
4. sing
5. and

Sing-along On each sign, write a Basic Word that has the letters that the singer is singing. Order of answers may vary.

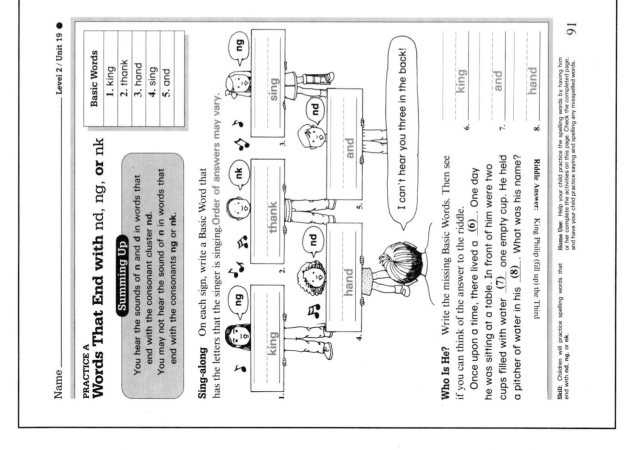

1. king
2. thank
3. sing
4. hand
5. and

I can't hear you three in the back!

Who Is He? Write the missing Basic Words. Then see if you can think of the answer to the riddle.

Once upon a time, there lived a __(6)__. One day he was sitting at a table. In front of him were two cups filled with water __(7)__ one empty cup. He held a pitcher of water in his __(8)__. What was his name?

6. king
7. and
8. hand

Riddle Answer: King Philip (fill up) the Third

Skill: Children will practice spelling words that end with **nd**, **ng**, or **nk**.

Home Use: Help your child practice the spelling words by having him or her complete the activities on this page. Check the completed page, and have your child practice saying and spelling any misspelled words.

Unit 19 Test: Words That End with nd, ng, or nk

Each item below gives three spellings of a word. Choose the correct spelling. Mark the letter for that word.

ANSWERS

Sample:
a. send   b. sen   c. seng   ● (b) (c)

Items 1–5 test Basic Words 1–5. Items 6–10 test Basic Words 6–10.

	a.	b.	c.	Answers
1.	ank	and	ang	(a) (b) (c)
2.	thangk	thang	thank	(a) (b) (c)
3.	king	kig	kingg	(a) (b) (c)
4.	sig	sing	sind	(a) (b) (c)
5.	hend	hant	hand	(a) (b) (c)
6.	think	thind	thinc	(a) (b) (c)
7.	lonk	logn	long	(a) (b) (c)
8.	enk	end	eng	(a) (b) (c)
9.	birng	brind	bring	(a) (b) (c)
10.	thing	thind	thign	(a) (b) (c)

PRACTICE C
Words That End with nd, ng, or nk

What's Wrong? Circle the four things that are wrong in this picture.

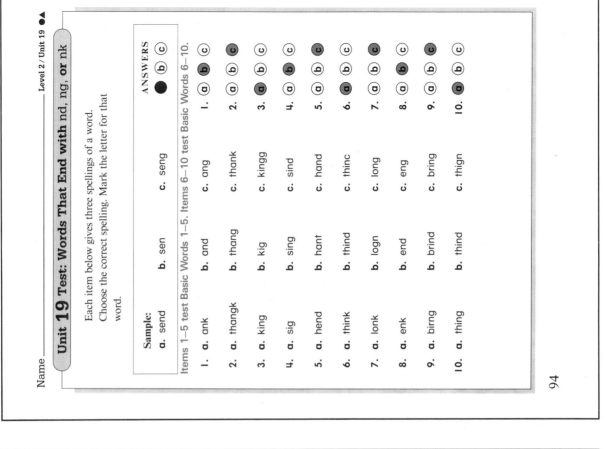

Challenge Words
1. grand
2. young

Theme Vocabulary
3. throne
4. castle
5. page
6. feast

Now write four sentences to tell what is wrong in the picture above. Use all the Challenge and Vocabulary Words in your sentences.   Sample answers:

1. The king is too *young*.

2. The *throne* is outside.

3. The *castle* door is on its side.

4. The *page* put the words *feast* and *grand* in the wrong order.

Skill: Children will practice spelling words that end with **nd, ng,** or **nk** and words related to the theme of castles and kings.

Home Use: Help your child practice the spelling words by having him or her complete the activities on this page. Check the completed page, and have your child practice saying and spelling any misspelled words.

Practice Master and Test Answers

231

Page 96

PRACTICE B
Words That End with s or es

Puzzle Play Write the Basic or Elephant Word for each clue. Use the letters in the boxes to spell the names of two ways to measure time.

Basic Words
1. dishes
2. dresses
3. bells
4. boxes
5. beaches
6. days
7. bikes
8. wishes
9. things
10. names
Elephant Word
🐘 children

1. what people are called by n a [m] e s

2. cans, _____, and bags b o x e s

3. boys and girls c h i l d r e [n]

4. rhymes with **rings** [t] h i n g s

5. strong hopes w i s [h] e s

6. machines with two wheels b i [k] e s

7. opposite of **nights** d [a] y s

8. things that ring b e [l] l s

9. places by the sea b e a [c] h e s

10. clothing for girls d [r] e s s e s

11. plates d i s h e [s]

Secret Words:

m o n t h s and y e a r s

Skill: Children will practice spelling words that end with s or es.

Home Use: Help your child practice the spelling words by having him or her complete the activities on this page. Check the completed page, and have your child practice saying and spelling any misspelled words.

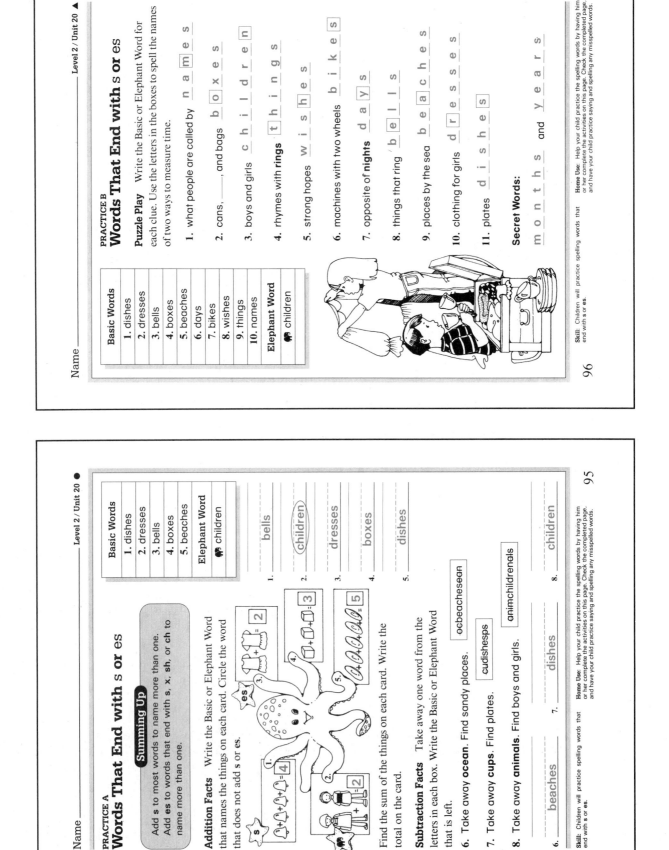

Page 95

PRACTICE A
Words That End with s or es

Summing Up

Add **s** to most words to name more than one.
Add **es** to words that end with **s**, **x**, **sh**, or **ch** to name more than one.

Basic Words
1. dishes
2. dresses
3. bells
4. boxes
5. beaches
Elephant Word
🐘 children

Addition Facts Write the Basic or Elephant Word that names the things on each card. Circle the word that does not add s or es.

1. bells
2. (children)
3. dresses
4. boxes
5. dishes

Subtraction Facts Take away one word from the letters in each box. Write the Basic or Elephant Word that is left.

Find the sum of the things on each card. Write the total on the card.

6. Take away **ocean**. Find sandy places. ocbeachesean

7. Take away **cups**. Find plates. cudishesps

8. Take away **animals**. Find boys and girls. animchildrenals

6. beaches   7. dishes   8. children

Skill: Children will practice spelling words that end with s or es.

Home Use: Help your child practice the spelling words by having him or her complete the activities on this page. Check the completed page, and have your child practice saying and spelling any misspelled words.

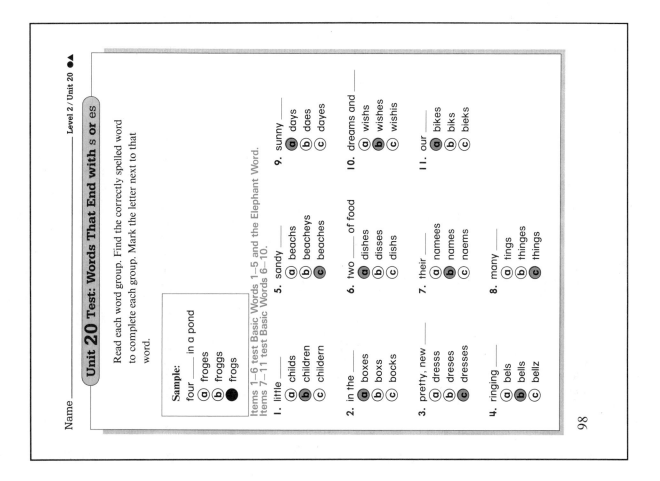

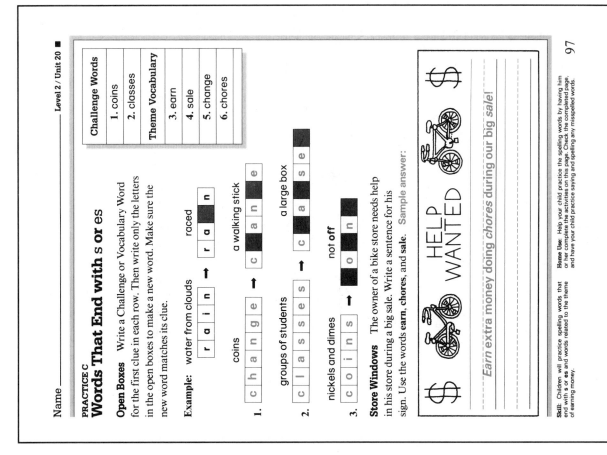

Name _____

Unit 20 Test: Words That End with s or es

Read each word group. Find the correctly spelled word to complete each group. Mark the letter next to that word.

Sample:

four ____ in a pond
- (a) froges
- (b) froggs
- (●) frogs

Items 1–6 test Basic Words 1–5 and the Elephant Word.
Items 7–11 test Basic Words 6–10.

1. little ____
- (a) childs
- (b) children
- (c) childern

2. in the ____
- (a) boxes
- (b) boxs
- (c) bocks

3. pretty, new ____
- (a) dresss
- (b) dreses
- (c) dresses

4. ringing ____
- (a) bels
- (b) bells
- (c) bellz

5. sandy ____
- (a) beachs
- (b) beacheys
- (c) beaches

6. two ____ of food
- (a) dishes
- (b) disses
- (c) dishs

7. their ____
- (a) namees
- (b) names
- (c) naems

8. many ____
- (a) fings
- (b) thinges
- (c) things

9. sunny ____
- (a) days
- (b) daes
- (c) dayes

10. dreams and ____
- (a) wishs
- (b) wishes
- (c) wishis

11. our ____
- (a) bikes
- (b) biks
- (c) bieks

98

Name _____

PRACTICE C
Words That End with s or es

Open Boxes Write a Challenge or Vocabulary Word for the first clue in each row. Then write only the letters in the open boxes to make a new word. Make sure the new word matches its clue.

Example: water from clouds → raced

r a i n → r a n

1. coins → a walking stick

c h a n g e → c a n e

2. groups of students → a large box

c l a s s e s → c a s e

3. nickels and dimes → not off

c o i n s → o n

Challenge Words
1. coins
2. classes

Theme Vocabulary
3. earn
4. sale
5. change
6. chores

Store Windows The owner of a bike store needs help in his store during a big sale. Write a sentence for his sign. Use the words **earn**, **chores**, and **sale**. Sample answer:

HELP WANTED

Earn extra money doing *chores* during our big *sale!*

Skill: Children will practice spelling words that end with s or es and words related to the theme of earning money.

Home Use: Help your child practice the spelling words by having him or her complete the activities on this page. Check the completed page, and have your child practice saying and spelling any misspelled words.

97

Practice Master and Test Answers

PRACTICE B
More Long o Spellings

Basic Words
1. boat
2. cold
3. go
4. slow
5. no
6. old
7. coat
8. grow
9. told
10. show

Elephant Words
toe
do

What Word Am I? Write a Basic or Elephant Word by writing a letter for each clue.

1. I am in **ten** but not in **den.**
   I am in **lot** but not in **let.**
   I am in **doe** but not in **dot.**   1. _t_ _o_ _e_

2. I am in **can** but not in **cap.**
   I am in **of** but not in **if.**   2. _n_ _o_

3. I am in **dig** but not in **pig.**
   I am in **fox** but not in **fix.**   3. _d_ _o_

4. I am in **on** but not in **an.**
   I am in **sly** but not in **sky.**
   I am in **cod** but not in **cot.**   4. _o_ _l_ _d_

5. I am in **cat** but not in **bat.**
   I am in **fog** but not in **fig.**
   I am in **beat** but not in **beet.**
   I am in **lost** but not in **lose.**   5. _c_ _o_ _a_ _t_

6. I am in **got** but not in **dot.**
   I am in **won** but not in **win.**   6. _g_ _o_

Proofreading 7–12. Find and cross out six Basic Words that are spelled wrong on these bumper stickers. Write each word correctly.   Order of answers may vary.

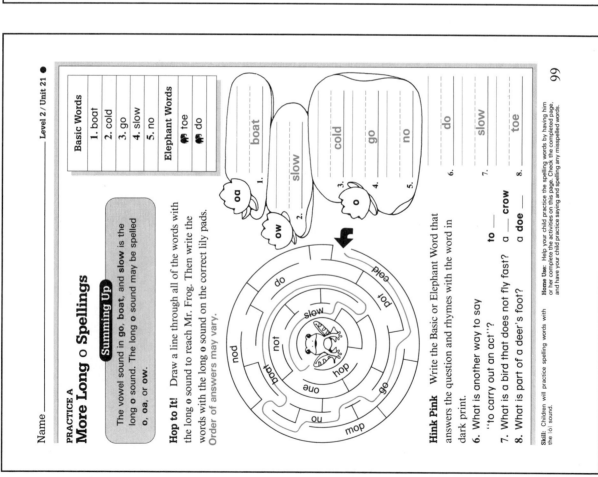

I Love My Old ~~Bolt~~

Help a Tree ~~Greel~~

Have I ~~Teold~~ You About My Cat?

Go ~~Slol~~

~~Cowld~~ Driver on Board!
Honk if You Can ~~Shoa~~ Me
How to Fix My ~~Heter~~.

7. _____ Boat
8. _____ Grow
9. _____ Slow
10. _____ Told
11. _____ Cold
12. _____ Show

Skill: Children will practice spelling words with the /ō/ sound.

Home Use: Help your child practice the spelling words by having him or her complete the activities on this page. Check the completed page, and have your child practice saying and spelling any misspelled words.

100

PRACTICE A
More Long o Spellings

Basic Words
1. boat
2. cold
3. go
4. slow
5. no

Elephant Words
toe
do

Stumming Up

The vowel sound in **go**, **boat**, and **slow** is the long **o** sound. The long **o** sound may be spelled **o**, **oa**, or **ow**.

Hop to It! Draw a line through all of the words with the long **o** sound to reach Mr. Frog. Then write the words with the long **o** sound on the correct lily pads. Order of answers may vary.

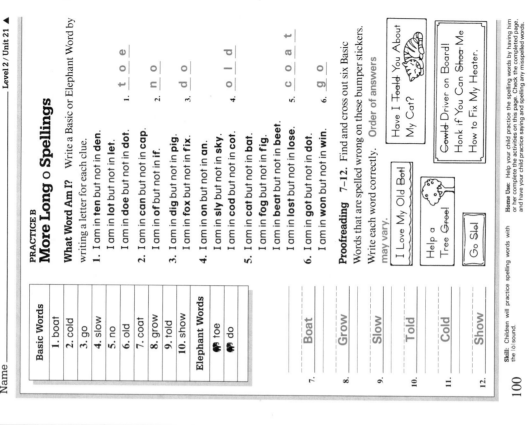

1. _____ boat
2. _____ slow
3. _____ cold
4. _____ go
5. _____ no
6. _____ do
7. _____ slow
8. _____ toe

Hink Pink Write the Basic or Elephant Word that answers the question and rhymes with the word in dark print.

6. What is another way to say "to carry out an act"?   to ___ a ___ **crow**

7. What is a bird that does not fly fast?   a ___ **crow**

8. What is part of a deer's foot?   a ___ **doe**

Skill: Children will practice spelling words with the /ō/ sound.

Home Use: Help your child practice the spelling words by having him or her complete the activities on this page. Check the completed page, and have your child practice saying and spelling any misspelled words.

99

234

Unit 21 Test: More Long o Spellings

Each item below gives three spellings of a word. Choose the correct spelling. Mark the letter for that word.

Sample:
a. so   b. soa   c. soe

ANSWERS
● b c

Items 1–7 test Basic Words 1–5 and the Elephant Words.
Items 8–12 test Basic Words 6–10.

1.	a. toa	b. toe	c. towe	1.	a ⬤b c
2.	a. noe	b. noa	c. no	2.	a b ⬤c
3.	a. cold	b. coald	c. cowld	3.	⬤a b c
4.	a. sloa	b. slow	c. slo	4.	a ⬤b c
5.	a. boat	b. bowt	c. bot	5.	⬤a b c
6.	a. goe	b. gow	c. go	6.	a b ⬤c
7.	a. dow	b. doh	c. do	7.	a b ⬤c
8.	a. old	b. oald	c. owld	8.	⬤a b c
9.	a. cowt	b. coat	c. cote	9.	a ⬤b c
10.	a. sho	b. showe	c. show	10.	a b ⬤c
11.	a. gro	b. grow	c. groe	11.	a ⬤b c
12.	a. told	b. towld	c. toald	12.	⬤a b c

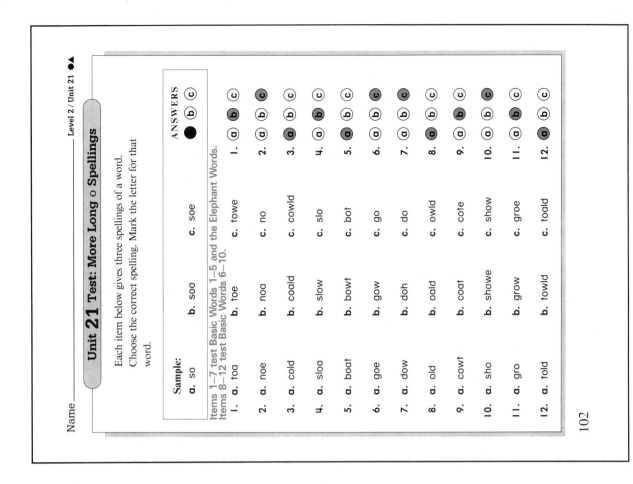

PRACTICE C
More Long o Spellings

Something Is Fishy   Help Hugo finish making a sign for Seaside Park. Write the Challenge and Vocabulary Words in the correct places. Then write a sentence for the sign.

Challenge Words
1. coast
2. rainbow

Theme Vocabulary
3. ocean
4. jellyfish
5. shrimp
6. crab

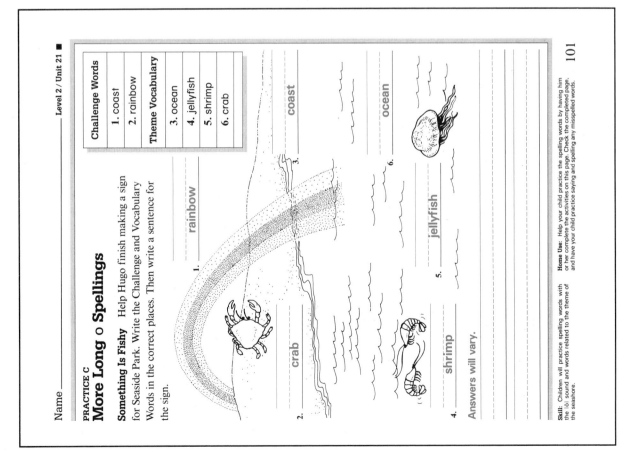

rainbow

coast

ocean

crab

jellyfish

shrimp

Answers will vary.

Skill: Children will practice spelling words with the /ō/ sound and words related to the theme of the seashore.

Home Use: Help your child practice the spelling words by having him or her complete the activities on this page. Check the completed page, and have your child practice saying and spelling any misspelled words.

Practice Master and Test Answers

PRACTICE B
The Vowel Sounds in moon and book

Basic Words
1. zoo
2. food
3. look
4. moon
5. book
6. soon
7. took
8. good
9. room
10. foot

Elephant Words
🐘 you
🐘 who

Hidden Words Find and circle the hidden Basic Word in each box. Then write the word.

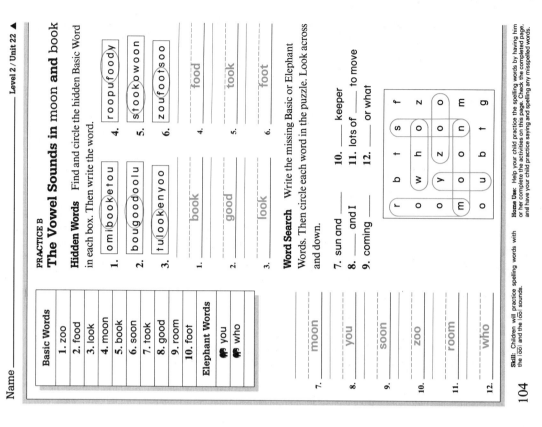

1. o m i b o o k e t o u   _____ book
2. b o u g o o d o o l u   _____ good
3. t u l o o k e n y o o   _____ look
4. r o o p u f o o d y   _____ food
5. s t o o k o w o o n   _____ took
6. z o u f o o t s o o   _____ foot

Word Search Write the missing Basic or Elephant Words. Then circle each word in the puzzle. Look across and down.

7. sun and _____   moon
8. _____ and I   you
9. coming _____   soon
10. _____ keeper   zoo
11. lots of _____   room
12. _____ or what   who

r	o	r	b	t	s	f
o	o	o	w	h	o	z
m	m	o	y	z	o	o
o	o	u	o	o	n	m
o	o	o	b	t	g	

Skill: Children will practice spelling words with the /o͞o/ and the /o͝o/ sounds.

Home Use: Help your child practice the spelling words by having him or her complete the activities on this page. Check the completed page, and have your child practice saying and spelling any misspelled words.

PRACTICE A
The Vowel Sounds in moon and book

Summing Up

The vowel sounds you hear in **moon** and **book** may be spelled oo.

Basic Words
1. zoo
2. food
3. look
4. moon
5. book

Elephant Words
🐘 you
🐘 who

Bookworm Fill in the missing letters to make Basic or Elephant Words. Color the books in which the vowel sound in **moon** is spelled oo. Circle the two books with a different spelling for this sound.

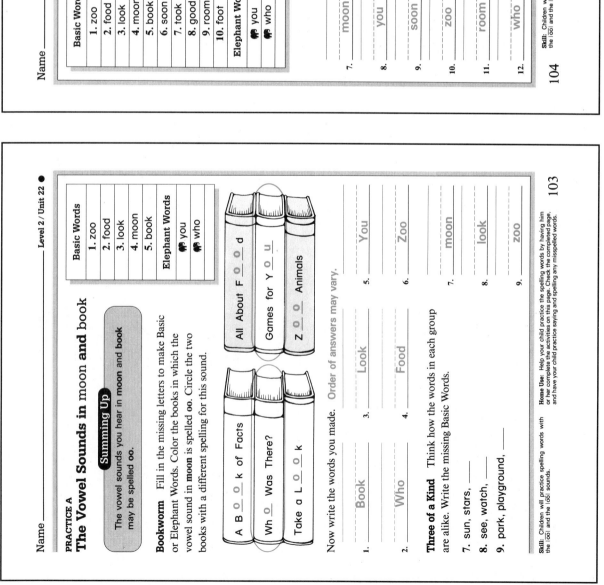

A B o o k of Facts

Wh o Was There?

Take a L o o k

All About F o o d

Games for Y o u

Z o o Animals

Now write the words you made. Order of answers may vary.

1. _____ Book
2. _____ Who
3. _____ Look
4. _____ Food
5. _____ You
6. _____ Zoo

Three of a Kind Think how the words in each group are alike. Write the missing Basic Words.

7. sun, stars, _____   moon
8. see, watch, _____   look
9. park, playground, _____   zoo

Skill: Children will practice spelling words with the /o͞o/ and the /o͝o/ sounds.

Home Use: Help your child practice the spelling words by having him or her complete the activities on this page. Check the completed page, and have your child practice saying and spelling any misspelled words.

236

Unit 22 Test: The Vowel Sounds in moon and book

Read each word group. Find the correctly spelled word to complete each group. Mark the letter next to that word.

Sample:

a ___ tooth
● **a** loose
ⓑ looz
ⓒ luse

Items 1–7 test Basic Words 1–5 and the Elephant Words.
Items 8–12 test Basic Words 6–10.

1. a new ___
   a bowk
   b bhok
   c book ⬤

2. at the ___
   a zoo ⬤
   b zew
   c zou

3. her favorite ___
   a fude
   b food ⬤
   c foud

4. why and ___
   a hoo
   b whoo
   c who ⬤

5. to ___ at
   a lewk
   b look ⬤
   c luk

6. the ___ and stars
   a moon ⬤
   b mune
   c mewn

7. for ___ and me
   a yeww
   b you ⬤
   c yoo

8. a ___ time
   a good ⬤
   b guud
   c goud

9. a ___ at home
   a roum
   b rume
   c room ⬤

10. on one ___
    a fut
    b foot ⬤
    c fout

11. a long walk ___
    a took ⬤
    b tuk
    c tooc

12. one day ___
    a sune
    b suun
    c soon ⬤

106

PRACTICE C
The Vowel Sounds in moon and book

Hink Pink Write a Challenge or Vocabulary Word and a word that rhymes with it to answer each question.

1. What is a large deer that is not tied up?

   a ___loose___ ___moose___

2. What is food that does not make noise?

   a ___quiet___ ___diet___

3. What is a sport that is not wild?

   a ___tame___ ___game___

Challenge Words
1. hoof
2. moose
Theme Vocabulary
3. tame
4. diet
5. groom
6. perch

Change a Letter Change one letter in each picture's name to write a Challenge or Vocabulary Word.

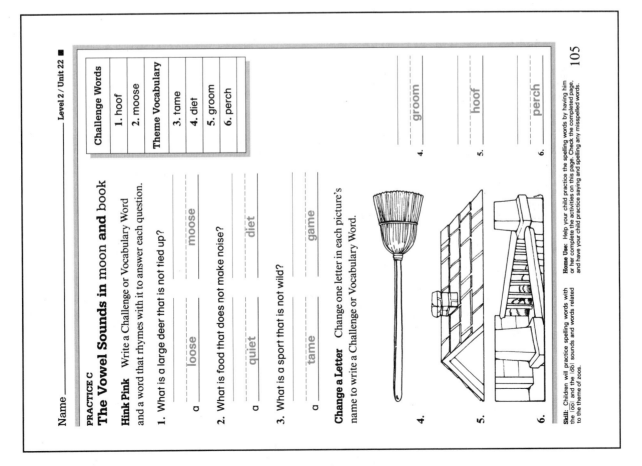

4. ___groom___

5. ___hoof___

6. ___perch___

Skill: Children will practice spelling words with the |ōō| and the |ŏŏ| sounds and words related to the theme of zoos.

Home Use: Help your child practice the spelling words by having him or her complete the activities on this page. Check the completed page, and have your child practice saying and spelling any misspelled words.

105

PRACTICE A
Homophones

Summing Up

Homophones are words that sound alike but do not have the same spelling or the same meaning.

Basic Words
1. plane
2. plain
3. tail
4. tale
Elephant Words
🐘 to
🐘 too
🐘 two

Moo Clues Write the missing Basic or Elephant Words to finish each set. The words in each set are homophones.

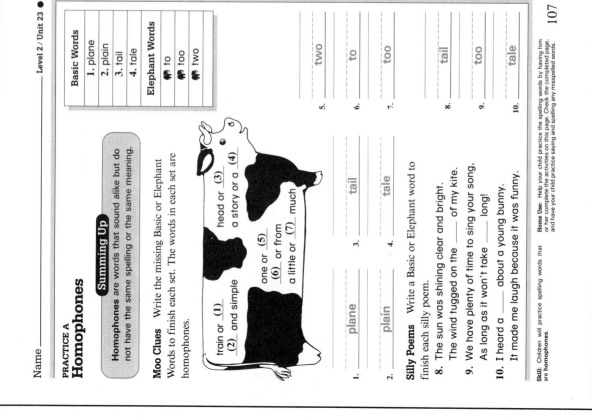

train or _(1)_
_(2)_ and simple

head or _(3)_
a story or a _(4)_

one or _(5)_
_(6)_ or from
a little or _(7)_ much

1. _plane_   3. _tail_

2. _plain_   4. _tale_

5. _two_

6. _to_

7. _too_

Silly Poems Write a Basic or Elephant word to finish each silly poem.

8. The sun was shining clear and bright.
The wind tugged on the ___ of my kite.

9. We have plenty of time to sing your song,
As long as it won't take ___ long!

10. I heard a ___ about a young bunny.
It made me laugh because it was funny.

8. _tail_

9. _too_

10. _tale_

Skill: Children will practice spelling words that are **homophones**.

Home Use: Help your child practice the spelling words by having him or her complete the activities on this page. Check the completed page, and have your child practice saying and spelling any misspelled words.

PRACTICE B
Homophones

Basic Words
1. plane
2. plain
3. tail
4. tale
5. rode
6. road
7. hole
8. whole
Elephant Words
🐘 to
🐘 too
🐘 two

Crossword Clues Write a Basic or Elephant Word for each clue.

Across

2. a place for cars
3. the opposite of **from**
4. a story

Down

1. something that flies
2. drove in a car

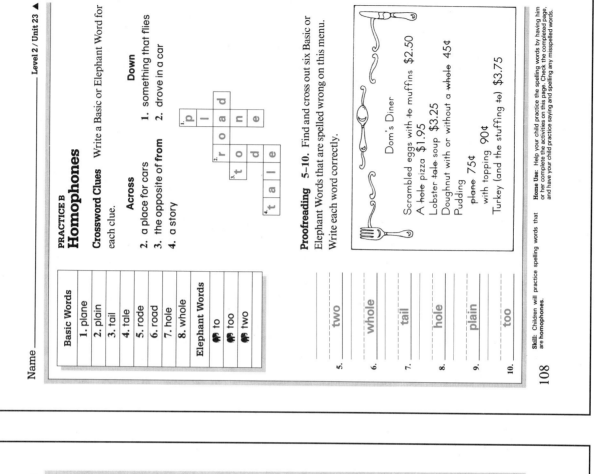

Proofreading 5–10. Find and cross out six Basic or Elephant Words that are spelled wrong on this menu. Write each word correctly.

Dom's Diner

Scrambled eggs with ~~te~~ muffins $2.50
A ~~hole~~ pizza $1.95
Lobster ~~tale~~ soup $3.25
Doughnut with or without a ~~whole~~ 45¢
Pudding
~~plane~~ 75¢
with topping 90¢
Turkey (and the stuffing ~~te~~) $3.75

5. _two_

6. _whole_

7. _tail_

8. _hole_

9. _plain_

10. _too_

Skill: Children will practice spelling words that are **homophones**.

Home Use: Help your child practice the spelling words by having him or her complete the activities on this page. Check the completed page, and have your child practice saying and spelling any misspelled words.

238

Unit 23 Test: Homophones

Read each sentence. Is the underlined word spelled right or wrong? Mark your answer.

	Right	Wrong
Sample: I can sea a bird in the sky.	○	●

Items 1–7 test Basic Words 1–4 and the Elephant Words.
Items 8–11 test Basic Words 5–8.

	Right	Wrong
1. Angelo can sing well two.	○	●
2. We made a very plane dinner.	○	●
3. Rosie told us a funny tale.	●	○
4. Are you going to Sandra's party?	●	○
5. Fred watched the plain fly by.	○	●
6. My dog chases his own tail.	●	○
7. Would Irene like too go with us?	○	●
8. Carl road the horse to work.	○	●
9. The mask covered her whole face.	●	○
10. Vera and I live on the same rode.	○	●
11. There is a big hole in my shoe.	●	○

110

PRACTICE C

Homophones

Flying High Write the missing Challenge and Vocabulary Words. Find out about the pilots.

1. Eli and Ruby ____ over the ocean.
2. Nell and Ira ____ on the runway.
3. Eli is the only ____ wearing glasses.
4. Ruby just flew ____ a cloud.
5–6. Ira wears a pack that a ____ member ____ to him.

Challenge Words
1. threw
2. through
Theme Vocabulary
3. pilot
4. glide
5. land
6. crew

1. glide   3. pilot   5. crew
2. land   4. through 6. threw

Now write the correct name of each pilot. Use the sentences above to help you.

Eli   Ruby

Ira   Nell

109

Skill: Children will practice spelling words that are **homophones** and words related to the theme of things that fly.

Home Use: Help your child practice the spelling words by having him or her complete the activities on this page. Check the completed page. and have your child practice saying and spelling any misspelled words.

Practice Master and Test Answers

Unit 24 Review: Test A

Read each sentence. One of the underlined words in each sentence is spelled wrong. Mark the letter for that word.

Sample:
Mom wants to lok at my painting.
         a b

ANSWERS
ⓐ ●

This test reviews Basic Words 1–5 and Elephant Words from Units 19–23.

1. That book is in one of the boxs.
   a   b
2. I will thenk the cook for this food.
      a   b
3. Bev will tell yoo a funny tale.
         a   b
4. Can I ride to the moon in a boet?
   a   b
5. Did the kign fly in his plane?
      a
6. It is very coald and windy today.
      a
7. Touch your toe with your hend.
   a   b
8. Will you go to buy new dishs?
      a   b
9. There are noe beaches near here.
      a
10. All of the childran went to the zoo.
    a   b
11. I like to wear plain dresss.
    a   b
12. My puppy's tail is not tooo long.
    a   b

1.	ⓐ	ⓑ
2.	ⓐ	ⓑ
3.	ⓐ	ⓑ
4.	ⓐ	ⓑ
5.	ⓐ	ⓑ
6.	ⓐ	ⓑ
7.	ⓐ	ⓑ
8.	ⓐ	ⓑ
9.	ⓐ	ⓑ
10.	ⓐ	ⓑ
11.	ⓐ	ⓑ
12.	ⓐ	ⓑ

Unit 24 Review: Test B

Read each sentence. One of the underlined words in each sentence is spelled wrong. Mark the letter for that word.

Sample:
How many wishs did you make?
        a   b

ANSWERS
● ⓑ

This test reviews Basic Words 6–10 and Elephant Words from Units 19–23.

1. Will Maria bring her warm cowt?
      a   b
2. It took four dayes to get there.
   a   b
3. Harvey toald me their names.
      a   b
4. Do you thenk two cars will fit?
      a   b
5. The whole rume was painted green.
      a   b
6. They use their biks on the road.
     a   b
7. Betty should sew up that hole sune.
   a   b
8. Please sho the note to Krisi.
     a   b
9. Do this theng by the end of the day.
      a   b
10. What do you grow in your garden?
    a   b
11. Ask them whoe rode on the bus.
    a   b
12. Did you bring good thinges to eat?
    a   b

1.	ⓐ	ⓑ
2.	ⓐ	ⓑ
3.	ⓐ	ⓑ
4.	ⓐ	ⓑ
5.	ⓐ	ⓑ
6.	ⓐ	ⓑ
7.	ⓐ	ⓑ
8.	ⓐ	ⓑ
9.	ⓐ	ⓑ
10.	ⓐ	ⓑ
11.	ⓐ	ⓑ
12.	ⓐ	ⓑ

PRACTICE B
More Long i Spellings

Basic Words
1. sky
2. find
3. night
4. high
5. fly
6. try
7. light
8. dry
9. right
10. kind

Elephant Words
eye
buy

Send a Message Use the code below to write Basic and Elephant Words.

1	2	3	4	5	6	7	8	9	10	11
d	e	f	i	k	l	n	r	s	t	y

1. 10·8·11 **try**
2. 2·11·2 **eye**
3. 3·6·11 **fly**
4. 9·5·11 **sky**
5. 3·4·7·1 **find**
6. 1·8·11 **dry**

In the Family Write the Basic or Elephant Word that is the opposite of the word in dark print.

7. Mr. Opposite has **dark** hair.
   Mrs. Opposite's hair is _____. **light**
8. Mr. Opposite writes with his **left** hand.
   Mrs. Opposite writes with her _____ hand. **right**
9. Mr. Opposite is sometimes **mean**.
   Mrs. Opposite is often _____. **kind**
10. Mr. Opposite likes to walk during the **day**.
    Mrs. Opposite likes to walk at _____. **night**
11. Mr. Opposite has a **low** voice.
    Mrs. Opposite's voice is _____. **high**
12. Mr. Opposite wants to **sell** the old car.
    Mrs. Opposite wants to _____ a new one. **buy**

Skill: Children will practice spelling words with the /ī/ sound.
Home Use: Help your child practice the spelling words by having him or her complete the activities on this page. Check the completed page, and have your child practice saying and spelling any misspelled words.

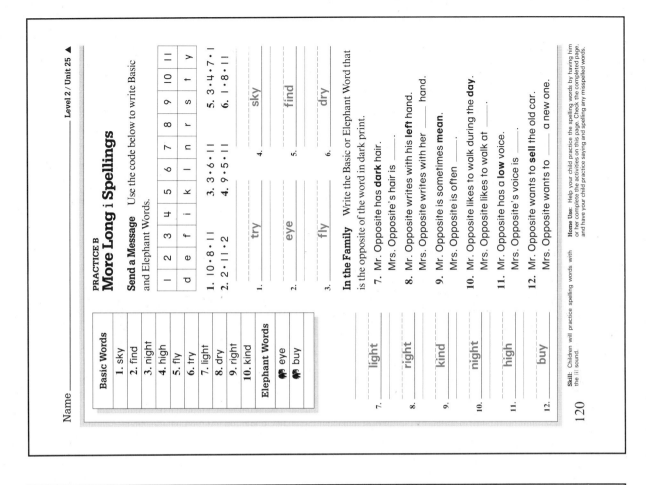

PRACTICE A
More Long i Spellings

> **Summing Up**
> The vowel sound in **sky**, **find**, and **night** is the long i sound. The long i sound may be spelled **y**, **i**, or **igh**.

Basic Words
1. sky
2. find
3. night
4. high
5. fly

Elephant Words
eye
buy

Catch a Fly Help the bug make its web. Write the letter or letters that spell the long i sound to finish each Basic Word.

sk **y**
h **i** g h
fl **y**
n **i** g h t
f **i** nd

Now write each word from the web under the correct bug.
Order of answers may vary.

1. sky
2. fly
3. high
4. night
5. find

Fill-In Fun Write the missing Basic or Elephant Words.

6. _____ and ear **eye**
7. _____ a kite **fly**
8. _____ and sell **buy**

Skill: Children will practice spelling words with the /ī/ sound.
Home Use: Help your child practice the spelling words by having him or her complete the activities on this page. Check the completed page, and have your child practice saying and spelling any misspelled words.

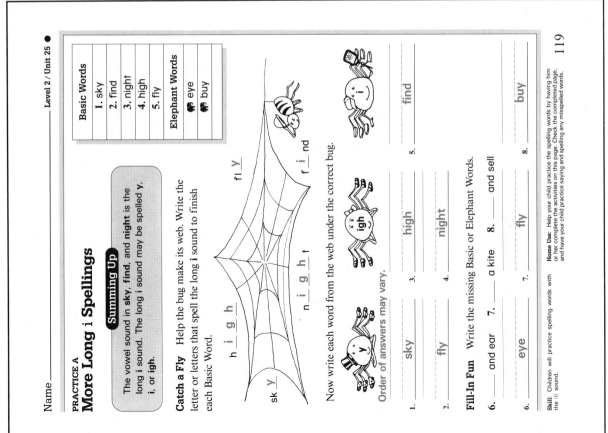

Practice Master and Test Answers

241

Unit 25 Test: More Long i Spellings

Each item below gives three spellings of a word.
Choose the correct spelling. Mark the letter for that word.

Sample:

a. cri b. cry c. crigh

Items 1–7 test Basic Words 1–5 and the Elephant Words.
Items 8–12 test Basic Words 6–10.

	a.	b.	c.
1.	a. fly	b. fli	c. fligh
2.	a. nyt	b. night	c. nite
3.	a. bigh	b. bi	c. buy
4.	a. hy	b. hye	c. high
5.	a. skie	b. sky	c. skigh
6.	a. eigh	b. eie	c. eye
7.	a. find	b. fynd	c. fighnd
8.	a. ryt	b. right	c. rit
9.	a. try	b. tri	c. trigh
10.	a. drigh	b. dry	c. dri
11.	a. lyt	b. liht	c. light
12.	a. kind	b. kynd	c. kighnd

ANSWERS

a ● c

	a	b	c
1.	●	b	c
2.	a	●	c
3.	a	b	●
4.	a	b	●
5.	a	●	c
6.	a	b	●
7.	●	b	c
8.	a	●	c
9.	●	b	c
10.	a	●	c
11.	a	b	●
12.	●	b	c

PRACTICE C

More Long i Spellings

Future Times Write a headline for each news story.
Use all the Challenge and Vocabulary Words. Use
capital letters correctly. Sample answers:

Challenge Words
1. flight
2. behind
Theme Vocabulary
3. Mars
4. space
5. planet
6. Pluto

Future Times
Thursday March 23, 2050

_____ Crew Gets Ready for *Flight* to *Mars* _____

PALM SPRINGS—Buzz Smith,
Gloria Tate, and Donna Carty
are getting ready for a trip to
the red planet. The trip will last
several months.

_____ Plants Found on *Planet Pluto* _____

KENNEDY SPACE CENTER—
Explorers have brought back
several tiny plants from the
planet farthest from the sun.

_____ Weather Station Is Left *Behind* in *Space* _____

The spaceship **Stardust**
returned to Earth today
after leaving a weather
station among the stars.

Skill: Children will practice spelling words with the |i| sound and words related to the theme of stars and planets.

Home Use: Help your child practice the spelling words by having him or her complete the activities on this page. Check the completed page, and have your child practice saying and spelling any misspelled words.

242

Name _____

PRACTICE B
The Final Sound in puppy

Rhyme Time Help name the people in the play. Write the Basic Word that rhymes with the word in dark print. Begin each word with a capital letter.

Basic Words
1. puppy
2. baby
3. lucky
4. happy
5. very
6. lady
7. funny
8. silly
9. many
10. only
Elephant Word
🍪 cookie

1. _Lucky_ **Ducky**

2. _Silly_ **Billy**

3. _Funny_ **Bunny**

4. _Lady_ **O'Grady**

5. _Happy_ **Pappy**

Proofreading 6–11. Find and cross out six Basic or Elephant Words that are spelled wrong on these greeting cards. Write each word correctly.

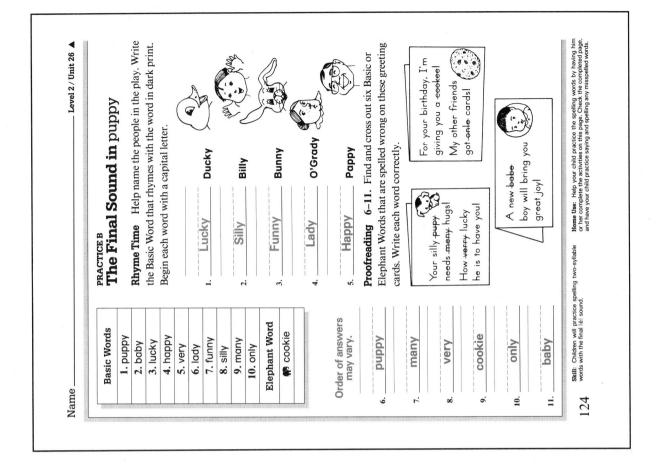

For your birthday, I'm giving you a ~~cookeel~~
My other friends got ~~onle~~ cards!

Your silly ~~pupy~~ needs ~~meny~~ hugs!

How ~~verry~~ lucky he is to have you!

A new ~~babe~~ boy will bring you great joy!

Order of answers may vary.

6. _puppy_

7. _many_

8. _very_

9. _cookie_

10. _only_

11. _baby_

Skill: Children will practice spelling two-syllable words with the final (ē) sound.

Home Use: Help your child practice the spelling words by having him or her complete the activities on this page. Check the completed page, and have your child practice saying and spelling any misspelled words.

Name _____

PRACTICE A
The Final Sound in puppy

Summing Up
The words **puppy** and **baby** have two syllables. The long **e** sound at the end of a two-syllable word may be spelled **y**.

Basic Words
1. puppy
2. baby
3. lucky
4. happy
5. very
Elephant Word
🍪 cookie

Crossword Fun Write a Basic or Elephant Word for each clue.

Across

2. glad
4. a young dog
5. a small, sweet cake

Down

1. a very young child
3. having good luck

Crossword:
1. b
2. h a p p y
   b
3. l p u p p y
     c
4. p u p p y
     o
5. c o o k i e
     y

Chart-a-Word Color the box under the letter or letters to finish each Basic Word. Write the words.

	y	py	by
6. hap			
7. luck			
8. ba			
9. ver			
10. pup			

Circle the letter that spells the long **e** sound in each word you wrote.

6. happ(y)
7. luck(y)
8. bab(y)
9. ver(y)
10. pupp(y)

Skill: Children will practice spelling two-syllable words with the final (ē) sound.

Home Use: Help your child practice the spelling words by having him or her complete the activities on this page. Check the completed page, and have your child practice saying and spelling any misspelled words.

Practice Master and Test Answers

243

Unit 26 Test: The Final Sound in puppy

Read each word group. Find the correctly spelled word to complete each group. Mark the letter next to that word.

Sample:

a _____ picture
- (a) prettie
- (b) pritty
- (●) pretty

Items 1–6 test Basic Words 1–5 and the Elephant Word.
Items 7–11 test Basic Words 6–10.

1. a _____ ending
- (a) happy
- (b) happe
- (c) hapi

2. a crying _____
- (a) babie
- (b) baby
- (c) baybe

3. a _____ quiet day
- (a) veery
- (b) veree
- (c) very

4. from the _____ jar
- (a) cooki
- (b) kooke
- (c) cookie

5. your _____ day
- (a) lucki
- (b) lucky
- (c) luckiy

6. a playful _____
- (a) puppy
- (b) puppi
- (c) puppie

7. a _____ song
- (a) sillie
- (b) silly
- (c) sili

8. a _____ story
- (a) funny
- (b) fune
- (c) funni

9. in _____ one day
- (a) onle
- (b) ownly
- (c) only

10. few or _____
- (a) meny
- (b) many
- (c) manie

11. a young _____
- (a) lady
- (b) ladie
- (c) ladi

PRACTICE C
The Final Sound in puppy

Take a Close Look Look at Pictures 1 and 2. Circle five things in Picture 2 that are different from Picture 1.

Challenge Words
1. furry
2. noisy
Theme Vocabulary
3. piglet
4. kid
5. tadpole
6. hatch

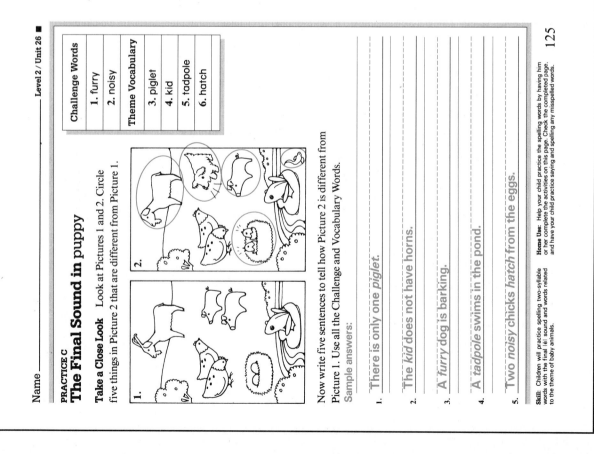

1.

2.

Now write five sentences to tell how Picture 2 is different from Picture 1. Use all the Challenge and Vocabulary Words.
Sample answers:

1. There is only one *piglet.*

2. The *kid* does not have horns.

3. A *furry* dog is barking.

4. A *tadpole* swims in the pond.

5. Two *noisy* chicks *hatch* from the eggs.

Skill: Children will practice spelling two-syllable words with the final /ē/ sound and words related to the theme of baby animals.

Home Use: Help your child practice the spelling words by having him or her complete the activities on this page. Check the completed page, and have your child practice saying and spelling any misspelled words.

PRACTICE B
The Vowel Sound in cow

Basic Words
1. town
2. house
3. out
4. down
5. cow
6. now
7. found
8. how
9. mouse
10. brown

Elephant Words
🐘 could
🐘 should

Hink Pink   Write two Basic Words that rhyme to answer each question.

1–2. What is a home for a small animal?
a _____ mouse _____ house

3–4. What is a village that is painted a dark color?
a _____ brown _____ town

Cow Catcher   Help Farmer Brown find her cow. Draw a line joining eight Basic and Elephant Words in ABC order. Then write those words in ABC order.

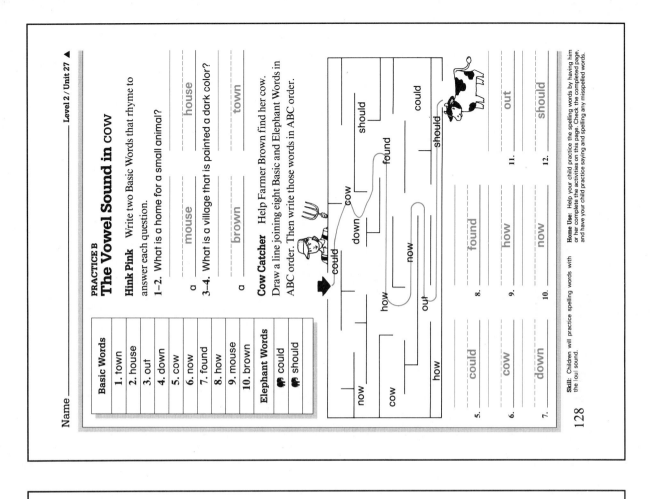

5. _____ could
6. _____ cow
7. _____ down
8. _____ found
9. _____ how
10. _____ now
11. _____ out
12. _____ should

Skill: Children will practice spelling words with the /ou/ sound.

Home Use: Help your child practice the spelling words by having him or her complete the activities on this page. Check the completed page, and have your child practice saying and spelling any misspelled words.

128

PRACTICE A
The Vowel Sound in cow

Basic Words
1. town
2. house
3. out
4. down
5. cow

Elephant Words
🐘 could
🐘 should

Summing Up
The words **town** and **house** have the same vowel sound. The vowel sound may be spelled **ow** or **ou**.

Queen of the Seas   Fill in the missing letters to finish each word. Then write the words that have the vowel sound in **town** and **house**.
Order of answers may vary.

c o_ u_ ld   sh o_ u_ ld   t o_ w_ n   d o_ w_ n   o_ u_ t   c o_ w   h o_ u_ se

1. _____ town
2. _____ out
3. _____ cow
4. _____ down
5. _____ house

Now color the spaces for the words with the vowel sound in **town** and **house**. Find the hidden picture.

6. _____ should
7. _____ house
8. _____ could

Scrambled Riddles   Unscramble the underlined Basic or Elephant Word in each riddle. Write the word. Then see if you can think of the answer to each riddle.

6. Why holdus dentists like potatoes?
7. What kind of shoue weighs the least?
8. How locud you make seven even?

Riddle Answers: 6. They are always filling. 7. a lighthouse
8. Take away the s.

Skill: Children will practice spelling words with the /ou/ sound.

Home Use: Help your child practice the spelling words by having him or her complete the activities on this page. Check the completed page, and have your child practice saying and spelling any misspelled words.

127

Practice Master and Test Answers

Unit 27 Test: The Vowel Sound in cow

Each item below gives three spellings of a word. Choose the correct spelling. Mark the letter for that word.

Sample:

a. cloun   b. clown   c. clouln

ANSWERS
(a) ● (c)

Items 1–7 test Basic Words 1–5 and the Elephant Words.
Items 8–12 test Basic Words 6–10.

				ANSWERS
1.	a. owt	b. out	c. outt	(a) (b) ●
2.	a. cow	b. cou	c. kow	● (b) (c)
3.	a. howse	b. hous	c. house	(a) (b) ●
4.	a. should	b. showd	c. shoud	● (b) (c)
5.	a. toun	b. town	c. towen	(a) ● (c)
6.	a. cood	b. cuwd	c. could	(a) (b) ●
7.	a. doun	b. down	c. doown	(a) ● (c)
8.	a. brone	b. brounn	c. brown	(a) (b) ●
9.	a. how	b. hou	c. houe	● (b) (c)
10.	a. fownd	b. found	c. fowend	(a) ● (c)
11.	a. nou	b. nawe	c. now	(a) (b) ●
12.	a. mouse	b. mowse	c. mawz	● (b) (c)

PRACTICE C
The Vowel Sound in cow

House for Sale Write ads to help sell the homes below. Use all the Challenge and Vocabulary Words. Use a separate sheet of paper if you need more room.

Challenge Words
1. couch
2. crowded
Theme Vocabulary
3. cottage
4. igloo
5. trailer
6. palace

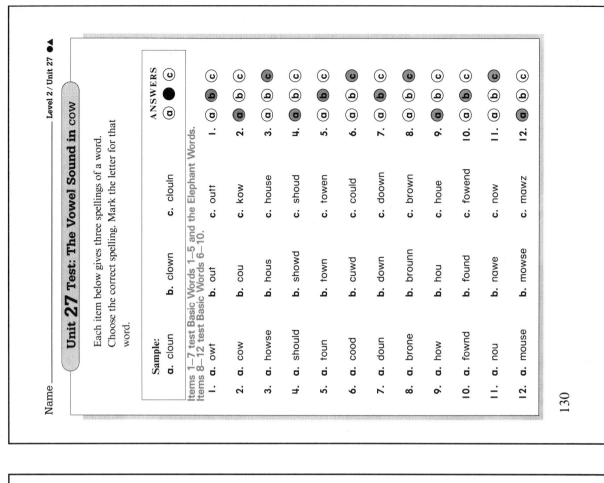

1. **For Sale**

2. **For Sale**

3. **For Sale**

4. **For Sale**

Sample answers:

Keep cool in a new *igloo!*

This *cottage* was made for you. Your *couch* will fit right in!

A *trailer* is perfect for people who are on the go!

Are you feeling *crowded?* Here is a *palace* with lots of room!

Skill: Children will practice spelling words with the /ou/ sound and words related to the theme of places to live.

Home Use: Help your child practice the spelling words by having him or her complete the activities on this page. Check the completed page, and have your child practice saying and spelling any misspelled words.

PRACTICE A
Compound Words

Summing Up

A **compound word** is a word that is made up of two shorter words.

Basic Words
1. bathtub
2. bedtime
3. myself
4. someone
5. maybe

Compound Maze Draw a line to join the two words that make up each Basic Word. Lines in maze may vary.

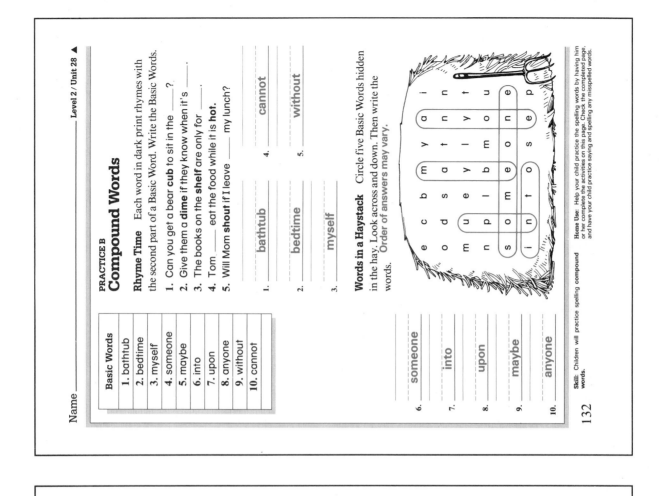

bed
some
bath
may
my

tub
self
time
one
be

Look at the Basic Words you made. Write a word for each clue.

1. another word for **perhaps** _____ maybe
2. a person _____ someone
3. me, ___, and I _____ myself
4. when you go to sleep _____ bedtime
5. where you get clean _____ bathtub

Dot-to-Dot What do you get whenever you sit in the bathtub? To find the answer, connect the dots to spell three Basic Words. Then write the words.

6. _____ bedtime
7. _____ someone
8. _____ myself

Skill: Children will practice spelling **compound** words.

Home Use: Help your child practice the spelling words by having him or her complete the activities on this page. Check the completed page, and have your child practice saying and spelling any misspelled words.

131

PRACTICE B
Compound Words

Basic Words
1. bathtub
2. bedtime
3. myself
4. someone
5. maybe
6. into
7. upon
8. anyone
9. without
10. cannot

Rhyme Time Each word in dark print rhymes with the second part of a Basic Word. Write the Basic Words.

1. Can you get a bear **cub** to sit in the ___? _____
2. Give them a **dime** if they know when it's ___. _____
3. The books on the **shelf** are only for ___. _____
4. Tom ___ eat the food while it is **hot**. _____
5. Will Mom **shout** if I leave ___ my lunch? _____

1. _____ bathtub
2. _____ bedtime
3. _____ myself
4. _____ cannot
5. _____ without

Words in a Haystack Circle five Basic Words hidden in the hay. Look across and down. Then write the words. Order of answers may vary.

```
e  c  b  m  y  a  i
o  d  s  a  t  n  n
m  e  y  l  y  o  u
n  p  i  b  m  o  e
s  o  m  e  o  n  e
i  n  t  o  s  e  p
```

6. _____ someone
7. _____ into
8. _____ upon
9. _____ maybe
10. _____ anyone

Skill: Children will practice spelling **compound** words.

Home Use: Help your child practice the spelling words by having him or her complete the activities on this page. Check the completed page, and have your child practice saying and spelling any misspelled words.

132

Unit 28 Test: Compound Words

Read each word group. Find the correctly spelled word to complete each group. Mark the letter next to that word.

Sample:
bright _____
ⓐ sunshin
ⓑ sonshine
● sunshine

Items 1–5 test Basic Words 1–5. Items 6–10 test Basic Words 6–10.

1. yes, no, or _____
   ⓐ mabee
   ● maybe
   ⓒ mayby

2. a story at _____
   ⓐ bettime
   ⓑ bedtim
   ● bedtime

3. for _____ else
   ⓐ somone
   ● someone
   ⓒ sumwun

4. me, _____, and I
   ⓐ myself
   ⓑ miself
   ● mysself

5. out of the _____
   ⓐ bathub
   ⓑ battub
   ● bathtub

6. once _____ a time
   ● upon
   ⓑ oupon
   ⓒ uphon

7. _____ a word
   ⓐ witout
   ● without
   ⓒ widthoud

8. to ask _____
   ⓐ anywun
   ⓑ enyone
   ● anyone

9. _____ the room
   ● into
   ⓑ intwo
   ⓒ entoo

10. _____ have one
    ⓐ canot
    ● cannot
    ⓒ kenknot

PRACTICE C
Compound Words

Staying in Shape Draw a picture to finish this story. Then write sentences to tell what happens in each picture. Use all the Challenge and Vocabulary Words.

Challenge Words
1. playground
2. nobody
Theme Vocabulary
3. jog
4. fit
5. muscles
6. shape

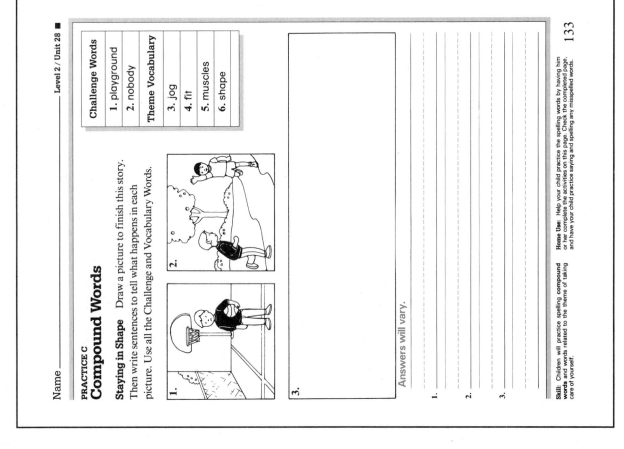

1.

2.

3.

Answers will vary.

1. _____
2. _____
3. _____

Skill: Children will practice spelling **compound words** and words related to the theme of taking care of yourself.

Home Use: Help your child practice the spelling words by having him or her complete the activities on this page. Check the completed page, and have your child practice saying and spelling any misspelled words.

Name

PRACTICE B
Contractions

Basic Words
1. I'll
2. we've
3. don't
4. you're
5. isn't
6. didn't
7. you'll
8. I've
9. hasn't
10. we'll

Elephant Word
🐘 can't

Letter Bugs   Write a contraction for each pair of words. Circle the letter or letters that you left out.

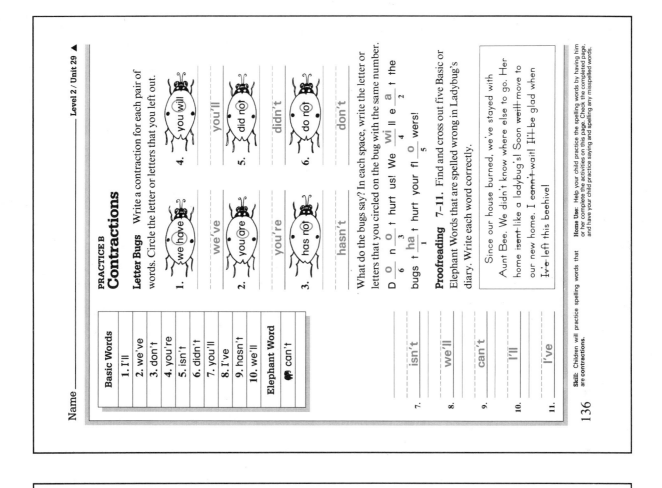

1. we have → **we've**

2. you are → **you're**

3. has not → **hasn't**

4. you will → **you'll**

5. did not → **didn't**

6. do not → **don't**

What do the bugs say? In each space, write the letter or letters that you circled on the bug with the same number.

D $\underline{O}$ n $\underline{O}$ t hurt us! We $\underline{wi}$ ll e $\underline{a}$ t the
  6   3   4   2

bugs t $\underline{ha}$ t hurt your fl $\underline{o}$ wers!
         1   5

Proofreading 7–11.   Find and cross out five Basic or Elephant Words that are spelled wrong in Ladybug's diary. Write each word correctly.

> Since our house burned, we've stayed with Aunt Bee. We didn't know where else to go. Her home isent like a ladybug's! Soon we'ill move to our new home. I cann't wait! I'll be glad when I've left this beehive!

7. __isn't__

8. __we'll__

9. __can't__

10. __I'll__

11. __I've__

136

Skill: Children will practice spelling words that are **contractions**.

Home Use: Help your child practice the spelling words by having him or her complete the activities on this page. Check the completed page, and have your child practice saying and spelling any misspelled words.

Name

PRACTICE A
Contractions

Summing Up

A **contraction** is a short way of writing two words. An **apostrophe** takes the place of the letter or letters that are left out.

Basic Words
1. I'll
2. we've
3. don't
4. you're
5. isn't

Elephant Word
🐘 can't

Contractions at Work   Help Ted's Sign Company fill six new orders. Write a contraction for the words on the brushes above each sign.

1. cannot → You **can't** use this door.

2. is not → This shop **isn't** open.

3. I will → **I'll** vote!

4. do not → Please **don't** feed the animals!

5. we have → Sorry, **we've** gone to lunch.

6. You are → **You're** here.

Skill: Children will practice spelling words that are **contractions**.

Home Use: Help your child practice the spelling words by having him or her complete the activities on this page. Check the completed page, and have your child practice saying and spelling any misspelled words.

135

Practice Master and Test Answers

249

Unit 29 Test: Contractions

Each item below gives three spellings of a word. Choose the correct spelling. Mark the letter for that word.

Sample:
a. letts   b. l'ets   c. let's

Items 1–6 test Basic Words 1–5 and the Elephant Word.
Items 7–11 test Basic Words 6–10.

1. a. isnt   b. izn't   c. isn't
2. a. don't   b. dowent   c. do'nt
3. a. weve   b. we've   c. w'eve
4. a. can'nt   b. ca'nt   c. can't
5. a. you're   b. yure   c. yo're
6. a. I'le   b. Il'l   c. I'll
7. a. hosent   b. hasn't   c. has'nt
8. a. yull   b. you'll   c. you'l
9. a. I've   b. Ive   c. Iv
10. a. di'dnt b. didnt   c. didn't
11. a. weel   b. we'll   c. w'ell

ANSWERS

	a	b	c
Sample	a	●	
1.	a	b	c
2.	a	b	c
3.	a	b	c
4.	a	b	c
5.	a	b	c
6.	a	b	c
7.	a	b	c
8.	a	b	c
9.	a	b	c
10.	a	b	c
11.	a	b	c

PRACTICE C
Contractions

Challenge Words
1. they're
2. wouldn't

Theme Vocabulary
3. flea
4. moth
5. beetle
6. crawl

Groups of Three   Draw another thing that fits in each group. Write a sentence telling how the things in the group are alike. Use all the Vocabulary Words.
Sample answers:

1.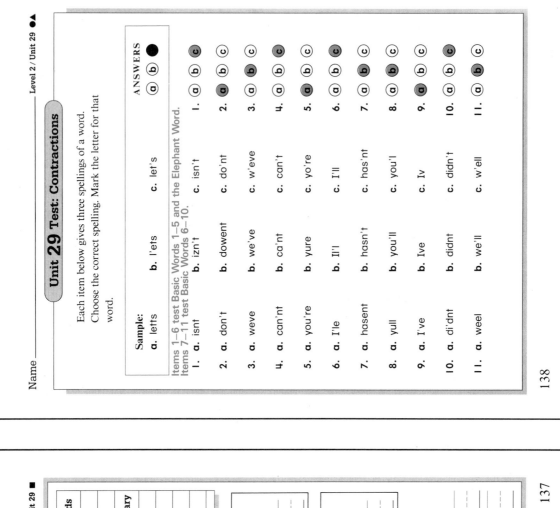

A flea, a frog, and a rabbit can jump.

2.

A moth, a bat, and a bird can fly.

3.

A beetle, a turtle, and a snake can crawl.

Riddle   Write the missing Challenge Words. Then write the answer to the riddle.

When _____ babies, they have gills so they can live in water. Then they grow lungs. Without lungs these green hoppers _____ be able to live on land. What are they?

4. _____ they're

5. _____ wouldn't

Answer: f r o g s

Skill: Children will practice spelling words that are **contractions** and words related to the theme of insects.

Home Use: Help your child practice the spelling words by having him or her complete the activities on this page. Check the completed page, and have your child practice saying and spelling any misspelled words.

Unit 30 Review: Test A

There are three words beside each number. One of the words is spelled wrong. Mark the letter next to that word.

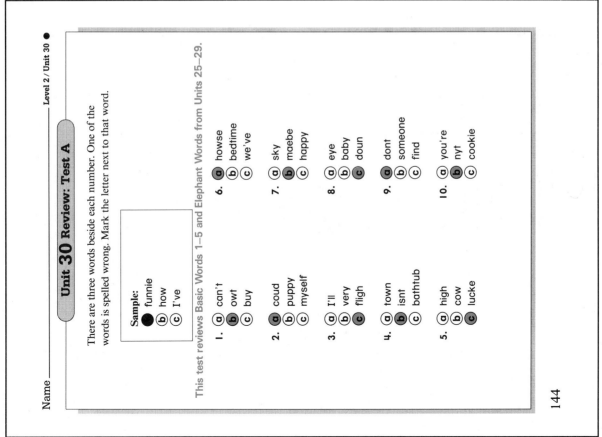

Sample:
- ● funnie
- ⓑ how
- ⓒ I've

This test reviews Basic Words 1–5 and Elephant Words from Units 25–29.

1. ⓐ can't
   ● owt
   ⓒ buy

2. ● coud
   ⓑ puppy
   ⓒ myself

3. ⓐ I'll
   ⓑ very
   ● fligh

4. ⓐ town
   ● isnt
   ⓒ bathtub

5. ⓐ high
   ⓑ cow
   ● lucke

6. ● howse
   ⓑ bedtime
   ⓒ we've

7. ⓐ sky
   ● maebe
   ⓒ happy

8. ⓐ eye
   ⓑ baby
   ● doun

9. ● dont
   ⓑ someone
   ⓒ find

10. ⓐ you're
    ● nyt
    ⓒ cookie

Unit 30 Review: Test B

There are three words beside each number. One of the words is spelled wrong. Mark the letter next to that word.

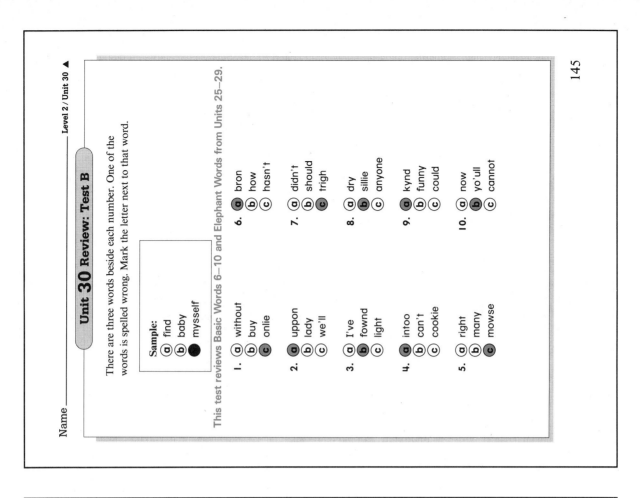

Sample:
- ⓐ find
- ⓑ baby
- ● mysself

This test reviews Basic Words 6–10 and Elephant Words from Units 25–29.

1. ● without
   ⓑ buy
   ⓒ onlie

2. ● uppon
   ⓑ lady
   ⓒ we'll

3. ⓐ I've
   ● fownd
   ⓒ light

4. ● intoo
   ⓑ can't
   ⓒ cookie

5. ⓐ right
   ⓑ many
   ● mowse

6. ● bron
   ⓑ how
   ⓒ hasn't

7. ⓐ didn't
   ⓑ should
   ● trigh

8. ⓐ dry
   ● sillie
   ⓒ anyone

9. ● kynd
   ⓑ funny
   ⓒ could

10. ⓐ now
    ● yo'ull
    ⓒ cannot

Practice Master and Test Answers

251

Name _____

PRACTICE B
The Vowel + r **Sound in** car

Picture Math   Write the word for each clue.

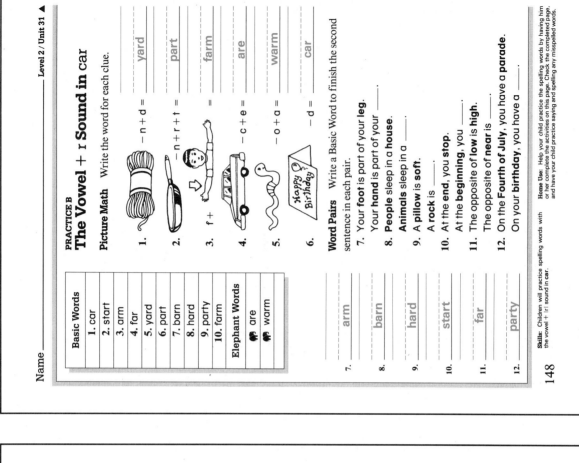

Basic Words
1. car
2. start
3. arm
4. far
5. yard
6. part
7. barn
8. hard
9. party
10. farm
Elephant Words
✦ are
✦✦ warm

1. − n + d = _____ yard
2. − n + r + t = _____ part
3. f + − c + e = _____ farm
4. = _____ are
5. − o + a = _____ warm
6. − d = _____ car

Word Pairs   Write a Basic Word to finish the second sentence in each pair.

7. Your **foot** is part of your **leg**.
   Your **hand** is part of your _____.   arm

8. **People** sleep in a **house**.
   Animals sleep in a _____.   barn

9. A **pillow** is **soft**.
   A **rock** is _____.   hard

10. At the **end**, you **stop**.
    At the **beginning**, you _____.   start

11. The opposite of **low** is **high**.
    The opposite of **near** is _____.   far

12. On the **Fourth of July**, you have a **parade**.
    On your **birthday**, you have a _____.   party

Skills: Children will practice spelling words with the vowel + |r| sound in **car**.

Home Use: Help your child practice the spelling words by having him or her complete the activities on this page. Check the completed page, and have your child practice saying and spelling any misspelled words.

148

Name _____

PRACTICE A
The Vowel + r **Sound in** car

Stumming Up
You hear a vowel + r sound in **car** and **start**.
This sound is spelled **ar**.

Basic Words
1. car
2. start
3. arm
4. far
5. yard
Elephant Words
✦ are
✦✦ warm

All Aboard!   Write the missing words. Find the words you wrote that have the vowel + **r** sound in **car**. Draw a line under the letters that spell that vowel sound.

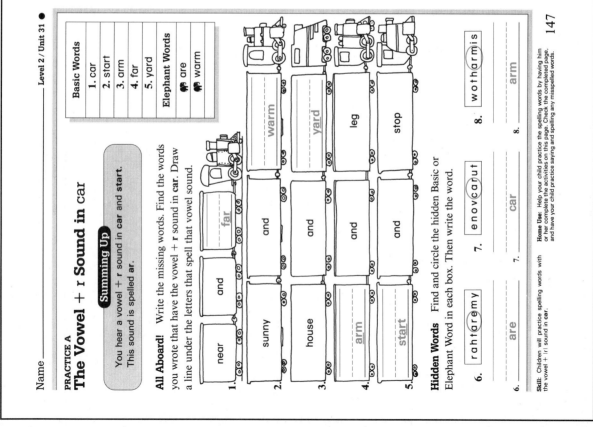

1. near and far
2. sunny and warm
3. house and yard
4. arm and leg
5. start and stop

Hidden Words   Find and circle the hidden Basic or Elephant Word in each box. Then write the word.

6. r a h t **a r e** m y   _____ are
7. e n o v **c a r** u t   _____ car
8. w o t h **a r m** i s   _____ arm

Skill: Children will practice spelling words with the vowel + |r| sound in **car**.

Home Use: Help your child practice the spelling words by having him or her complete the activities on this page. Check the completed page, and have your child practice saying and spelling any misspelled words.

147

PRACTICE C
The Vowel + r Sound in car

Crossword Clues Write the Challenge and Vocabulary Words in the puzzle. Then write a clue for each **Across** word and each **Down** word.

Challenge Words
1. large
2. carpet

Theme Vocabulary
3. hood
4. motor
5. trunk
6. traffic

```
      ²t r u n k
h
m o t o r   ⁴l
o         a
³d         f   r
           f   g
          i
          ⁵c a r p e t
```

Across

Answers will vary.

2. _____

3. _____

5. _____

Down

1. _____

2. _____

4. _____

Skill: Children will practice spelling words with the vowel + |r| sound in **car** and words related to the theme of automobiles.

Home Use: Help your child practice the spelling words by having him or her complete the activities on this page. Check the completed page, and have your child practice saying and spelling any misspelled words.

Unit 31 Test: The Vowel + r Sound in car

Read each sentence. Find the correctly spelled word to complete each sentence. Mark the letter next to that word.

Sample:
Fill the glass _____.

ANSWERS
(a) jur ● jar (c) jer

Items 1–7 test Basic Words 1–5 and the Elephant Words.
Items 8–12 test Basic Words 6–10.

1. May we _____ to play?
(a) stirt (b) stert ● start

2. Bert travels near and _____.
● far (b) fer (c) furr

3. We _____ the winners!
(a) ar (b) arr ● are

4. I like my old _____.
(a) kar ● car (c) cor

5. Marty works in the _____.
● yard (b) yarde (c) yerd

6. Dora has a _____ blanket.
(a) warme ● warm (c) wurm

7. Move your left _____.
(a) arme (b) arn ● arm

8. Is that _____ or soft?
(a) haad ● hard (c) hird

9. Come to my birthday _____.
● party (b) parti (c) pardy

10. The cow is in the red _____.
(a) bern (b) barrn ● barn

11. Paul has a _____ in the play.
(a) pard ● part (c) parte

12. My class will visit a _____.
● farm (b) farn (c) ferm

PRACTICE A
The Vowel + r Sound in store

Summing Up
You hear a vowel + **r** sound in **corn** and **store**.
This sound is spelled **or** or **ore**.

Basic Words
1. store
2. corn
3. for
4. more
5. or

Elephant Words
four
your

Good Knight! Write the missing letters to finish each Basic Word. Then write the words on the correct flags. Order of answers may vary.

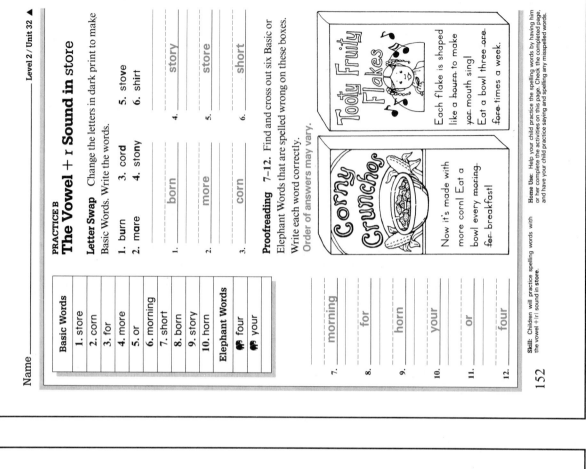

c _o_ r n
m _o_ r _e_
f _o_ r
st _o_ r _e_

or
1. corn
2. for

ore
3. more
4. store

Crossword Clues Write a Basic or Elephant Word for each clue.

Across
7. one more than three
9. a shop
10. something you eat

Down
5. the opposite of less
6. one ____ the other
8. belonging to you

Skill: Children will practice spelling words with the vowel + |r| sound in **store**.

Home Use: Help your child practice spelling words by having him or her complete the activities on this page. Check the completed page, and have your child practice saying and spelling any misspelled words.

PRACTICE B
The Vowel + r Sound in store

Basic Words
1. store
2. corn
3. for
4. more
5. or
6. morning
7. short
8. born
9. story
10. horn

Elephant Words
four
your

Letter Swap Change the letters in dark print to make Basic Words. Write the words.

1. burn
2. mare
3. cord
4. stony
5. stove
6. shirt

1. born
2. more
3. corn
4. story
5. store
6. short

Proofreading 7–12. Find and cross out six Basic or Elephant Words that are spelled wrong on these boxes. Write each word correctly. Order of answers may vary.

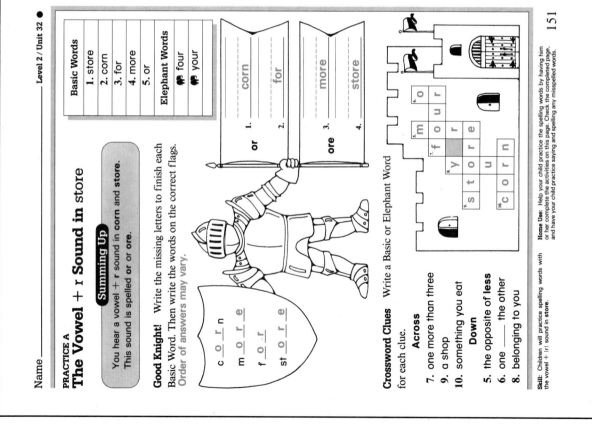

Corny Cruncher
Now it's made with more corn! Eat a bowl every moring for breakfast!

Tooty Fruity Flakes
Each flake is shaped like a horn to make your mouth sing! Eat a bowl three ore times a week.

7. morning
8. for
9. horn
10. your
11. or
12. four

Skill: Children will practice spelling words with the vowel +|r| sound in **store**.

Home Use: Help your child practice the spelling words by having him or her complete the page. Check the completed page, and have your child practice saying and spelling any misspelled words.

Name _____

PRACTICE C
The Vowel + r Sound in store

Mixed-up Market Circle the four things that are wrong in this picture.

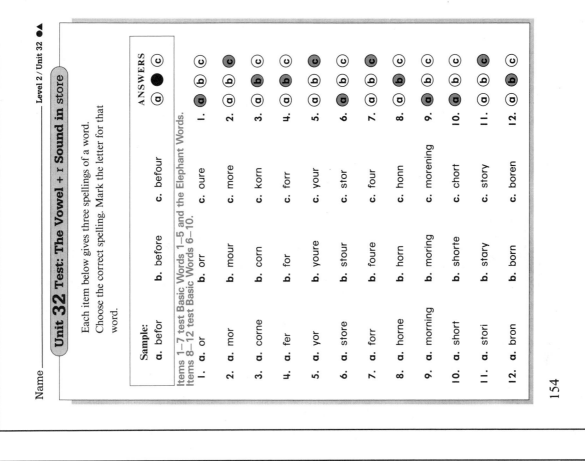

Challenge Words
1. afford
2. before
Theme Vocabulary
3. dairy
4. counter
5. price
6. cart

Now write sentences to tell what is wrong in the picture above. Use all the Challenge and Vocabulary Words in your sentences.
Sample answers:

Milk and butter belong with the *dairy* foods. The *price* of food

is too high. No one could *afford* to shop here. A *cart* is on top

of the *counter*. The man should shop *before* he pays.

153

Skill: Children will practice spelling words with the vowel + |r| sound in **store** and words related to the theme of supermarkets.

Home Use: Help your child practice the spelling words by having him or her complete the activities on this page. Check the completed page, and have your child practice saying and spelling any misspelled words.

Name _____

Unit 32 Test: The Vowel + r Sound in store

Each item below gives three spellings of a word. Choose the correct spelling. Mark the letter for that word.

Sample:
a. befor   b. before   c. befour

ANSWERS
a ● c

Items 1–7 test Basic Words 1–5 and the Elephant Words.
Items 8–12 test Basic Words 6–10.

#	a.	b.	c.	Answers
1.	a. or	b. orr	c. oure	a **b** c
2.	a. mor	b. mour	c. more	a b **c**
3.	a. corne	b. corn	c. korn	a **b** c
4.	a. fer	b. for	c. forr	a **b** c
5.	a. yor	b. youre	c. your	a b **c**
6.	a. store	b. stour	c. stor	**a** b c
7.	a. forr	b. foure	c. four	a b **c**
8.	a. horne	b. horn	c. honn	a **b** c
9.	a. morning	b. moring	c. morening	**a** b c
10.	a. short	b. shorte	c. chort	**a** b c
11.	a. stori	b. stary	c. story	a b **c**
12.	a. bron	b. born	c. boren	a **b** c

154

PRACTICE B
Words That End with er

Basic Words

1. flower
2. water
3. under
4. over
5. better
6. sister
7. brother
8. mother
9. father
10. after

Billy Goat Books Write the missing Basic Word for each book title. Begin each word with a capital letter.

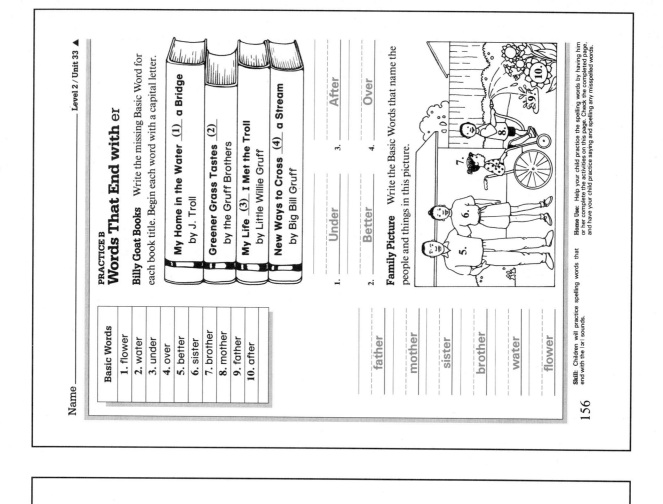

My Home in the Water __(1)__ **a Bridge**
by J. Troll

Greener Grass Tastes __(2)__
by the Gruff Brothers

My Life __(3)__ **I Met the Troll**
by Little Willie Gruff

New Ways to Cross __(4)__ **a Stream**
by Big Bill Gruff

1. ____ Under ____   3. ____ After ____

2. ____ Better ____   4. ____ Over ____

Family Picture Write the Basic Words that name the people and things in this picture.

____ father ____

____ mother ____

5. ____ sister ____

6. ____ brother ____

7. ____ water ____

10. ____ flower ____

Skill: Children will practice spelling words that end with the |ər| sounds.

Home Use: Help your child practice the spelling words by having him or her complete the activities on this page. Check the completed page, and have your child practice saying and spelling any misspelled words.

PRACTICE A
Words That End with er

Basic Words

1. flower
2. water
3. under
4. over
5. better

Summing Up

The sound at the end of **flower** and **water** is a vowel + **r** sound. This sound is spelled **er**.

Word Maze Draw a line to join the two syllables that make up each Basic Word. Use a different colored crayon for each word.

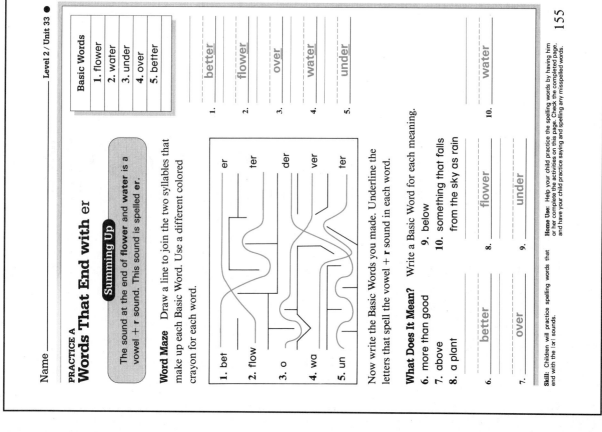

1. bet   er
2. flow   ter
3. o   der
4. wa   ver
5. un   ter

Now write the Basic Words you made. Underline the letters that spell the vowel + **r** sound in each word.

1. ____ better ____

2. ____ flower ____

3. ____ over ____

4. ____ water ____

5. ____ under ____

What Does It Mean? Write a Basic Word for each meaning.

6. more than good
7. above
8. a plant
9. below
10. something that falls from the sky as rain

6. ____ better ____

7. ____ over ____

8. ____ flower ____

9. ____ under ____

10. ____ water ____

Skill: Children will practice spelling words that end with the |ər| sounds.

Home Use: Help your child practice the spelling words by having him or her complete the activities on this page. Check the completed page, and have your child practice saying and spelling any misspelled words.

256

Unit 33 Test: Words That End with er

Read each word group. Find the correctly spelled word to complete each group. Mark the letter next to that word.

Sample:

a very hot _____
- (a) sommer
- (b) sumer
- ● summer

Items 1–5 test Basic Words 1–5. Items 6–10 test Basic Words 6–10.

1. up and _____
- (a) ower
- (b) over
- (c) ovver

2. cool, fresh _____
- (a) water
- (b) watter
- (c) warter

3. for _____ or worse
- (a) beter
- (b) better
- (c) battur

4. a pretty red _____
- (a) floer
- (b) flowr
- (c) flower

5. down and _____
- (a) under
- (b) ander
- (c) undr

6. father and _____
- (a) mothr
- (b) muther
- (c) mother

7. sister or _____
- (a) bruther
- (b) brother
- (c) brouther

8. before and _____
- (a) after
- (b) aftar
- (c) aftr

9. my little _____
- (a) sistr
- (b) sester
- (c) sister

10. son and _____
- (a) fawther
- (b) father
- (c) fathar

158

PRACTICE C
Words That End with er

Word Change Write the Challenge or Vocabulary Word for each clue. Then follow the directions to change that word to another word.

1. Write a Vocabulary Word that means **a plant that has just begun to grow**.

2. Change the second vowel to a consonant to write a word that means the opposite of **tall**.

1. ___shoot___   2. ___short___

3. Write a Challenge Word that means **to bring together**.

4. Change one consonant to write a word that means **a male parent**.

3. ___gather___   4. ___father___

Challenge Words
1. gather
2. center
Theme Vocabulary
3. soil
4. petals
5. shoot
6. hoe

What Class Think how the words in each group are alike. Write the missing Challenge or Vocabulary Word. In the box next to each group, write a word or words that tell about all the things in the group.

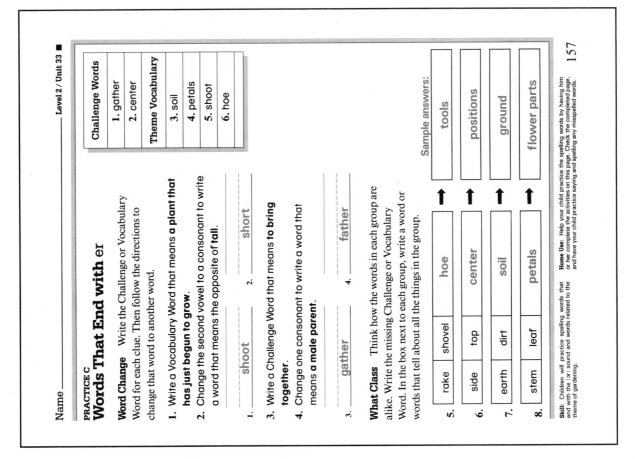

Sample answers:

5.	rake	shovel	hoe	→	tools
6.	side	top	center	→	positions
7.	earth	dirt	soil	→	ground
8.	stem	leaf	petals	→	flower parts

157

Skill: Children will practice spelling words that end with the /ər/ sound and words related to the theme of gardening.

Home Use: Help your child practice the spelling words by having him or her complete the activities on this page. Check the completed page, and have your child practice saying and spelling any misspelled words.

Practice Master and Test Answers

257

Name _____

PRACTICE B
Words That End with ed or ing

Crossword Fun   Write a Basic or Elephant Word for each clue.

Across
2. ended
7. walked
8. hit a ball
9. held with a pin
10. putting your arms around someone
11. becoming

Down
1. slapped hands together
2. visiting stores
3. did not hit
4. moving quickly
5. saying in words
6. resting on the lower part of your body

Basic Words
1. batted
2. running
3. clapped
4. stopped
5. getting
6. shopping
7. stepped
8. hugging
9. pinned
10. sitting
Elephant Words
🐘 missed
🐘 telling

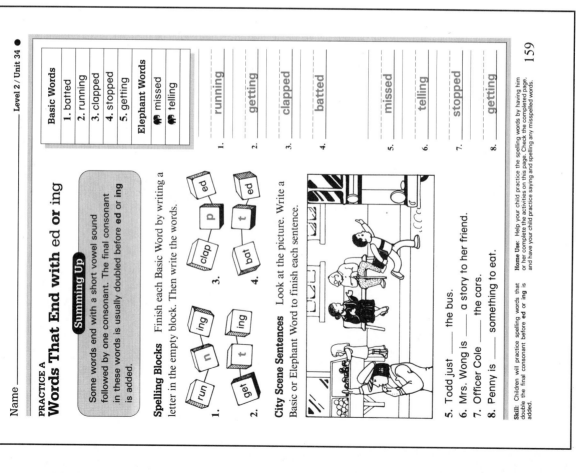

Crossword answers: ¹c l a p p e d; ²s t o p p e d; ⁵s i t t i n g; ⁶b a t t e d; ³m i s s e d; ⁴r u n n i n g; ⁷s t e p p e d; ⁸h u g g i n g; ⁹p i n n e d; ¹⁰h u g g i n g; ¹¹g e t t i n g

160

Skill: Children will practice spelling words that double the final consonant before **ed** or **ing** is added.

Home Use: Help your child practice the spelling words by having him or her complete the activities on this page. Check the completed page, and have your child practice saying and spelling any misspelled words.

Name _____

PRACTICE A
Words That End with ed or ing

Summing Up

Some words end with a short vowel sound followed by one consonant. The final consonant in these words is usually doubled before **ed** or **ing** is added.

Basic Words
1. batted
2. running
3. clapped
4. stopped
5. getting
Elephant Words
🐘 missed
🐘 telling

Spelling Blocks   Finish each Basic Word by writing a letter in the empty block. Then write the words.

1. run | n | ing _____
   clap | p | ed
2. get | t | ing _____
   bat | t | ed

1. __running__
2. __getting__
3. __clapped__
4. __batted__

City Scene Sentences   Look at the picture. Write a Basic or Elephant Word to finish each sentence.

5. Todd just ____ the bus.   __missed__
6. Mrs. Wong is ____ a story to her friend.   __telling__
7. Officer Cole ____ the cars.   __stopped__
8. Penny is ____ something to eat.   __getting__

159

Skill: Children will practice spelling words that double the final consonant before **ed** or **ing** is added.

Home Use: Help your child practice the spelling words by having him or her complete the activities on this page. Check the completed page, and have your child practice saying and spelling any misspelled words.

Level 2 / Unit 34 ●▲

PRACTICE C
Words That End with ed or ing

The Name of the Game Write the missing Challenge or Vocabulary Word for each clue.

1. Maria said, "I was _____ when I hurt my foot."
2. Suki said, "The _____ was six to five when I hit a home run."
3-4. Abby said, "I _____ the puck into the net and scored a _____."
5-6. Pat said, "The _____ between my friend and me ended in a _____."

Challenge Words
1. jogging
2. flipped

Theme Vocabulary
3. score
4. tie
5. goal
6. match

1. ___jogging___   3. ___flipped___

2. ___score___   4. ___goal___

5. ___match___

6. ___tie___

Now use the clues to write the correct name under each girl. Then write the name of the sport she plays.

Sports	
baseball	hockey
tennis	running

___Pat___   ___Maria___   ___Suki___   ___Abby___

___tennis___   ___running___   ___baseball___   ___hockey___

Skill: Children will practice spelling words that double the final consonant before **ed** or **ing** is added and words related to the theme of sports.

Home Use: Help your child practice the spelling words by having him or her complete the activities on this page. Check the completed page, and have your child practice saying and spelling any misspelled words.

161

Unit 34 Test: Words That End with ed or ing

Each item below gives three spellings of a word. Choose the correct spelling. Mark the letter for that word.

Sample:

a. wening   b. winning   c. wineng

ANSWERS

Sample: (a) ● (c)

Items 1–7 test Basic Words 1–5 and the Elephant Words.
Items 8–12 test Basic Words 6–10.

1. a. mised   b. mesed   c. missed
2. a. getting   b. gitting   c. geting
3. a. beted   b. batted   c. battad
4. a. ranning   b. runink   c. running
5. a. clapped   b. klapped   c. claped
6. a. telind   b. telling   c. teeling
7. a. stoped   b. stopped   c. staped
8. a. hugging   b. hugeing   c. huging
9. a. steped   b. stepped   c. stepped
10. a. sitting   b. siting   c. seting
11. a. pinnd   b. pened   c. pinned
12. a. shoping   b. shopping   c. choping

1. (a) (b) ●
2. ● (b) (c)
3. (a) ● (c)
4. (a) (b) ●
5. (a) ● (c)
6. (a) ● (c)
7. (a) ● (c)
8. ● (b) (c)
9. (a) ● (c)
10. ● (b) (c)
11. (a) (b) ●
12. (a) ● (c)

162

Practice Master and Test Answers

259

PRACTICE A
More Words with ed or ing

Summing Up

Some words end with the vowel-consonant-**e** pattern. The final **e** in these words is dropped before **ed** or **ing** is added.

Basic Words
1. liked
2. hoping
3. baked
4. using
5. chased

Odd One Out Cross out the shape that is different from the others in the row. Write a Basic Word with the letters that are left.

1. b a k ⊗ + e d   1. _____ baked

2. l i ⊠ + e ⊲   2. _____ liked

3. u s ⊠ + i n g   3. _____ using

4. h o p ⊠ + i n g   4. _____ hoping

A Better Letter Write the missing Basic Words to finish this letter.

January 16, 1991

Dear Mitch,

I went to the circus last night! It was funny when the clowns ran and __(5)__ each other. An elephant picked one clown up by __(6)__ its trunk! I __(7)__ it so much that I want to go again. I was __(8)__ you could come with me next time.

Your friend,
Liz

5. _____ chased

6. _____ using

7. _____ liked

8. _____ hoping

Skill: Children will practice spelling words that drop the final **e** before **ed** or **ing** is added.   **Home Use:** Help your child practice spelling words by having him or her complete the activities on this page. Check the completed page, and have your child practice saying and spelling any misspelled words.

PRACTICE B
More Words with ed or ing

Basic Words
1. liked
2. hoping
3. baked
4. using
5. chased
6. making
7. closed
8. hiding
9. named
10. riding

Proofreading 1–4. Find and cross out four Basic Words that are spelled wrong in this news story. Write each word correctly.

Chip Baker was namd Cook of the Year. He baked 1000 cookies in two hours. Everyone liked the cookies. Next year he will be makeing a new kind of cookie, useing nuts. He is hopeing the new cookies will be even better.

1. _____ named   3. _____ using

2. _____ making   4. _____ hoping

Word Search Write a Basic Word for each clue. Then find the word in the puzzle and circle it.

5. cooked   8. shut
6. covering up   9. moving on a bike
7. enjoyed   10. followed

5. _____ baked

6. _____ hiding

7. _____ liked

8. _____ closed

9. _____ riding

10. _____ chased

k	e	l	c	l	o	s	e	d	v
v	p	u	r	i	d	i	n	g	q
l	e	b	a	k	e	d	r	n	c
c	h	a	s	e	d	t	w	i	e
o	b	h	i	d	i	n	g	f	s

Skill: Children will practice spelling words that drop the final **e** before **ed** or **ing** is added.   **Home Use:** Help your child practice the spelling words by having him or her complete this page. Check the completed page, and have your child practice saying and spelling any misspelled words.

Level 2 / Unit 35 ●▲

Unit 35 Test: More Words with ed or ing

Read each word group. Find the correctly spelled word to complete each group. Mark the letter next to that word.

Sample:
___ a trip
- (a) tacing
- ● taking
- (c) takeng

Items 1–5 test Basic Words 1–5. Items 6–10 test Basic Words 6–10.

1. boiled or ___
- (a) bakked
- (b) backeg
- (c) baked

2. ___ your head
- (a) using
- (b) ussig
- (c) uzing

3. ___ that book
- (a) likked
- (b) liked
- (c) liket

4. wishing and ___
- (a) hoping
- (b) hopeink
- (c) hopeng

5. ___ up a tree
- (a) chasd
- (b) chassed
- (c) chased

6. ___ and seeking
- (a) hideing
- (b) hiding
- (c) hidding

7. a dog ___ Frank
- (a) namd
- (b) nammed
- (c) named

8. ___ a mud pie
- (a) making
- (b) macking
- (c) makeind

9. ___ the door
- (a) closd
- (b) clozed
- (c) closed

10. ___ a horse
- (a) riddign
- (b) riding
- (c) rideig

166

Level 2 / Unit 35 ■

PRACTICE C
More Words with ed or ing

Eddie's Decisions Read each problem. Write what you think Eddie decided to do to be a good friend. Use all the Challenge and Vocabulary Words.
Sample answers:

Challenge Words
1. teasing
2. decided

Theme Vocabulary
3. neighbor
4. share
5. welcome
6. invite

1. A new child moved into a house near Eddie. What did Eddie decide to do?

1. _Eddie decided to welcome his new neighbor._

2. Eddie's friend forgot her lunch. What did Eddie decide to do?

2. _Eddie decided to share his lunch with her._

3. Eddie's friend Sam was crying because Eddie made fun of him. What did Eddie decide to do?

3. _Eddie decided to stop teasing him._

4. A friend was left out of a game that Eddie was playing. What did Eddie decide to do?

4. _Eddie decided to invite the friend to play._

165

Skill: Children will practice spelling words that drop the final **e** before **ed** or **ing** is added and words related to the theme of friendship.

Home Use: Help your child practice the spelling words by having him or her complete the activities on this page. Check the completed page, and have your child practice saying and spelling any misspelled words.

Practice Master and Test Answers

261

Unit 36 Review: Test A

Read the three word groups. Find the underlined word that is spelled wrong. Mark the letter for that word.

Sample:
- ● the silly storry
- (b) at the farm
- (c) making bread

This test reviews Basic Words 1–5 and Elephant Words from Units 31–35.

1. (a) corne on the cob
   (b) are at home
   (c) clapped their hands

2. (a) baked beans
   (b) a pretty flowar
   (c) over the top

3. (a) feeling better
   (b) a strong arm
   (c) runing the race

4. (a) mor careful
   (b) getting ready
   (c) using my pen

5. (a) under the table
   (b) a gift for you
   (c) batid the ball

6. (a) missed the bus
   (b) in our yared
   (c) four years old

7. (a) yes or no
   (b) hopeing for
   (c) from the start

8. (a) telling the truth
   (b) a blue car
   (c) at the stour

9. (a) cool watir
   (b) chased the ball
   (c) stopped the car

10. (a) too farr away
    (b) liked the book
    (c) on a warm day

Unit 36 Review: Test B

Read the three word groups. Find the underlined word that is spelled wrong. Mark the letter for that word.

Sample:
- ● his old cor
- (b) more or less
- (c) wishing and hoping

This test reviews Basic Words 6–10 and Elephant Words from Units 31–35.

1. (a) after dinner
   (b) a better part
   (c) yur turn

2. (a) my big brothir
   (b) four new friends
   (c) hugging my doll

3. (a) early in the morning
   (b) makeing my lunch
   (c) farm animals

4. (a) siting on the grass
   (b) a horn to blow
   (c) hard to do

5. (a) from my fathe
   (b) a good hiding place
   (c) pinned the sleeve

6. (a) riding my bike
   (b) with your mother
   (c) a storry to tell

7. (a) at the party
   (b) teling time
   (c) closed the door

8. (a) shourt or tall
   (b) in the barn
   (c) her older sister

9. (a) shopping for food
   (b) warrm clothing
   (c) born today

10. (a) missed the bus
    (b) a boy named Fred
    (c) steped on the rug

End-of-Year Test

There are three words beside each number. One of the words is spelled wrong. Mark the letter next to that word.

Sample:
- ● **a** carr
- ⓑ baked
- ⓒ brown

Items 1–13 test Basic Words 1–5 and Elephant Words in Cycles 1–6.
Items 14–25 test Basic Words 6–10 and Elephant Words in Cycles 1–6.

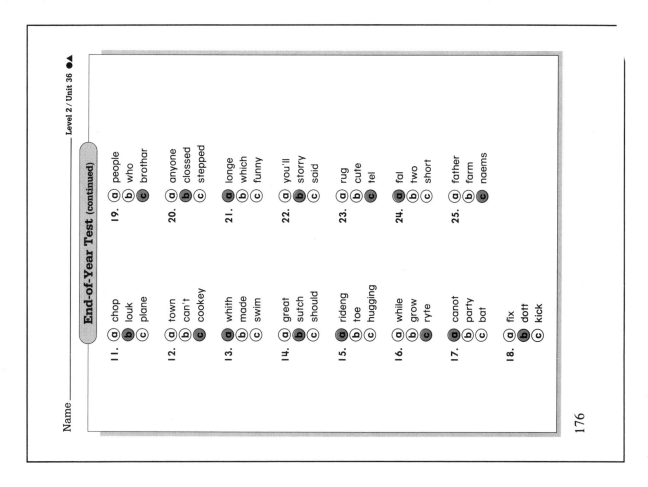

1. ⓐ king
   ● **b** tayle
   ⓒ boat

2. ⓐ very
   ⓑ myself
   ● **c** ar

3. ⓐ better
   ⓑ hoping
   ● **c** childran

4. ● **a** ey
   ⓑ but
   ⓒ of

5. ● **a** club
   ⓑ trale
   ⓒ please

6. ⓐ boxes
   ⓑ moon
   ● **c** howse

7. ⓐ fly
   ● **b** you'r
   ⓒ store

8. ● **a** mised
   ⓑ as
   ⓒ pet

9. ⓐ is
   ⓑ nine
   ● **c** noze

10. ● **a** adde
    ⓑ pick
    ⓒ saw

(continued)

End-of-Year Test (continued)

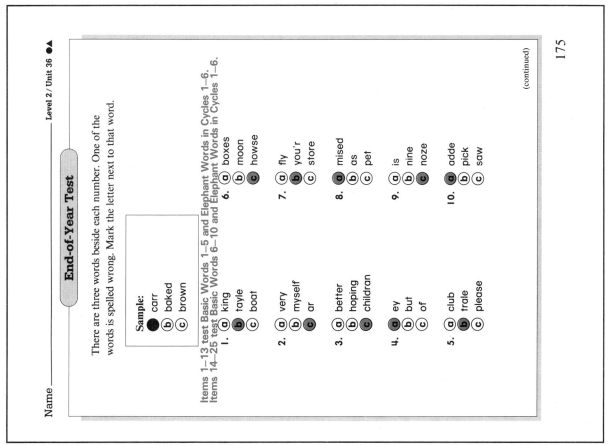

11. ⓐ chop
    ● **b** louk
    ⓒ plane

12. ⓐ town
    ⓑ can't
    ● **c** cookey

13. ● **a** whith
    ⓑ made
    ⓒ swim

14. ⓐ great
    ● **b** sutch
    ⓒ should

15. ● **a** rideng
    ⓑ toe
    ⓒ hugging

16. ⓐ while
    ⓑ grow
    ● **c** ryte

17. ● **a** canot
    ⓑ party
    ⓒ bat

18. ⓐ fix
    ● **b** dott
    ⓒ kick

19. ⓐ people
    ⓑ who
    ● **c** brothar

20. ⓐ anyone
    ● **b** clossed
    ⓒ stepped

21. ● **a** longe
    ⓑ which
    ⓒ funny

22. ⓐ you'll
    ● **b** storry
    ⓒ said

23. ⓐ rug
    ⓑ cute
    ● **c** tel

24. ● **a** fal
    ⓑ two
    ⓒ short

25. ⓐ father
    ⓑ farm
    ● **c** naems